EXILES *of* ERIN

LYNN HOLLEN LEES is Associate
Professor of History at the University of
Pennsylvania. A graduate of Swarthmore
College, she holds M.A. and Ph.D. degrees
from Harvard University. She formerly
taught at Mount Holyoke College and
Smith College, and in 1978–1979 was a
visiting fellow of the Department of Eco-
nomic and Social History, University of
Leicester, England.

There came to the beach a poor Exile of Erin,
The dew on his thin robe was heavy and chill,
For his country he sigh'd when at twilight repairing,
To wander alone by the wind-beaten hill;
But the day-star attracted his eye's sad devotion,
For it rose o'er his own native Isle of the ocean,
Where soon in the fire of his youthful emotion,
He sang the bold anthem of Erin go bragh.
*   —"The Exile of Erin"*

I'll stay no more in Dublin
To live upon potatoes fare,
But I'll go up to London.
Arrah! Pat, won't you come, my dear?

Arrah! come, come away,
My Irish blade.
Arrah! come, come away.
*   —"The Irishman's Ramble to London"*

EXILES *of* ERIN

IRISH MIGRANTS IN VICTORIAN LONDON

LYNN HOLLEN LEES

CORNELL UNIVERSITY PRESS
ITHACA, NEW YORK

Library of Congress Cataloging in Publication Data
(For library cataloging purposes only)

Lees, Lynn.
  Exiles of Erin.

  Bibliography: p.
  Includes index.
  1. Irish in London—History. 2. Rural-urban migration—England—London.
  3. London—History—1800-1950. I. Title.
DA676.9.I75L43   942.1′2′0049162   78-11046
ISBN 0-8014-1176-9

For my mother and father

Contents

Maps

Illustrations

Tables

Figures

Acknowledgments

The long process of writing this book has been eased by the advice and encouragement of many friends and colleagues. David Landes provided much helpful criticism and moral support. Sheridan Gilley and the late H. J. Dyos were regular sources of references and suggestions, and Frank Carney took time from his own work to initiate me into Irish archives and the mysteries of prefamine Irish demography. Etienne Van de Walle, Peter Laslett, and John Modell have offered helpful criticism of my work on Irish family organization. My discussions of Irish popular religion profited from the comments and lively interest of colleagues at the Shelby Cullom Davis Center at Princeton University; during my stay there, Ira Berlin, Robert Bezucha, Herbert Gutman, James Obelkevich, and Lawrence Stone helped to make my research and revisions pleasurable and productive. I also wish to thank Richard Dunn, Paul Hohenberg, Andrew Lees, Charles Rosenberg, and Charles Tilly for their careful reading of earlier drafts of the book and their help in refining them. Remaining errors are of my own making. My thanks also go to Abraham Mora and Katherine Rieff, who worked with me as computer programmers at the facilities of the Philadelphia Social History Project, and to Sally Gordon and Marilyn Budzanoski, who served as research assistants on parts of the project.

My work was made much easier than it might have been by the unfailing help I received at several English and Irish libraries. I am most grateful to the staffs of the British Library, the Holborn Public Library, the Westminster Archive, the Cork County Library, the Public Record Office, the National Library of Ireland, and the Marist Archive in Rome. The priests of St. Mary of the Angels, Bayswater; St. Anne, Underwood Road; the Church of the Most Holy Trinity, Dockhead; and St. Patrick's, Soho, generously permitted me to consult parish records. The Society of Marist Fathers, the Cork Archives Council, and the rector of St. Giles in the Fields have kindly allowed me to quote from manuscripts and letters in their possession. Sections of Chapter 4 originally appeared in *Victorian Studies,* and I am grateful for the permission of the editor to use them here.

Finally, I must express my appreciation to the Henry Foundation, the National Endowment for the Humanities, and the American Philosophical Society, which provided funding for research trips and computer programming. Mount Holyoke College gave me both a sabbatical and a research grant, and the Shelby Cullom Davis Center invited me to spend a semester there in 1975 to continue my writing. The list of my debts is long; I only hope that the final product of my work merits the help it has received. To all, I say thank you.

LYNN HOLLEN LEES

Philadelphia

EXILES *of* ERIN

Introduction

Thousands of Irish men and women sailed into English ports during the nineteenth century. The Irish had been touring and settling in England for hundreds of years; but after 1815 migration intensified and assumed a predominantly urban character. Although some Irish came to wander as itinerant laborers and many moved on to North America, those who stayed moved into Britain's largest cities — London, Manchester, Liverpool, Glasgow. During the desperate years of the potato famine, thousands arrived monthly; in 1847, 300,000 descended on Liverpool alone, attempting by flight to save themselves from starvation.[1] One-half million Irish-born had settled in England and Wales by 1851, and four-fifths of them lived in towns of more than 10,000 people. For a society that had received no large-scale migration since the Norman Conquest, this influx of Irish amounted to an urban invasion.

The arrival of the Irish intensified the effects of English movement from country to town, at that time in full swing under the pressure of rapid industrialization. And the Irish seemed to bring with them a host of intense social problems to compound the difficulties of the cities that received them. "When the outskirts of a rapidly increasing town . . . become the seat of an Irish colony, who invariably fasten on the cheapest, that is, the worst and most unhealthy situations, bringing with them their

1. Of this number, 130,000 then emigrated from Liverpool; see R. Lawton, "Irish Immigration to England and Wales in the Mid–Nineteenth Century," *Irish Geography* 4, no. 1 (1959):48.

uncleanly and negligent habits, often more suited to a country rather than a town life, and herding in large numbers in the same house, so that several families frequently occupy each room from the cellar to the garret, the whole presents an appearance of filth, neglect, confusion, discomfort, and insalubrity, which it would be vain to seek in any English town inhabited solely by the natives of the place," claimed the Royal Commission investigating the Irish poor in Great Britain.[2] When the housing, medical services, and sanitation in workers' neighborhoods were already abominable, when the local government had neither the power nor the personnel to tackle social problems, the contagion of Irish manners was much feared. The Irish strained facilities and social relationships already hard pressed by the effects of industrial and demographic revolutions.

But if the Irish threatened the city, the reverse is also true; routines of Irish village and country life had to give way to those of an urban, industrial culture, and migrants had to accommodate themselves to the rhythms and settings of the city, where clock time replaced sun time and multistory apartments supplanted thatched cottages. Increasingly after 1815, those who came to England were Catholic peasants who had been driven from their land by successive crop failures. Such people seemingly had few resources to ease the transition from rural to urban life. Many spoke only Irish or imperfect English, and very few had the capital necessary to set up a shop or to buy an apprenticeship for their sons. They were newcomers to a complex, hierarchical society that did not highly reward the skills of potato raising and animal tending. Yet despite many fears and dire prognostications, both the English and the Irish survived the dislocations caused by Celtic movement into Britain. Indeed, by the end of the nineteenth century, Irish migration was attracting little attention. By that time it seemed far less threatening, since its volume fell off sharply after the 1850s. Those who remained in England made adjustments to their new life. The nature of those adjustments and the manner in which they were accomplished are the central themes of this book.

2. Great Britain, *Parliamentary Papers* (Commons), "Report on the State of the Irish Poor in Great Britain," 1836, 34:xlii:

When analyzing the migration of ethnic minorities and their assimilation into urban populations, historians have used two basic models, one stressing disorganization and one denying it. Until recently the influence of Georg Simmel and the Chicago school of sociologists has been decisive for historians in the United States. Since the classic work by the sociologist William I. Thomas and his collaborator, Florian Znaniecki, on Polish peasants in Europe and America, migration has often been pictured as a dislocating, painful experience. Combining certain ideas derived from Georg Simmel, Louis Wirth, and Robert Park — in particular those stressing the disorienting psychological effects of cities — with Robert Redfield's sharply opposed ideal types of rural and urban life, historians have tended to reinforce the view of migrants as people overwhelmed by transplantation from a traditional society.[3] Once removed from the stable folk communities of their birth, migrants supposedly have found it difficult to live in an urban environment; many have shown their alienation by becoming alcoholics, thieves, prostitutes. Among historians, Oscar Handlin most clearly uses this model. He argues that migrants in the city were "overwhelmed by the fear of being lost." They found themselves isolated from kin and community; their failure to adjust to American urban society is reflected in their high rates of mental illness, crime, and juvenile delinquency.[4]

The view that migration into a city led individuals into disorganized or pathological behavior has been strongly challenged, however. Oscar Lewis, for example, has criticized both the adequacy of Redfield's rural and urban ideal types and Wirth's

3. William I. Thomas and Florian Znaniecki, *The Polish Peasant in Europe and America*, 2 vols. (New York, 1927); Georg Simmel, "The Metropolis and Mental Life," in *Classic Essays on the Culture of Cities*, ed. Richard Sennett (New York, 1969); Robert Park, "Human Migration and the Marginal Man," *American Journal of Sociology* 33 (1928):881–893; Louis Wirth, "Urbanism as a Way of Life," *American Journal of Sociology* 44 (1938):1–24; Robert Redfield, "The Folk Society," *American Journal of Sociology* 52 (1947):293–308. For a recent reprinting of these essays, see Sennett, ed., *Classic Essays*.
4. Oscar Handlin, "Immigration in American Life: A Reappraisal," in *Immigration and American History*, ed. Henry Steele Commager (Minneapolis, 1961), pp. 12, 17–18, 20, and *The Newcomers: Negroes and Puerto Ricans in a Changing Metropolis* (Cambridge, Mass., 1959), pp. 98, 103. See also Handlin's *The Uprooted* (New York, 1951).

theory of secondary urban relationships. Lewis stresses the continuity between the rural and urban lives of recently urbanized
Mexican peasants. Both he and Herbert Gans write of "urban
villagers," immigrants segregated from the city by residence in
relatively stable lower- or working-class neighborhoods, who
have re-created the strong kinship networks supposedly characteristic only of rural communities.[5] Studies of migration to both
American and African cities have also altered the picture of the
rootless newcomer by stressing the importance of chain migration
in bringing groups of related or acquainted people to the same
destination and the role of aid from kin in finding jobs and
housing.[6] Both of these factors substantially decrease the isolation
of migrants and increase their resources for meeting the economic
and social challenges of urban life. While upwardly mobile
migrants may choose to ignore their ethnic or tribal background,
others find in it a resource and the basis for membership in an
urban community. The creation of a subculture offers migrants a
viable method of adapting to a city.

The migrant Irish chose to create ethnic subcultures abroad.
Rather than adopt the beliefs and customs of their host populations, they adapted their Irish heritage to life in foreign cities.[7]
Contrary to the predictions of the Chicago theorists, they found
that they could maintain the cohesion of their ethnic cultures in
urban settings, despite their need to develop an urban life-style.
Claude Fischer suggests that cities intensify the ability of an
ethnic group to develop a distinctive subculture. The larger the
city, the greater the chance that a given ethnic group will be large
enough to support a full range of institutions to protect and
elaborate the subculture. And the larger the city, the greater the
variety of subcultures whose conflicts and differences help

5. Oscar Lewis, "The Folk-Urban Ideal Type," in *The Study of Urbanization*, ed. Philip Hauser and Leo Schnore (New York, 1965), pp. 491–500, and *La
Vida* (New York, 1966); Herbert J. Gans, *The Urban Villagers* (New York, 1962).

6. Charles Tilly and C. Harold Brown, "On Uprooting, Kinship, and the
Auspices of Migration," in *An Urban World*, ed. Charles Tilly (Boston and
Toronto, 1974), pp. 109–133; John S. MacDonald and Leatrice D. MacDonald,
"Chain Migration, Ethnic Neighborhood Formation, and Social Networks," in
ibid., pp. 226–235; Philip Mayer, *Townsmen or Tribesmen* (Oxford, 1961).

7. Forms of adaptation to American society are discussed in Milton M.
Gordon, *Assimilation in American Life: The Role of Race, Religion, and
National Origins* (New York, 1964), especially pp. 62–63, 72–73.

members to deepen and define their loyalties to their group.[8] London offers an excellent laboratory for the observation of these processes at work. Its size, density, and volume of immigration made it the largest center of Irish settlement in Great Britain. The 107,000 Irish migrants who had moved to London by 1861 formed the critical mass for a complex set of cultural and political institutions and ethnic neighborhoods. Within the framework of Victorian London, we can observe the Irish during decades of both high mobility and relative stability and can trace their geographic, economic, and social movement. When they are compared with their English counterparts and their Irish kin who remained at home, they provide a portrait of an urban ethnic subculture as it changed over time and diverged from that of both rural Ireland and urban England.

The themes of this inquiry are more usually explored by anthropologists and sociologists than by historians. Indeed, the sources and methods of social scientists who study contemporary groups make it far easier for them than for historians to assess the social changes triggered by migration from village to town. Those of us who study the past are quite effectively barred from interviewing our subjects or living among them. Yet in the last few decades historians have broadened enormously the range of concerns within the discipline and have explored dozens of approaches and sources that enable them to "do social history from below." The methods of the demographer, the archaeologist, and the folklorist can be used to illuminate various aspects of the social and cultural life of nineteenth-century workers and peasants. People who left neither letters nor personal papers were listed in birth, marriage, and death registers and tallied by census takers. They paid taxes, built houses, took jobs, talked to doctors and priests, bought books and ballads. All of these encounters generated documents or artifacts that have survived. While the events of any one life may remain obscure, many patterns of mass social life can be reconstructed by the use of such materials.

To observe the complex pattern of ethnic redefinition and cultural diffusion among the London Irish, we must periodically

8. Claude S. Fischer, "Toward a Subcultural Theory of Urbanism," *American Journal of Sociology* 80, no. 6 (May 1975):319–341.

narrow our vision from the metropolis to the Irish neighborhood. As Oscar Lewis quite correctly insists, "social life is not a mass phenomenon."[9] Only at the level of the Roman Catholic parish, the apartment house, the club, and the family can the development of an ethnic subculture be seen. In order to have precise data on these tiny units of urban Irish society, I drew a systematic sample of Irish households from the manuscript census schedules for London in 1851 and 1861. Needing information on major Irish neighborhoods, I selected the three census subdistricts with the highest proportion of Irish-born; these were the very old areas of Irish settlement in St. Giles in the Fields and Whitechapel and the riverside parish of St. Olave, Southwark. Wishing also to collect data on suburban Irish neighborhoods, I selected two more subdistricts in western and southern London (St. John, Notting Hill; St. George, Camberwell) where the proportion of Irish-born was relatively low and whose economic bases differed from those of centrally located Irish areas. In each of these subdistricts, a systematic sample of every third household with an Irish-born member was selected. Information was then coded, punched onto IBM cards, and processed by computer. Since the sample was deliberately biased toward heavily Irish districts of central London, the results cannot be shown statistically to be representative of the entire London Irish population. Additional information on the way the sample was designed and the way data were collected and presented is provided in Appendix A.

This book begins by examining social and economic conditions in the several regions of Ireland during the late eighteenth and early nineteenth centuries in an effort to discover who the migrants were. I then move to an analysis of the people who settled in London, looking at their regional origins, demographic characteristics, and occupational distribution. Their settlement patterns and geographic movements, set alongside a portrait of an Irish working-class neighborhood, form the subject of Chapter 3, while Chapter 4 is devoted to analysis of the role of the Irish in the London labor market. In order to study the private as well as the public side of Irish social life, I

9. Oscar Lewis, "Further Observations on the Folk–Urban Continuum and Urbanization, with Special Reference to Mexico City," in *The Study of Urbanization*, ed. Hauser and Schnore, p. 497.

then shift attention to the Irish family in Chapters 5 and 6. Here the demographic characteristics of Irish families and house-holds, their marriage patterns, and the structure of family authority and power both in prefamine Ireland and in London in 1851 are compared in an effort to chart transformations resulting from movement into the city. The changes in Irish religious and cultural life that followed migration, particularly those shaped by the Roman Catholic church, are the focus of Chapter 7. The final section of the book treats the shift in Irish political behavior from factional fights and marauding bands to participation in trade unions, political parties, and nationalist groups. Within this framework, the Irish are traced from their farms and hamlets in the early nineteenth century to their urban villages in the back streets of London on the eve of a new century.

CHAPTER 1

"Poor Pat Must Emigrate"

In popular ballads that circulated in Ireland, England, and the United States during the nineteenth century, migrants announced their reasons for leaving home.

> Oh, farewell to poor old Erin's Isle, I now must leave you for awhile,
> The rent and taxes are so high, I can no longer stay.
> From Dublin Quay I sailed away, and landed here but yesterday.
> My shoes and brogues and my shirt are all that's in my kit.
> I have just called in to let you know the sights I've seen before I go.[1]

"For to live poor I can't endure. / There's nothing here but misery," a balladeer complained.[2] "Children aren't pigs, you know, for they can't pay the rent," sang Pat Molloy, a ballad hero from a family of thirteen, who had to leave for England and make his own way.[3] In the mythology of Irish migration, poverty, famine, and overpopulation drove peasants into exile.

Social scientists who analyze Irish migration have used the same explanations. Poverty looms largest in older historical works. Oscar Handlin writes of "the uprooted" and describes evictions, agricultural distress, and the collapse of Irish industry in the early nineteenth century, which in his opinion triggered mass move-

---

1. "Poor Pat Must Emigrate," in *The Mercier Book of Old Irish Street Ballads*, ed. James N. Healy (Cork, 1969), vol. 4, pp. 62–63.
2. "Lamentation for the Loss of Ireland," in ibid., p. 78.
3. "Pat Molloy," Baring-Gould Collection, British Library, vol. 2, p. 215.

ments overseas.[4] To William Forbes Adams, "the compelling motive behind this great shift of population . . . was distress."[5] Even the most recent account of transatlantic migration, Philip Taylor's *The Distant Magnet*, identifies "population pressure" along with poverty and "a problem of social organization" as the underlying causes of Irish movement overseas.[6] Geographers and economists also stress poverty and famine as the main triggers of migration.[7]

Most of the historiography of Irish migration in fact uses a model derived from Malthus: population increased faster than the means of subsistence, so the extra mouths had to leave. Crop failures account for the timing of their exit. The picture of Irish economic organization that emerges from all but the most recent works is a simplified one in which the defects of legal arrangements and the injustice of governmental regulations are highlighted. The system of land tenure and English manipulation of tariffs supposedly destroyed any feeble impulses toward economic progress. Meanwhile the mass of the population multiplied, subdivided their farms, and lived on potatoes until natural disaster forced them either to emigrate or to starve.[8] Accounts of the potato famine, during which thousands fled from starvation and disease, confirm these Malthusian and economic determinist models. Yet to let the events of an atypical period serve to explain a population movement that began several centuries earlier and which still continues today is to let drama substitute for the analysis of a historical process.

Impoverishment and overpopulation certainly stimulated Irish emigration, but any model that accounts for this phenomenon by

4. Oscar Handlin, *The Uprooted* (New York, 1951), and *Boston's Immigrants: A Study in Acculturation*, rev. ed. (Cambridge, Mass., 1959), pp. 31, 38–41, 43.

5. William Forbes Adams, *Ireland and the Irish Emigration to the New World from 1815 to the Famine* (New Haven and London, 1932), p. 2.

6. Philip Taylor, *The Distant Magnet: European Emigration to the U.S.A.* (New York, 1971), p. 32.

7. T. W. Freeman, *Pre-Famine Ireland: A Study in Historical Geography* (Manchester, 1957), p. 39; Brinley Thomas, *Migration and Economic Growth: A Study of Great Britain and the Atlantic Economy* (London, 1954), p. 72.

8. Marcus Lee Hansen, *The Atlantic Migration, 1607–1860*, new ed. (New York, 1961), pp. 201–208; Handlin, *Boston's Immigrants*, pp. 43–51; George O'Brien, *The Economic History of Ireland from the Union to the Famine* (London, 1921), pp. 3, 208–209.

reference to such factors alone is highly misleading. Much Irish migration resulted directly from the fact that Ireland was less developed than other countries of the Atlantic economy. More jobs at higher pay were available in industrializing areas. Lacking work at home, the Irish joined a mass movement into English and American cities. If jobs had been available in Cork, they would have converged there. An adequate explanation of Irish emigration must therefore consider several factors in addition to poverty and population density.

Models of migration based solely on economic determinants neglect cultural factors that can either speed or impede migration. Not all Irish were equally ready to emigrate. The poorest were not the first to leave; indeed, exodus from the most backward and densely populated regions in the west lagged far behind that from the wealthier counties of Ulster and Leinster until long after the famine. A decision to leave Ireland was made on the basis of knowledge of the outside world, interest in it, and ease of entry into it. As Gino Germani and R. C. Taylor have suggested, analyses of migration should consider not only the structural characteristics of the areas of origin and destination but also the perceptions and motives of individuals and the means by which migration takes place.[9]

Economic and cultural changes at home and abroad produced a setting in which migration became an attractive choice for many Irish. In comparison with England, Ireland in the early nineteenth century was densely populated and poor. Housing remained primitive, agriculture backward, and industry almost nonexistent except in Dublin and in the region around Belfast. Despite relative economic underdevelopment, the Irish population had grown rapidly during the late eighteenth century as potato cultivation spread. By switching from a grain to a potato diet, peasants could support themselves on approximately one-fifth of the land they had previously needed. Farms could then be subdivided among children, permitting them to remain on the land. Subdivision of farms had reached an extreme level by the

9. Gino Germani, "Migration and Acculturation," in *Handbook for Social Research in Urban Areas,* ed. Philip Hauser (Paris, 1964), pp. 159–178; R. C. Taylor, "Migration and Motivation," in *Migration,* ed. J. A. Jackson, Sociological Studies no. 2 (Cambridge, 1969), p. 132.

time of the potato famine of the late 1840s. Holdings originally called "a cow's grass" had been subdivided into "a cow's foot," then "a cow's toe," and eventually "a sheep's foot," one-sixteenth part of the original land. The average density of arable land in Connaught and Munster was over 330 persons per square mile. The census of 1841 showed that 45 percent of all Irish farms were of five to fifteen acres; an additional 10 percent of all farming families held less than one acre of land. Population was clearly pressing on resources in many regions.[10]

These measures of rural poverty and overpopulation must be set in their regional context. By 1800 there were in Ireland at least two economies, a modernizing sector in the north and east and a highly traditional one in the west and southwest. Much of the coastal territory from Belfast to Cork, as well as the central plain, produced goods for English markets. In 1841 the Dublin lowlands contained relatively large farms that produced grain and cattle and were connected with the capital by good transportation facilities. Mixed farming also dominated the southeast. The land in the central plain, particularly in the eastern and southeastern portions, was the best tilled and the highest valued in Ireland. In contrast to the rest of the country, Leinster was enclosed by 1800, and farms there were generally larger than in other regions. In addition, demographic pressures were lower in Leinster than in the west. Population was less dense than in Connaught and western Munster, and it was kept so by the demographic decisions of the local population. Both age at first marriage and the incidence of celibacy were higher in eastern counties than in western ones by the 1840s.[11]

Ulster maintained its relative prosperity in a different way. Its major crops were flax, grain, and potatoes; its chief manufacture

10. Freeman, *Pre-Famine Ireland*, pp. 32, 54–55; M. Morineau, "La Pomme de terre au XVIIIe siècle," in *Annales: Economies, Sociétés, Civilisations* 25, no. 6 (November–December 1970):1768.

11. P. Lynch and J. Vaizey, *Guinness's Brewery in the Irish Economy, 1759–1876* (Cambridge, 1960), pp. 9, 17; J. H. Johnson, "The 'Two Irelands' at the Beginning of the Nineteenth Century," in *Irish Geographical Studies*, ed. Nicolas S. Stephens and Robin E. Glasscock (Belfast, 1970), pp. 224, 227–228, 239; Freeman, *Pre-Famine Ireland*, pp. 18, 55, 110, 112, 168–185; Barbara Lewis Solow, *The Land Question and the Irish Economy, 1870–1903* (Cambridge, Mass., 1971), p. 105.

was textiles. Farm sizes were small, 43 percent consisting of 1 to 5 acres and only 4 percent consisting of more than 30 acres; yet the persistence of domestic textile production meant that farming and industry remained complementary occupations: tenants had an additional source of income. The most densely populated area was therefore the least poor. During the eighteenth century the region had entered a stage of "proto-industrialization" and produced textiles, chiefly linen, for export.[12] Although the removal of tariffs on English imports led to a marked contraction of domestic spinning and weaving as well as growing specialization in the Belfast area after 1825, the census of 1841 still recorded 270,495 domestic spinners and 90,436 weavers (30 percent of the nonagricultural employed population of the region). The growth of textile factories and the progress of other industries in Belfast and the Lagan Valley gave the rural population a prospect of alternative employment because of industrial growth in eastern Ulster.[13]

The provinces of Munster and Connaught were touched far less by the forces of modernization. The mountainous west contained the most densely populated parts of the country, except for the linen-producing sections of Ulster, but also the fewest towns. Communications in the west were poorly developed; there were fewer roads and coach services there than in other provinces, and only one canal linked the region with Leinster. Except for Cork and Limerick, coastal towns exported little produce, although agriculture was the occupation of over four-fifths of the employed males in Connaught and three-quarters in Munster in 1841. The area, in fact, was dominated by subsistence agriculture of an exceptionally primitive sort. Only in eastern Munster did commercial farming on the many large desmesnes and grazing farms make much progress before the famine.[14]

Traditional Irish culture had its centers in the mountainous

12. The term is defined in Franklin F. Mendels, "Proto-industrialization: The First Phase of the Industrialization Process," *Journal of Economic History* 32, no. 2 (March 1972):241. Freeman, *Pre-Famine Ireland*, p. 54.
13. Freeman, *Pre-Famine Ireland*, pp. 76–77, 270–273; Henry David Inglis, *A Journey throughout Ireland during the Spring, Summer, and Autumn of 1834*, 3rd ed., 2 vols. (London, 1835), vol. 2, pp. 248–262, 272–283; Conrad Gill, *The Rise of the Irish Linen Industry* (Oxford, 1925), pp. 21–23.
14. Freeman, *Pre-Famine Ireland*, pp. 18, 26, 77, 110, 112.

1. Provinces and counties of Ireland, 1851

coastal areas of Munster and Connaught. Here English had penetrated the least: a majority of the population still spoke Irish in 1851, in contrast to the inhabitants of Leinster and Ulster, where the proportion of Irish speakers was under 25 percent.[15] By the eighteenth century, when single-family farms and enclosed fields dominated in Leinster and the rest of the central plain, an older system of partnership farming of an infield and an outfield — sometimes involving transhumance or seasonal movement to distant pastureland — survived in the west. These kin-based farm clusters, or clachans, were broken up in the east by improving landlords, but they survived and grew in the west under the pressure of rising population.[16] Although Estyn Evans believes that this system was "in decay" by the nineteenth century, rapid change was deferred until after the famine, and clachans had by no means disappeared even in 1900. They were concentrated in what Desmond McCourt calls a "crescentic belt of receding native culture," generally on marginal land in the north, west, and south. These family communes in which land was periodically redistributed to maintain a rough equality in shares as population size changed provided a flexible kin-based framework for the maintenance of traditional agricultural techniques and folk customs.[17] A shift to a more labor-intensive crop, the potato, gave the members work and increased the productivity of the land to accommodate increased numbers.

Ireland in the nineteenth century may have been a relatively backward society, but it was not a static one. The two Irelands were dynamic systems in which domestic industry, agricultural techniques, and the balance between grain and potatoes or between grain and cattle shifted according to demand in urban markets and the size of the farming unit. It was less the backward-

15. Ruth Dudley Edwards, *An Atlas of Irish History* (London, 1973), p. 230.

16. Indeed, because Ireland practiced partible inheritance, an Einzelhof settlement, in the absence of regulatory pressure from the landlord or demographic restriction of the family, could itself become a clachan in two generations; see R. H. Buchanan. "Rural Settlement in Ireland," in *Irish Geographical Studies*, ed. Stephens and Glasscock, pp. 152–153; Desmond McCourt, "The Dynamic Quality of Irish Rural Settlement," in *Man and His Habitat: Essays Presented to Emyr Estyn Evans*, ed. R. H. Buchanan et al. (New York, 1971), pp. 131, 137–139.

17. E. Estyn Evans, *Irish Folkways* (New York, 1957), pp. 23–24; McCourt, "Dynamic Quality," pp. 139–141, 147.

ness of this dynamic system than changes in it and in the economies of other countries during the late eighteenth and the first half of the nineteenth century that provided the setting for migration. Several major strains that put pressure on Irish society can be identified. Most important were population increase, growing commercialization of agriculture, and protoindustrialization. As these processes went on in Ireland, England industrialized. Irish markets were flooded with English goods, and English demand for Irish agricultural products increased. These changing market conditions made changes within the Irish economy and society inevitable. The result was the collapse of Irish domestic industry, an increased rate of farm consolidation, and changes in agricultural techniques, all of which lowered the demand for labor in Ireland. Together these changes laid the groundwork for mass exodus. Dramatic events such as the potato famines and political troubles merely changed the incidence of migration; they cannot be seen as the basic causes of the process.

The direction of modernization in Ireland went from east to west, and the change threatened the subsistence economy of the peasant, based as it was on the cultivation of potatoes and corn by means of spades and a very light plow requiring the labor of two men. This form of agriculture, one of the most labor-intensive known, spread during the eighteenth century as rising English corn prices and population increases led to a shift in Ireland away from livestock rearing. But after the Napoleonic Wars, the relative profitability of grazing increased. As early as the 1830s, rising amounts of livestock were exported to England. The impact of changing prices and lower transport costs made dairying and cattle raising increasingly profitable. Finally, after the famine, when corn production plummeted, Irish agriculture became strongly oriented toward dairying and the raising of livestock.[18]

The beginning of this process in Munster can be seen in the Reverend Horatio Townsend's survey of Cork in 1815. The prevailing agricultural technique was still spade cultivation of potatoes and grain, but around Bandon and Cork he met improving landlords, and in the baronies of Kinalea and Kerricurrihy

18. Freeman, *Pre-Famine Ireland*, p. 68; K. H. Connell, *The Population of Ireland, 1750–1845* (Oxford, 1950), p. 116; Solow, *Land Question*, pp. 94–99.

gentlemen farmers had introduced seed drills, artificial grasses, and improved plows. One farm even had a threshing machine. Tillage in the area, he noted, was increasing daily and improving in quality as crop rotations became more sophisticated and more fertilizer was used. Modernization proceeded slowly but inexorably in southern counties. The vast estates of the Duke of Devonshire, which were allegedly miserable and badly cultivated in 1815, had been improved greatly by the mid-1830s. By 1845 farmers in remote districts of Cork were bringing Scottish iron plows to plowing competitions sponsored by agricultural societies. Crop rotations changed in several areas to include turnips, drilled potatoes, carrots, and beans; more sheep and dairy cattle were grazed per unit of pasture. Local agriculture became increasingly oriented toward foreign markets.[19]

But unemployment of major proportions accompanied this growing commercialization of agriculture. While the consolidation of farms by improving landlords forced many small occupiers to join the ranks of the landless laborers, the shift away from spade cultivation made Irish agriculture less labor intensive.[20] As farming technology improved in Ireland, the demand for labor decreased. Population growth and economic change combined to increase the numbers of the underemployed and the landless. Among the poorer peasants, rural population density increased and farm sizes shrank. At a time when cottiers and small holders were becoming less self-sufficient and more dependent on sources of cash to buy goods and pay rising rents, the prospering sectors of Irish agriculture were not providing jobs in sufficient numbers. George Cornewall Lewis estimated in 1835 that only a third of all Irish laborers could count on steady employment. The reports of the Royal Commission on the State of the Poorer Classes in Ireland document the vast extent of rural unemploy-

19. Rev. Horatio Townsend, *A General and Statistical Survey of the County of Cork*, 2 vols. (Cork, 1815), vol. 1, pp. 197–198, 207, 356–357, 372, 409, 490; vol. 2, pp. 8–29, 48, 53–54, 85, 87–88; Inglis, *Journey throughout Ireland*, vol. 1, pp. 165–166; Johnson, "'Two Irelands,'" p. 228; Edward Wakefield, *An Account of Ireland, Statistical and Political*, 2 vols. (London, 1812), vol. 1, p. 250; James S. Donnelly, Jr., *The Land and the People of Nineteenth-Century Cork: The Rural Economy and the Land Question* (London and Boston, 1975), pp. 37–40.

20. For an account of farm consolidation in Cork before the famine, see Donnelly, *Land and People*, pp. 54–61.

ment by 1835: in parish after parish, cottiers could not find regular work even during the harvest. Permanent jobs were rare. As the cash economy made deep inroads into the Irish countryside, the need to find wage labor to pay the rent and supplement the produce of inadequate holdings turned peasants into a rural proletariat.[21]

The economic position of the cottier or small farmer also worsened as a result of the increasing inability of wives and daughters to supplement family income by means of textile production. During the first half of the nineteenth century domestic industry gradually collapsed in areas outside the Ulster textile districts. In the late 1770s Arthur Young had found widespread production of yarn in Connaught and Munster as well as in rural Ulster. Among the poor, he noted, "spinning is the general business of the women." In addition to cloth, both linen and woolen thread were produced for merchants, who shipped it to English or Ulster weavers. Although linen production had been concentrated in the northeast since the early eighteenth century, markets for the sale of unbleached linen were to be found throughout the northwest in 1815, and linen thread was regularly sold at Connaught fairs. In Cork in 1815, occupiers in the west commonly raised flax, and linens and woolens were manufactured to be sold at fairs. Townsend found that "the trade of weaving, of course, is very general, as well throughout the country as in towns and villages."[22]

After the Napoleonic Wars and the union of England and Ireland, the flagging Irish domestic textile industry began to decline. Attempts to introduce the factory production of cotton failed while linen production shifted increasingly into factories around Belfast, where by 1841 there were more than twenty flax-spinning mills. The importation of English cottons undercut the

21. O'Brien, *Economic History of Ireland*, pp. 10–13.

22. Arthur Young, *A Tour in Ireland . . . in 1776, 1777, and 1778*, 2 vols. (London, 1780), vol. 1, pp. 369–372; L. M. Cullen, *Anglo-Irish Trade, 1660–1800* (Manchester, 1968), pp. 55–57; Freeman, *Pre-Famine Ireland*, p. 83; Johnson, "'Two Irelands,'" pp. 230–231; Gill, *Rise of the Irish Linen Industry*, pp. 122–129; Townsend, *General and Statistical Survey*, vol. 1, pp. 257, 311–312; Wakefield, *Account of Ireland*, pp. 683, 690–691, 709–711; Great Britain, *Parliamentary Papers* (Commons), "Reports from the Select Committee on the State of Ireland," 1825, 8:693.

market for Irish cloth, and when all duties were removed in 1824, the remaining markets for Irish woolens and other homespun cloth contracted sharply. Weavers' wages plummeted during the 1830s. Spinning, however, remained a by-occupation of women in some parts of Ireland until the famine; the census recorded over half a million people with this occupation in 1841, and 40 percent of the 12,180 women and girls residing on estates owned by Trinity College in county Kerry in 1845 called themselves spinners. Although some domestic textile production survived until after the famine, it provided at best an unreliable source of additional family income, leaving those who had depended on a mixture of farming and spinning or weaving for their livelihood without adequate means of support. Remaining in their home communities became increasingly difficult.[23]

In a more highly industrialized and urbanized society, the underemployed population could have migrated a short distance to a town and found work. Unfortunately, Irish cities were few and far between. In 1841 only nine towns had more than 15,000 people, and rates of urban growth were far lower in Ireland than in England or the United States. At a time when cities grew explosively in industrializing countries, Irish towns stagnated. Even during the 1840s, when hundreds of thousands of Irish were leaving their homes in search of work and food, the Irish urban population grew by only 7 percent. Most Irish cities drew only a few outsiders from beyond county boundaries. The rest of their residents were natives or had migrated from within the county.

The Irish avoided their own cities because there were few jobs to be found there. Except for Dublin and Belfast, most Irish cities were sleepy market towns or ports. Their industries consisted mainly of simple crafts, breweries, and flour mills, each of which employed only a few people. Dublin in 1841 had several woolen and worsted factories, as did one or two towns in the south. But in general small urban industries such as potteries, tanneries, and

23. Freeman, *Pre-Famine Ireland*, pp. 87–88; Gill, *Rise of the Irish Linen Industry*, pp. 126, 129; Gearoid O Tuathaigh, *Ireland before the Famine, 1798–1848* (Dublin and London, 1972), p. 118; *Census of Ireland for 1841*, p. 440; "County Kerry: College Estates," Muniments 5, ser. 78, Trinity College, Dublin, pp. 53–56.

glassmaking firms declined in the quarter century before the famine, after protective tariffs were removed. Only in the textile-making area of Ulster was there a growing demand for labor.[24] The tiny proportion of the Irish population that did live in cities shared the same problems of unemployment and underemployment that afflicted the countryside. Travelers' accounts stressed the poverty of the urban Irish and described urban laborers in terms that differed only slightly from their images of rural cottiers.[25]

Although few Irish moved into Irish cities, migration abroad became increasingly attractive, easy, and inexpensive during the first half of the nineteenth century. After 1818, regular steamboat connections between British and Irish towns multiplied, and by the 1820s unregulated traffic in substandard ships flourished between the smaller Irish ports and North America. The standard fare from Ireland to Quebec had declined to thirty shillings by 1831, and after 1834 a flood of remittances to finance passages reached Ireland. Belfast shipping agents reported that as much as one-third of the tickets to the United States in that year had been prepaid in America. By 1830, therefore, transportation abroad was easily and cheaply available.[26]

Migration in the first half of the nineteenth century became an increasingly feasible and rational response to the strains and dislocations of Irish social and economic life. The decision to leave, however, required that potential migrants perceive that their interests would be better served abroad and that they be willing to give up the social and cultural world in which they were raised. When famine intervened, many had no alternative to flight, but in more normal times they had to want to go abroad.

The Decision to Leave

The psychological preconditions of migration spread rapidly in Ireland during the first half of the nineteenth century. As knowledge of the outside world increased, so did awareness that

24. Freeman, *Pre-Famine Ireland*, p. 27.
25. Inglis, *Journey throughout Ireland*, pp. 35, 51–52, 104–105.
26. Adams, *Ireland and the Irish Emigration*, pp. 111–115, 143–145, 150, 160–161, 180–181.

conditions were better elsewhere. Many Irish had, or acquired during this time, aspirations for a different life, and evidence of opportunities abroad was easy to find.

The organization of a national school system in the 1830s and the concomitant spread of the English language not only increased literacy but brought knowledge of a wider English-speaking world to rural Ireland. Ports and provincial towns had their own newspapers, which printed announcements of ship sailings, emigration schemes, and sometimes advertisements for jobs abroad. As early as 1816 these papers carried emigrants' letters listing wages, prices, and conditions of work in other countries. Printers published handbills and broadside ballads about migration and had them circulated in the surrounding area. Posters touting emigration schemes appeared on town walls. The ports and larger county towns were both agencies of social change and disseminators of news about migration.[27] How far into the countryside their influence reached is difficult to estimate, but farmers and their wives went into local towns regularly to market produce. Irish roads and canals made travel relatively easy. Although the Irish railroad network was small and concentrated in the east until after 1850, elaborate coach services linked most provincial towns by the 1830s. By 1841 only a few remote coastal areas in western Kerry, Donegal, Mayo, and Londonderry were more than ten miles from some form of public transport.[28]

Knowledge of England, America, and Europe was clearly spreading in Ireland during the first three decades of the nineteenth century. Thousands of young men had served in the English army during the Napoleonic Wars, and seasonal migration to England increased after 1815 with the advent of cheap, fast steamboat service. Letters home from the growing number of migrants multiplied. Some were even published and circulated as guides for emigrants.[29] When weavers' families in Bandon, Cork, corresponded in the 1820s with relatives in Nova Scotia, they traded information on the cost of living and asked for detailed

27. Ibid., pp. 77–78.
28. Freeman, *Pre-Famine Ireland*, pp. 107–109, 111–115.
29. *Emigrants' Guide* (Westport, 1832), quoted in Adams, *Ireland and the Irish Emigration*, p. 180.

listings of the tools that would be needed in Canada. Behind all their remarks can be discerned the hope for a better life and a sense that conditions in Ireland would not improve. James Huston wrote in 1826 to his uncle, Robert Eedy, "We do not lose sight of going to America as soon as it is possible for us," and in 1827, "There is scarcely any prospect of bettering one's condition in this country."[30]

Similar aspirations for a new life could be found among Irish laborers. The commissioners who investigated the Irish poor in Great Britain wrote in 1836 of migrants' wishes to "improve their condition." A Wexford laborer who had gone to Liverpool asserted that most of his countrymen thought that "if they came to England, their fortunes would be made," because of the higher wages. They expected to be able to find jobs for their children. Those already in England sent back reports that encouraged the belief that a man could easily earn enough for subsistence.[31] More and more Irish probably acquired the wish for a different and a better life during the first half of the nineteenth century as migration became an established fact of social life.

Those seeking to leave Ireland had two choices: seasonal migration to Great Britain or permanent emigration to any one of several English-speaking countries. Seasonal migration to Britain provided an important outlet for those who could not find work at home. During the eighteenth century, Irishmen gradually displaced the Scottish and Welsh laborers who had done much of England's harvesting. Although seasonal movement from Ireland decreased during the French wars because of temporary home demand for agricultural labor and military service, it revived after 1815, when the amount of land devoted to pastures increased. Seasonal labor was diverted to England. Since the difference between the numbers of workers required in summer and in winter in grain-growing areas was great, and was in fact accelerated by adoption of the threshing machine, English farmers in many areas had an intermittent need for extra labor that could not

30. James Huston, Bandon, Ireland, to Robert Eedy, Chaleur Bay, New Bandon, Nova Scotia, March 24, 1826; James Huston, Ballinadee, to Robert Eedy, New Bandon, Nova Scotia, July 29, 1827; both in Cork Archives Council, folder V9.
31. Great Britain, *Parliamentary Papers* (Commons), "Report on the State of the Irish Poor in Great Britain," 1836, 34:vi.

be met by parish residents. Kent hop growers regularly employed large numbers of Irish in the peak season, and the market gardeners around London used Irish labor in the summer as early as 1803.[32]

The first tabulation of this movement came in 1841, when officials counted 57,651 persons sailing to Great Britain from Irish ports during the spring and summer to work temporarily as agricultural laborers. This is a minimum figure, for it was thought that "no inconsiderable number" had embarked from other spots on the coast. Almost all of the recorded migrants were young men: about 30,000 were males between the ages of sixteen and thirty-five. Only 2,000 children and 6,000 women made the trip; therefore, few of these seasonal workers brought their families with them. Most returned home after the harvest.[33]

The incidence of seasonal migration varied dramatically from county to county, and was highest in Connaught and Ulster. In the wheat-growing area of eastern Ireland and in parts of Munster, where the proportion of farms larger than thirty acres was higher than in the rest of Ireland, extra harvest employment was available to local laborers. The incidence of seasonal migration in Munster was particularly low — less than 1 percent of the Munster population in 1841. Connaught, which supplied almost half of the registered seasonal migrants, experienced rates of migration many times higher — 2.7 percent of the Mayo population and 2.1 percent of Roscommon residents. If the average size of the Irish household in 1841 (5.65 persons) is taken into account, these rates become even more striking. In Mayo there was one seasonal migrant for every 6.6 households, in Roscommon one for every 8.3 households, while in Cork only one person for every 227 households left seasonally. Short-term migration was a particularly suitable solution to the employment problem in areas where there were many small holders and few large farms to provide work. In contrast to the prevailing pattern in the south, less than a quarter of the population was landless in most counties of the north and west. Connaught cottiers commonly

32. O'Brien, *Economic History of Ireland*, pp. 52–53; Barbara Kerr, "Irish Immigration into Great Britain, 1798–1838," B. Litt. thesis, Oxford University, 1938, p. 29.
33. *Census of Ireland for 1841*, xxvi-xxvii.

held a scrap of land, and they were not willing to abandon it permanently. Short-term migration permitted them to remain in Ireland and to pay the rent. In parts of Cork, however, landless laborers made up more than 50 percent of the population. These people had less incentive to take seasonal work in England because there was little for them to return home to.[34] The incidence of seasonal migration before the famine was therefore tied to land distribution and local Irish economic structures.

Permanent emigration before the famine also varied by county and by social status. Unfortunately, quantitative evidence of the regional and social incidence of migration before the famine is very limited.[35] We know, however, that the geographic and social origins of emigrants changed over time. A movement that began among Scotch-Irish artisans and small farmers in the north spread first to the farmers in the east and southeast and finally reached the landless laborers and cottiers of the west and southwest. Those who led the way were the ones hit first by economic competition from Britain, not the landless or the cottiers who were initially isolated from the fever to leave by their language, their culture, and their relative lack of dependence on commercial agriculture.

During the eighteenth century a regular but small number of Scotch-Irish sailed from Belfast and Londonderry to the American colonies and to Britain. By 1790, around 250,000 Scotch-Irish lived in the United States, and many thousands more resided in Scotland and England. The rate of emigration to North America

34. S. H. Cousens, "The Regional Pattern of Emigration during the Great Irish Famine," *Transactions and Papers of the Institute of British Geographers*, no. 28 (1960), p. 130.

35. Ideally, an analysis of emigration would specify the birthplaces, occupations, ages, and sexes of those who moved overseas. Unfortunately, none of this information was recorded by the British authorities until 1852; thereafter they listed only the nationalities, ages, and sexes of migrants and the ports between which they sailed. Even then, however, Irish immigrants were ignored, as they were citizens of the United Kingdom. After 1831, meager British port records can be supplemented by census tabulations of inhabitants' birthplaces in the various countries where the Irish settled. For a discussion of the statistical material available on Irish migration, see N. H. Carrier and J. R. Jefferey, *External Migration: A Study of the Available Statistics*, Studies on Medical and Population Subjects no. 6 (London, 1953). Detailed information on Scandinavian emigrants is available in Khristian Hvidt. *Flight to America: The Social Background of 300,000 Danish Emigrants* (New York, 1975).

increased sharply after 1816, and 20,000 came in 1818. Only the relatively well-to-do could have made a transatlantic crossing at this time, since in 1816 the minimum fare from Belfast to Quebec was £6 plus the cost of provisions. Since between one-half and two-thirds of the Belfast passengers went in family groups, the total cost would have been substantial. Newspaper reports confirm this estimate of the travelers' affluence. They identified emigrants as "the strong and active farmers," "tradesmen, shopkeepers, and even professional men." Large numbers of Ulster farmer-weavers also left in 1816 and 1817, when wages in the American textile industry were two to four times higher than those in Ireland and when job prospects were good. When the ending of tariff protection for Irish textiles and crafts came in the early 1820s, more and more artisans and textile workers left the country. In Bandon, Cork, the number of weavers declined from 2,000 in 1815 to about 150 in 1841. Then as grain prices fell, more and more farmers from Leinster joined the exodus.[36]

Using a standard death rate, figures on internal migration, and the decline over time in the population under twenty-one years of age, S. H. Cousens has calculated the proportion of each county's residents who migrated between 1821 and 1841. Ulster and neighboring counties in Leinster and Connaught suffered by far the heaviest losses, a fact that Cousens ascribes to the contraction of the textile industry in an area where a tenant family could raise passage money by selling their interest in the land to the family that took over their lease. At the same time in the centers of subsistence agriculture in the west and south, rates of emigration were low in comparison with those in the more progressive counties of the central plain. Munster showed comparatively little seasonal or overseas migration in this period; it was primarily from the more fertile farming areas of Leinster that outward movement took place in the 1820s and 1830s. Therefore, the more dynamic sectors of the Irish economy furnished the human

36. Adams, *Ireland and the Irish Emigration*, pp. 69–70, 93, 104, 107; Oliver MacDonagh, *A Pattern of Government Growth, 1800–1860* (London, 1961), pp. 22–24; Maldwyn Jones, *American Immigration* (Chicago, 1960), p. 22; Great Britain, *Parliamentary Papers* (Commons), "Select Committee on the State of Ireland," 1825, 8:135; Ó Tuathaigh, *Ireland before the Famine*, p. 119.

material for the first wave of migration overseas.[37] By the 1840s
the zone of highest outflow had shifted south and west to parts of
Leinster and eastern Connaught; it reached eastern Munster in
the 1850s. The link between the land and the peasantry of the far
west was not broken until long after the famine.

Emigration reached its peak during and immediately after the
potato famine. Between 1846 and 1854 approximately 1.75 million Irish left the country. The pattern of migration in a time of
crisis differed somewhat from that of earlier decades, but the
heaviest flows abroad still came from the central and eastern
counties. S. H. Cousens explains the incidence of migration in
the late 1840s largely in terms of local levels of destitution.
Emigration was least in areas where pauperism was either negligible or extremely high. In the former case, people lacked an
incentive to leave; in the latter, they lacked the means. Where
nonagricultural sources of employment were available — in
Ulster, for example — pauperism, poor rates, and consequently
migration were kept at low levels. Where poor rates were much
higher, tenants were discouraged from staying by heavy taxation,
and if a farmer had a cash crop to sell, he could afford passage
abroad. Where these conditions obtained — in most of Leinster,
for example — between 12 and 20 percent of the population
emigrated between 1846 and 1851. The ratepayers in areas of
commercial farming led the flight to America. Only one-third to
one-half as many people left counties with the highest proportion
of landless laborers — Cork, Tipperary, Waterford, and Kilkenny
— as left the Leinster counties, where more families occupied
small farms. Moreover, the poor who did manage to leave chose
different destinations. Exodus to the United States was too
expensive for most laborers during the famine. Migration to
England was of course possible, and many thousands from
Munster walked to eastern ports and crossed the Irish Sea.[38]

After 1851, the proportion of the landless who migrated over-

37. S. H. Cousens, "The Regional Variations in Emigration from Ireland
between 1821 and 1841," *Transactions and Papers of the Institute of British
Geographers* 37 (1965):22–29.

38. Eire, Commission on Emigration and Other Population Problems,
1948–1954, *Report* (Dublin, 1955), p. 119; Cousens, "Regional Pattern of Emigration," pp. 122–123, 126.

seas increased. As economic conditions improved and the rural population declined in size, more of the poor could raise passage money. In addition, the level of remittances reached an average of £850,000 per year between 1848 and 1887, and much of this money was used to finance emigration. Immediate pressures on small holders decreased, while the incentive to leave remained strong for those at the bottom of the economic scale. The increase in the average size of farms that took place after the famine indicates that many who had held only small scraps of land either died or had left the country by 1861. Emigration was exceptionally heavy from parts of Munster with many large farms and a relatively large proportion of landless laborers during the decade after the famine.[39] Yet in the west, where landlords did not forbid the establishment of new farms on marginal land after the famine, cottiers remained and the population continued to increase. Cousens concludes, "The clinging to the land was a social and not an economic phenomenon. . . . From a preliminary survey of the 1871 census it is clear that the break between peasant and land in the poorer parts of the west had not yet occurred. . . . Neither famine nor eviction loosed the hold of the peasantry in much of the west."[40] Areas where the Irish language remained in use, where subsistence farming continued, and where urbanization was least advanced furnished few migrants until the twentieth century. Only after 1900 did Connaught's share of total emigration swell markedly. Since that time, the pattern of exodus has remained remarkably stable. The counties with the highest rates of net emigration have continued to be in Connaught, western Munster, and Donegal, the far western section of Ulster.

No simple Malthusian or economic model can account for the Irish pattern of emigration. Rates of migration from the poorest and the most densely crowded counties lagged far behind those of more prosperous areas of commercial farming. Emigrants were people touched by social and economic changes who had the

39. S. H. Cousens, "Emigration and Demographic Change in Ireland, 1851–1861," *Economic History Review* 14, 2d ser. (August 1961–April 1962):275, 277, 285; Robert E. Kennedy, Jr., *The Irish: Emigration, Marriage, and Fertility* (Berkeley, 1973), pp. 92–95; Eire, Commission on Emigration, *Report*, pp. 130–131, 325; Arnold Schreier, *Ireland and the American Emigration, 1850–1900* (Minneapolis, 1958), pp. 104–110.
40. Cousens, "Emigration and Demographic Change," p. 288.

resources, the will, the information, and the aspirations to move abroad. Where more traditional economic and social structures remained relatively intact, emigration was much less frequent. Social and economic changes were more responsible than poverty or overpopulation for the Irish exodus.

CHAPTER 2

Destinations:
Those Who Chose London

The Irish moved abroad during the first half of the nineteenth century at an accelerating pace. By 1840 more than a million Irish lived outside the country's borders, and during the next decade over a million and a quarter more joined them. Subsequently, migration has continued, although at a much lower level, producing a regular decline in Ireland's population. This sustained exodus has been part of a much wider pattern of rural-to-urban migration within a developing Atlantic economy. The Irish chose to live in foreign cities. Established routes of transportation channeled them abroad to a limited number of destinations, most of them in North America. Between 1876 and 1921, 84 percent of all Irish emigrants from the twenty-six counties of the republic sailed to the United States, and 8 percent chose to settle in Great Britain. But while most Irish went west rather than east, their level of emigration was so high that a small percentage of the flow abroad created large Irish communities in England. In 1841 the British census recorded 126,321 Irish in Scotland and 289,404 in England, most residing in the largest and fastest growing industrial towns. The London Irish numbered 75,000 in that year, while 105,916 resided in Lancashire cities. The Irish became an urban people when they left their homeland.[1]

1. These figures substantially understate the amount of movement into Great Britain; at least 500,000 Irish migrants were missed by port officials and census takers. See Cormac Ó Gráda, "A Note on Nineteenth-Century Irish Emigration Statistics," *Population Studies*, no. 29 (1975), pp. 145–148; for additional informa-

The Irish chose a wide variety of urban destinations, responding to economic, demographic, geographic, and familial influences. The comparative state of the business cycle in the United States and England affected the comparative level of emigration east and west, as did the price of fares. Before 1850 the more affluent migrants crossed the Atlantic, while the poorer could afford transportation only as far as Great Britain. Fares to North America were several pounds higher per person. Over time, however, this difference in American and British migrants' economic statuses lessened, since laborers' wages in Ireland rose after the famine, permitting more of them to pay for transatlantic passages. Moreover, in the growing practice of chain migration, one member of a family was sent abroad to earn the fares for others. By the middle of the 1870s, three-quarters of Irish emigrants to the United States were laborers. By this time the occupational distributions and levels of wealth of the Irish who crossed the Atlantic were probably quite similar to those of Irish settlers in England and Scotland.[2]

Sex and age also influenced a migrant's choice of destination. Before the famine, movement overseas was dominated by men, since Irish women could still find work within the country as servants. In addition, the severe economic pressures during the prefamine period led whole families to migrate simultaneously. The age structures of the Irish-born in Philadelphia and in London in 1851 indicate that families with young children were more likely to choose to travel to England than to the United States. The proportion of Irish-born under the age of fifteen was far lower in Philadelphia than in London. Not only were the economic constraints more limiting when the fares of several people had to be paid, but the perils of crossing the ocean in emigrant ships must have deterred many parents from subjecting their families to the trip. After 1850, however, the age and sex distributions of emigrants show a decrease in the proportion of children and of old people and an increase in the proportion of

tion on Irish patterns of movement, see John Archer Jackson, *The Irish in Britain* (London and Cleveland, 1963), pp. 13–14, and Robert E. Kennedy, Jr., *The Irish: Emigration, Marriage, and Fertility* (Berkeley, 1973), pp. 74–75.

2. Jackson, *Irish in Britain*, Table 9, p. 192; William Forbes Adams, *Ireland and Irish Emigration to the New World from 1815 to the Famine* (New Haven and London, 1932), pp. 194, 220.

unmarried women leaving the country. Over time, age and sex came to have a decreasing influence on the direction of emigration. The young and the single of both sexes came to dominate the migratory flow to both North American and British cities.[3]

Distance combined with transportation facilities also helped to influence destinations. The Irish who traveled to Great Britain moved eastward to the closest major port city. Most of those from Ulster went to Glasgow, while the Leinster Irish went directly east via Dublin to Liverpool and other Lancashire cities.[4] The major stream of emigrants from Munster went to Bristol and London via south-coast Irish ports. A similar distance gradient helped to stream transatlantic migration to Canada and to the northeastern United States.

But the influence of economics, demography, and distance were mediated through the ties of kinship and community. Personal contact with earlier emigrants gave individuals and families a favored destination where help in getting established was available. Chains of migrants went from Irish towns or rural parishes to Glasgow, to London, to Boston, to New York. Several weaving families from Bandon, Cork, followed one after the other to New Bandon, Nova Scotia. Links of kinship, occupation, and residence drew migrants to destinations where they had a claim on someone already settled there. The presence of kin and friends in England, as will be seen in the case of the London community, provided substantial reasons for ignoring the lure of a new life outside British control. Past settlement patterns influenced future ones. Irish migrant communities therefore differed in several ways. Their demographic, occupational, religious, and social composition, as well as their geographic origins, were not identical. The stream of migrants into the London community must be investigated in detail, therefore, if we are to discover what sorts of people chose to settle in the English capital.

3. Lynn H. Lees and John Modell, "The Irish Countryman Urbanized: A Comparative Perspective on the Famine Migration," *Journal of Urban History* 3, no. 4 (August 1977):391–408.

4. For material on the Irish in Scotland, see J. H. Handley, *The Irish in Scotland, 1798–1845*, new ed. (Cork, 1945). Arthur Redford, in his classic study *Labour Migration in England, 1800–1850*, 2d ed. (Manchester, 1964), discusses Irish migration into England.

Irish movement into London began several centuries ago. The presence of Irish beggars in England led to statutes ordering their expulsion in 1243 and again in 1413. A royal proclamation of the late 1680s complained that "in and about the city of London, and in parts in and about Her Majesty's court . . . there did haunt and repair a great multitude of wandering persons, many of whom were men from Ireland." The parish books of St. Giles in the Fields mention poor Irish residents for the first time in 1640, and their presence can be regularly documented thereafter.[5] By the eighteenth century, Irish enclaves were well established. Periodic reports of street fights, court cases, and applications for relief indicate the arrival in central London of an active Irish working-class population. By the 1770s, one in eleven married persons treated at the Westminster Dispensary came from Ireland, and mobs on the rampage during the Gordon Riots of 1780 identified the businesses of quite a few Irish shopkeepers and then attacked the premises.[6]

In 1814 a group of English philanthropists tried to count the Irish in London and found over 14,000 of them, but they added that they had probably missed half of the group. Their figure, in any case, is only a minimum, since they were looking for those in need of charity: irregularly employed laborers' families, the old, the sick, the disabled.[7]

Advances in transportation during the early nineteenth century made a trip to London increasingly easy. By 1825, several steamship companies that made regular trips to Irish ports had registered in the metropolis. Although the cost of direct transportation must have discouraged the poorest migrants, it was not prohibitive: 1,900 agricultural laborers sailed to London in the summer of 1841, most from Cork and Dublin. Fares fluctuated but were well below the cost of a trip to America. In the 1840s, competition between two companies on the Cork-to-London route briefly

5. John Parton, *Some Account of the Hospital and Parish of St. Giles in the Fields, Middlesex* (London, 1822), pp. 299–300; see also Kevin O'Connor, *The Irish in Britain*, rev. ed. (Dublin and London, 1974), p. 13.

6. M. Dorothy George, *London Life in the Eighteenth Century*, 2d ed. (London, 1930), pp. 117–120.

7. Great Britain, *Parliamentary Papers* (Commons), "Report on Mendicity in the Metropolis," 1814–1815, 3:Appendices 4 and 5, 90–95.

lowered deck fares to one shilling a head, with free bread offered as an added inducement. In 1848 the fare for deck passage was five shillings — still remarkably low. Fares to ports on the west coast of England were even lower. Coaches and, by 1841, railroads linked London to Liverpool and Bristol.[8]

Partly as a result of these changes in transportation, movement by the Irish into the metropolis increased rapidly during the 1820s and 1830s, decades of intensified emigration from Ireland. By 1841, between 75,000 and 80,000 Irish had settled in the English capital. Ten years later, the number had reached 109,000. (See Table 1.1.) In order to sustain these totals, a minimum of 46,000 Irish-born had to enter London during the decade of the potato famine. Between 1841 and 1851 the Irish accounted for 14 percent of the permanent migration into the metropolis from all places outside the city limits. Irish movement into the capital reached its peak during the years of mass Irish flight from hunger and disease. Thereafter, Irish migration into the metropolis gradually decreased, never exceeding 5 percent of the net decadal inflow during the rest of the nineteenth century. A regular decline in the number of resident Irish-born resulted. By 1891 only 66,000 Irish-born remained.[9]

The London Irish colony was much larger than the census tabulations indicated, however. Only the Irish-born were counted; the returns would have been swelled considerably by the addition of the second and third generations. Indeed, the English-born children of Irish parents made up 30 percent of a sample of Irish households in five London parishes in 1851, and by 1861 this rate had risen to 40 percent.[10] If these proportions are assumed to have prevailed throughout London, the minimum size of the London Irish community becomes 156,000 for 1851 and 178,000 for 1861. These figures still underestimate the size of the group,

8. Henry Mayhew, *London Labour and the London Poor*, 4 vols. (New York, 1968), vol. 1, p. 113; John Garwood, *The Million-Peopled City* (London, 1853), pp. 299–300; W. T. Jackman, *The Development of Transportation in Modern England,* 2 vols. (Cambridge, 1916), vol. 2, pp. 553, 564.

9. H. A. Shannon, "Migration and the Growth of London, 1841–1891," *Economic History Review* 5 (1935):84.

10. These and all other numerical references to the London Irish refer to a five-parish sample drawn from the London manuscript census schedules of 1851 and 1861. For information on the way the sample was selected, see Appendix A.

Table 1.1. Birthplaces of inhabitants of London, 1841–1891

	Census-year population (in thousands)											
	1841		1851		1861		1871		1881		1891	
Birthplace	Number	Percent	Number	Percent	Number	Percent	Number	Percent	Number	Percent	Number	Percent
London	1,264±25	64.9	1,457	61.7	1,741	62.1	2,056	63.2	2,414	63.3	2,778	66.0
Elsewhere in England	562±25	28.9	724	30.6	852	30.4	974	29.9	1,155	30.3	1,168	27.8
Scotland	26	1.3	30	1.3	36	1.3	41	1.3	50	1.3	53	1.3
Ireland	75	3.9	109	4.6	107	3.8	91	2.8	81	2.1	66	1.6
Abroad	20	1.0	43	1.8	68	2.4	92	2.8	112	2.9	144	3.4
Total	1,947	100.0	2,363	100.0	2,804	100.0	3,254	100.0	3,812	99.9	4,209	100.1

Source: H. A. Shannon, "Migration and the Growth of London, 1841–1891," *Economic History Review* 5, no. 2 (1935):81, 83.

inasmuch as they include only those descendants who lived in households with at least one Irish-born member. Others cannot be distinguished from residents of English ancestry. The decreasing size of the London Irish population reported in the census is therefore deceptive. The extent to which second- and third-generation Irish acknowledged their ethnic ties remains to be established, but their presence in the metropolis is undeniable. The Irish were easily the biggest and indeed the only large foreign group in London until the last quarter of the nineteenth century, when migration from eastern Europe and Russia created a substantial Jewish community.

Migration is a selective process. Neither the Irish who left Ireland nor those who settled in London were a random sample of the Irish population. The most common demographic differences between migrants and the total population of a city or a country occur in the composition by age and sex. Migrants usually possess in an extreme form characteristics of an urban population, but they often exhibit the reverse of certain national traits. In general, an excess of women among migrants creates a disproportionate number of females in cities; it also decreases the percentage of women in the area of origin. And because the young and the single predominate in both long- and short-distance moves, people between the ages of fifteen and thirty-four (64 percent among those leaving Ireland in 1852–1854, 70 percent in 1861–1871) are especially numerous among migrants. Although the effects of migration on the age and sex structure of an urban population vary with the size of the city, the distance of migration, and the local demand for labor, the net result among migrants is generally the same: a low ratio of men to women and a disproportionate number of young adults. The London Irish were no exception to this pattern, but their demographic structure in 1850 reveals some interesting modifications of it.[11]

Selective migration created a group in London unbalanced in both age composition and sex ratio. A steady movement of young adults into the capital and the concomitant aging of earlier

11. Adna Ferrin Weber, *The Growth of Cities in the Nineteenth Century*, Cornell University Reprints in Urban Studies (Ithaca, 1963), pp. 276–281; Brinley Thomas, *Migration and Economic Growth* (London, 1954), p. 73.

migrants produced a population heavily dominated by adults. The largest age groups were those between twenty and forty-five, which accounted for 53 percent of the total Irish-born population in 1851. At the same time, the effects of the extraordinary mass exodus during the potato famine can be seen in the demographic composition of the London Irish. The extreme pressures of eviction, famine, and disease forced families to flee the country. As a result, the London Irish community in 1851 included a relatively large proportion of children and adults over thirty-four among recent migrants. Of the 635 people sampled who can be identified as having left Ireland between 1846 and 1851, 43 percent were over the age of thirty-four and 17 percent were below the age of fifteen. The famine brought many who normally would not have migrated.

Selective migration also affected the sex ratios of the London Irish. Instead of the pattern common to closed populations — a steady movement from an excess of males at birth to a growing majority of females — the balance between Irish-born men and women in London shifted back and forth. In the five-parish sample, men outnumbered women among the Irish-born aged five to fourteen, forty-five to fifty-four, and seventy to eighty. Different patterns of migration for each sex explain this irregularity. Women, who could find work as domestic servants as adolescents, came to London at earlier ages than men. The largest cohort of Irish-born women in the metropolis was composed of those between twenty and twenty-four, but the largest group of men fell between the ages of thirty and thirty-four. Although women outnumbered men at all ages from fifteen to forty-five, an increasing level of migration into London by adult males reduced and finally overcame this disparity. A steady increase in the proportion of women was postponed until the age cohorts over fifty-five. The relative proportions of Irish-born males and females varied considerably, however, among London areas. The predominance of Irish women was most marked in affluent districts, where the demand for servants was highest. Just as in Paris, a large female labor force maintained the parishes of the rich. In poorer areas, where there was less demand for female labor, the excess of Irish women was far less. Men outnumbered women only in riverside parishes, where large numbers of them were drawn to work on the docks or on construction jobs. (See Table A.1, Appendix B.)

A large segment of the migrating Irish consisted of family groups. Among the 524 sampled households with residents under fourteen, 44 percent had at least one Irish-born child in 1851. Almost half of the sampled married couples with young children had married in Ireland and had started their families there. Of course, they did not always come to London together. John O'Neill, a Munster shoemaker, left his wife and children in Waterford while he established himself in London, but they soon joined him. Many family migrations took place in stages. As we have seen, families regularly sent one member ahead to England or the United States to earn passage money for the rest. A number of the Irish among the street people interviewed in the 1850s by Henry Mayhew, a London journalist, reported that the members of their families had migrated sequentially as the money for their transportation was accumulated.[12]

Irish families in London had not resided elsewhere in England for long periods of time. Perhaps the first member of a migration chain tried his or her luck in other areas before bringing kin to England, but a pattern of stage migration to London from a series of smaller English towns was not common. Only 5 percent of the 901 English-born children in the 1851 sample of Irish families were born outside the metropolis, while 95 percent were born in London. The few who had stopped for a time after arriving in England had lived in the south Midlands and the counties adjoining the capital: Surrey, Sussex, Oxford, Buckinghamshire, Berkshire. Although stage migrations to the capital from northern areas more than doubled by 1861, they still involved very few families; only 2 percent of migrants' English-born children were born north of Chester. The married who chose to settle in London came quickly to the capital, moving eastward through counties in south and central England. Their movement was less a gradual drift into London via smaller and simpler urban settlements than a purposeful journey from their homes in Ireland to the largest, most complex city in Great Britain.

12. John O'Neill, "Fifty Years' Experience of an Irish Shoemaker in London," *St. Crispin* 1 (1869):240–241, 254, 296; James H. Tuke, *A Visit to Connaught in the Autumn of 1847*, 2d ed. (London, 1848), pp. 46–47, 49; Mayhew, *London Labour*, vol. 1, pp. 115, 121.

We have established so far that most of the London Irish-born were young adults, that women slightly outnumbered men, and that many migrants brought their families with them, but we need to know far more about these people. Where were they born? What were their occupations in Ireland? Both John Garwood and the Reverend Samuel Garrett of Trinity Church, Lincoln's Inn Fields, said that most of the London Irish had come from Munster, and Garwood pointed especially to the counties of Cork and Kerry. Most of the Irish residing in Church Lane, St. Giles, in 1848 came from Cork.[13] Henry Mayhew thought that "the great immigration into London is from Cork"; most of the Irish crossing sweepers he met came from that county.[14] Some systematic information is available from census takers who, after asking inhabitants about their places of birth, recorded more than the word "Ireland" on their census forms. These partial returns cannot be shown to be representative of the entire Irish migrant population, but the profile of county origins they supply agrees with contemporary opinion. As London residents thought, by far the largest share of the Irish in their midst came from Munster, especially the county of Cork. Twenty percent of the sampled Irish-born in 1861 were assigned birthplaces, and two-thirds of these came from western Munster. Over 70 percent of the 857 Irish-born in London workhouses in 1871 for whom birthplaces were listed came from these same counties. Although emigration from Munster had been less heavy before the famine than that from Leinster and Ulster, movement out between 1821 and 1841, particularly by weavers and landless laborers, had been substantial. London was an easy alternative destination for those who could not afford the fare to the United States. Eastern Leinster also supplied a large proportion of the Irish who moved into the capital. Census and workhouse listings indicate that one-fifth to one-quarter of the London Irish came from this province.

It is not possible to establish the proportions of the London Irish that came from rural areas and from small villages or towns. Both sorts migrated to London; yet the Irish countryside probably

---

13. Garwood, *Million-Peopled City*, p. 304; Samuel Garrett, "The Irish in London," in *Motives for Missions* (London, 1853), p. 192; "Report of a Committee of the Statistical Society of London on . . . Church Lane, St. Giles," *Journal of the [Royal] Statistical Society* 11 (1848):16.

14. Mayhew, *London Labour*, vol. 1, pp. 109, 113; vol. 2, pp. 481–483.

furnished by far the greater part. The fact that at least 60,000 Irish moved into the metropolis between 1841 and 1861, a period of marked exodus of the landless from Munster, gives prima facie evidence that the rural component was substantial. Contemporaries confirm this judgment. Mayhew thought that most Irish construction workers and street sellers in London had worked on the land before migrating and reported the histories of some of these people to prove his point. As one of his informants put it:

I had a bit o'land, yer honor, in County Limerick. Well, it wasn't just a farrum, nor what ye would call a garden here, but my father lived and died on it — glory be to God! — and brought up me and my sister on it. It was about an acre, and the taties was well known to be good. But the sore times came, and the taties was afflicted, and the wife and me — I have no childer — hadn't a bite nor a sup, but wather to live on, and an igg or two. I filt the famine a-comin'. I saw people a-feedin' on the wild green things, and as I had not such a bad take, I got Mr. —— [he was the head master's agent] to give me 28s. for possession in quietness, and I sould some poultry I had. . . . The wife and me walked to Dublin, though we had betther have gone by the 'long say', but I didn't understand it thin, and we got to Liverpool. Then sorrow's the taste of worruk could I git, beyant oncte 3s. for two days of harrud porthering, that broke my back half in two. I was tould, I'd do betther in London, and so Glory be to God! I have — perhaps I have.[15]

This man was typical of many who gave up their small plots of land and resettled their families in England during the 1840s and 1850s.

The London Irish community did not, however, consist exclusively of people from rural backgrounds. There was a small but important movement by skilled workers and by middle-class people from Irish cities to the English capital. Many Irish craftsmen came to London. John O'Neill, a shoemaker who migrated to the capital in 1808, had lived in Waterford, a medium-sized port in the southeast of Munster. His circle of friends in London included several other Irish craftsmen from Waterford and Carrick, a neighboring town. Henry Mayhew met tailors from Cork and Dublin, as well as a shoemaker from Tralee, all of whom came to London looking for jobs. A young

15. Ibid., vol. 1, pp. 105–106.

Irish fruit seller told Mayhew of her family's migration to England: her father had been a Dublin mason who around 1830 had brought his wife and children to Liverpool and then on to London when he could find no work in the Merseyside area.[16]

A small but culturally significant number of upper- and middle-class Irish also came to London. Irish politicians and gentry came to London periodically for the social and parliamentary seasons. Aspiring actors, playwrights, and poets imitated the Goldsmiths and Garricks of the past and sought their fortunes in the English capital. George Bernard Shaw's mother, an Irish mezzo-soprano, followed her manager to London in 1863. Shaw joined her in 1876. The family of William Butler Yeats moved to London when Yeats was a child so that his father, Jack Yeats, could advance his career as a painter. A continuing stream of authors, journalists, and law students came to London seeking jobs and recognition. Barristers were of course dependent on the London Inns of Court for their legal training. London newspapers attracted others; the *Times* had a number of Irish employees during the middle and late nineteenth century, as did the *Morning Herald*. Around 1850 several reporters from the *Cork Examiner* joined the *Northern Daily Times* in Liverpool. London papers were the next step.[17]

Three sorts of Irish came to London, and vastly different prospects lay before them. A small number of middle-class Irish, many Protestant and culturally similar to the English, chose the metropolis for its professional and educational opportunities. They were likely to live in heavily English neighborhoods and could assimilate relatively easily into the London middle class. Craftsmen from Irish villages and small towns also traveled to London for training and job opportunities. These people would find it difficult but not impossible to join the social world of the London artisan and trade unionist. But the largest group and by far the most disadvantaged consisted of the rural laborers and

16. O'Neill, "Fifty Years' Experience," *St. Crispin* 1:240, 323, and 2:27, 54; Mayhew, *London Labour*, vol. 1, pp. 514, 522.

17. George Bernard Shaw, *Collected Letters*, ed. Dan H. Lawrence (London, 1965), pp. 3, 19; William Butler Yeats, *The Autobiography of William Butler Yeats* (New York, 1958), p. 16; Francis A. Fahey and D. J. O'Donaghue, *Ireland in London*, Evening Telegraph Reprints no. 7 (Dublin, 1887), pp. 153–154; Justin MacCarthy, *The Story of an Irishman* (London, 1904), pp. 82, 102–103, 115.

small farmers who lacked skills and urban experience. By choosing to enter the English urban hierarchy via its largest, most complex city, they compounded their social and economic difficulties.

CHAPTER 3

The Social Geography
of Irish London

London's housing and labor markets provided a framework within which migrants adapted to the city. Their choice of neighborhood and residence tied them into a local social system and determined the physical environment of their daily lives. Reconstruction of their position in London's social geography reveals important elements of the urban life-style of the Irish.

The Changing Pattern of Irish Settlement

The pattern of Irish settlement that evolved in London should be viewed as a form of adaptation to urban life. Newcomers had to choose a residence, and only certain options were open to them. Learning the nature of those options was the first step in accommodation to the city. Patterns of land use and the existing housing supply determined the areas into which it was possible to move. At the same time, economic constraints in the form of high rents and transport costs closed off large parts of the metropolis. In consequence, migrants usually moved into the older areas, where residential competition was least intense.[1]

Irish migrants first settled during the reigns of the Tudors in the more notorious, run-down quarters of London's inner ring, but they stayed outside the City, where guild rules blocked employment opportunities. From the reign of Elizabeth I, the

1. This model of ethnic separation is drawn from Stanley Lieberson, *Ethnic Patterns in American Cities* (New York, 1963), pp. 4–6.

whole area of St. Giles and Holborn was designated as the haunt of vagrants and other rogues and vagabonds, some of whom were Irish.[2] Other Irish chose Whitechapel, which long before the nineteenth century sheltered most of London's foreign population. The Irish there settled close to the port to live among the disreputable lodging houses, brothels, taverns, and dolly shops that choked the waterfront.[3] Once a few Irish had moved into these areas, later Irish immigrants had a great incentive to locate nearby. As more and more Irish came, they displaced earlier residents, who voluntarily left the area either in reaction to the Celtic influx or as a continuation of normal movement within London. The result was the establishment of small centers in courts and alleys where the concentration of Irish households rose to over 75 percent of the local population.

As migration intensified and London grew, the Irish spread far beyond their seventeenth- and early-eighteenth-century centers of residence, near but north of the Thames. By 1815 more than 700 of them lived in one small section of Marylebone, and more than 1,500 were located in Southwark and Bermondsey, south of the river.[4] Still, as late as 1850 most Irish had settled in the inner industrial district, the area between Westminster and Whitechapel, Holborn and Southwark. (See Map 2a.) Like newcomers to American cities, Irish immigrants to London moved into areas that provided both a demand for unskilled labor and a supply of relatively cheap housing. They and the foreign-born in London congregated where both density and death rates were high, predominantly in districts paralleling the Thames. They had created not a ghetto but a string of settlements tucked into the tumbledown corners of working-class London.

The scattered nature of this pattern of settlement must be stressed. By 1851 Irish migrants had moved into every registrar general's district of the metropolis. The populations of even the most remote districts contained several hundred Irish-born. In Lewisham and Woolwich, 2.8 percent of the population were

2. John Parton, *Some Account of the Hospital and Parish of St. Giles in the Fields, Middlesex* (London, 1822), pp. 299–300.
3. D. I. Munby, *Industry and Planning in Stepney* (London, 1951), p. 20; Millicent Rose, *The East End of London* (London, 1951), pp. 52, 55.
4. Great Britain, *Parliamentary Papers* (Commons), "Select Committee on Mendicity in the Metropolis," 1814–1815, 3:325.

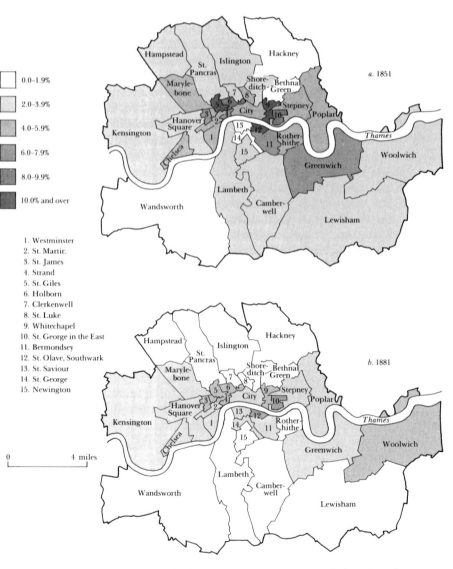

2. Distribution of London Irish-born as percentage of total population of London census districts, 1851 and 1881

Irish-born, in Hampstead 2.0 percent. At the same time, the population of none of the central districts was more than 15 percent Irish-born. Only in St. Giles in the Fields, St. Olave, Southwark, and Whitechapel did the Irish-born number more than 10 percent of all residents in 1851. (See Map 2a.)

These Irish colonies tucked into every corner of the metropolis simultaneously possessed the qualities of great mobility and great stability. The Irish held certain streets in central London and the East End with great tenacity for decades. Indeed, Charles Booth regularly found Irish colonies in 1900 in the same locations where they had been fifty years earlier. Nevertheless, within Irish areas the residents of any one dwelling changed rapidly. Joseph Oppenheim, who visited tenements in St. Giles in 1861 for the London City Mission, found that in one month half the families in Monmouth Court had been replaced.[5] Observers of the Irish poor thought that they moved constantly. In the words of one government school inspector assigned to London in the 1860s, they were "rolling stones" who gathered "but little of the moss of civilization."[6] Yet geographic mobility does not necessitate moving out of one's chosen neighborhood. The evidence does not support the stereotype of the poor as a free-floating underclass without roots in any one geographic area.

Both in England and in the United States nineteenth-century urban populations were highly mobile, but most moves involved only short distances. Peter Knights has shown that in Boston between 1830 and 1860 one household in three moved every year and that the foreign-born were nearly twice as mobile as natives. Yet the foreign-born moved primarily within the urban core before 1850. The need of the employed to live near their work kept mobile working families from moving very far.[7]

The same pattern held for the London Irish. The vast majority of the sampled second generation of all ages were born in the same parish where their parents resided in 1851 or 1861. Several

5. Joseph Oppenheim, unpublished "Visitors' Book," 1861–1862, St. Giles in the Fields, London, p. 70.

6. P. Le Page Renouf, "General Report for the Year 1865 on the Roman Catholic Schools in the Southern Division of England," *Report of the Committee of Council on Education* (London, 1866), p. 277.

7. Peter R. Knights, *The Plain People of Boston, 1830–1860: A Study in City Growth* (New York, 1971), pp. 61–62, 64–65.

families can be traced back and forth several times across the Southwark and Bermondsey boundary, but their residences remained within a radius of approximately one-half mile. Except when decreases in the supply of housing threatened a whole district, most changes of residence probably involved only a short-distance move. Charles Booth described this manner of relocation: "Such people never stay very long in any place: they are constantly shifting; they get evicted, their things are put into the streets, but they manage to borrow enough to get a room somewhere near, and get along somehow for a time."[8]

This pattern of rapid circulation within a small area was disrupted and altered by the many demolitions and so-called improvements carried on in the metropolis during the century. Threatened by railroads, street-widening schemes, and slum-clearance projects, few working-class parishes emerged unscathed. H. J. Dyos has estimated that 76,000 were displaced in London by railway construction between 1853 and 1901. When the Southeastern Railway and London Bridge Station were built, destruction of houses within the parish brought about a deceptive lowering of the density per acre: although the total population decreased, from 1841 to 1861 the average number of occupants per dwelling increased. Many would not or could not move beyond adjoining streets. Similarly, the demolitions in St. Giles for New Oxford Street were followed by a substantial rise in the population of remaining streets in the Rookery.[9] Some, of course, had to leave, owing in large part to the fact that before 1880 no provisions were made for the relocation of those evicted by these large construction projects. In consequence, Booth found a substantial movement from central London out to the far corner of Kensington as "the dregs" were thrown out of their rookeries. According to a study of Lambeth residential displacement, most of the

8. Charles Booth, *Life and Labour of the People of London*, ser. 3, *Religious Influences* (London, 1902), vol. 7, p. 263.
9. For a compilation of census returns for London districts and various measures of density and population change, see H. Price-Williams, "The Population of London, 1801–1881," *Journal of the [Royal] Statistical Society* 47 (1885):349–432. Also Horace Mann, "Statement of the Mortality Prevailing in Church Lane during the Last Ten Years . . .," *Journal of the [Royal] Statistical Society* 11 (1848):19–20; H. J. Dyos, "Railways and Housing in Victorian London," *Journal of Transport History* 2 (1955–1956):14–18.

residents who fled from the railway in 1858 moved at least one-half mile away.[10]

As London's economic geography changed, all groups tended to move to the periphery. (See Table 2.1.) By 1861 such inner districts as Westminster, the City, and St. Giles were experiencing steady population losses, although the metropolis as a whole was expanding at rates of more than 15 percent per decade.[11] The transformation of the center city from a manufacturing area to a commercial quarter led more and more of London's population to move to outer districts. Forced out by rising rents and demolition, or attracted by the socially segregated housing estates that sprouted like mushrooms in suburban areas, many chose to commute or to look for work outside the central districts. But if all were mobile, all were not equally so. The cost of transport kept the poorest in central London. Both the Irish and the foreign-born showed a smaller tendency than natives or English migrants to settle in outer metropolitan districts until at least 1880, although even for them relocation was inevitable. Throughout the 1860s the Marist fathers of Spitalfields complained bitterly that their flock was being driven away by the railroads and the influx of Eastern European Jews.[12] By 1881 the older Irish communities of the inner ring were fast disappearing; fewer than half as many Irish lived in St. Giles, Whitechapel, and Southwark as had done so twenty years earlier. (See Map 2b.)

These moves of longer distances were influenced by the structure of the London labor market and the geography of the city. London was divided into three distinct sections separated both by tradition and by physical barriers: the settled area south of the Thames, the West End, and the East End. The Thames effectively

10. For a survey of parliamentary action on rehousing workers, see London County Council, *Housing of the Working Class in London* (London, 1913). Percy J. Edwards, in *History of London Street Improvements* (London, 1898), pp. 59–71, describes conflicts over rehousing that developed out of the construction of Rosebury Avenue and the widening of Tooley Street, Southwark. See also Booth, *Life and Labour*, ser. 3, *Religious Influences*, vol. 3, pp. 141, 151–152; Henry Claxton Binford, "Residential Displacement by Railway Construction in North Lambeth, 1858–1861," unpublished master's thesis, University of Sussex, 1967, p. 4.

11. Price-Williams, "Population of London," pp. 388–395.

12. Father S. E. Chauvrain, "The Mission and Its Work," unpublished report, file "Historica," Archive of the Marist Fathers, Rome, n.d.

Table 2.1. Changing settlement patterns of London residents, 1851–1881: Distribution between central and peripheral districts, by birthplace

Birthplace	1851		1861		1881	
	Central district[a]	Peripheral district[b]	Central district[a]	Peripheral district[b]	Central district[a]	Peripheral district[b]
London	55.7%	44.3%	48.6%	51.4%	38.2%	61.8%
Elsewhere in Great Britain	48.3	51.7	41.3	58.7	29.3	70.7
Ireland	62.3	37.7	56.8	43.3	42.1	57.9
Other countries	67.1	32.9	64.6	35.4	40.2	59.8
All birthplaces	53.7%	46.3%	48.5%	51.5%	35.2%	64.8%

Source: Census of England, 1851 and 1861; Charles Booth, *Life and Labour of the People of London*, ser. 1, *Poverty*, vol. 3, pp. 114–117, 150–166.

[a] St. George Hanover Square, Westminster, St. Giles, Strand, Holborn, City, Shoreditch, Bethnal Green Whitechapel, St. George in the East, Stepney, Mile End.

[b] Hammersmith, Kensington, Chelsea, Marylebone, Hampstead, St. Pancras, Islington, Hackney, Poplar, Lambeth, Wandsworth, Camberwell, Greenwich, Lewisham, Woolwich.

stopped most movement from north to south, except for those who could afford to travel by coach or omnibus, and the distance from east to west kept workers within their own enclaves. Because the city was unified neither politically nor economically, workers responded to local rather than metropolitan conditions. Even the influence of trade associations was often limited to one geographic area. Not only was daily movement over long distances outside one of the three sections inhibited by ignorance and transport difficulties; in the long run circulation patterns were shaped by these same factors.[13]

The threefold division of London marked out the large areas within which Irish families were most likely to move. Once settled in the East End, they tended to remain there; typical changes of residence for the Whitechapel Irish were to and from Stepney or St. George in the East. Very few moved to Whitechapel after they had lived elsewhere in London. The south was a similarly closed area of circulation. Most of the Irish who came to St. Olave in Southwark or St. George in Camberwell from other parts of London had lived previously in riverside districts south of the Thames. The direction of movement was definitely toward the south: the Camberwell Irish had drifted into the district from areas closer to the river, while virtually no migrants' families in St. Olave came from parishes not adjoining the river. Movement between central London and the West End was more common than a transfer of population from the center to the east or south. Paths of circulation went both ways — into Kensington from all northern areas west of Hackney and into St. Giles from virtually every part of the west, center, and north. St. Giles not only sent migrants to other parts of London after they had lived for a time in the old Irish quarter but attracted a substantial number of people back into central London. The Irish moved therefore in a complex but regular pattern from the center to the periphery and sometimes back again to the oldest Irish settlements of the metropolis.[14]

13. E. J. Hobsbawm, "The Nineteenth-Century London Labour Market," in Centre for Urban Studies, *London: Aspects of Change* (London, 1961) pp. 7–9.

14. This description of Irish movement inside London is drawn from cross tabulations of current residences and the birthplaces of London-born children in the Irish households sampled in 1851 and 1861.

The pattern of Irish settlement in London, then, combines elements of both mobility and stability. The cast of characters changed constantly, as unknown numbers regularly left and entered the city. At the same time, the daily instability of working-class life produced a population that was highly mobile within small areas; unusual pressures triggered longer moves, usually within the three major geographic divisions of London. Yet how much changed for the Irish as they hopped from room to room? The hold of neighborhood and district remained strong. And as we shall see, the Irish repeated in their new locations their pattern of clustered settlements in working-class neighborhoods. As Booth said, "the pressure of poverty and want has made these poor people movable, but they are very gregarious, and wherever the unskilled labour, which is what they have to offer, is in demand, they readily form new communities."[15] Mobility did not produce geographic assimilation.

The Social Geography of Five Irish Neighborhoods

Robert Park made explicit a link between urban geography and social structure when he wrote that "physical distances so frequently are, or seem to be, the indexes of social distances."[16] In other words, the degree and type of geographic segregation reveals the nature of social segregation. In mid-nineteenth-century London, the pattern of ethnic residential settlement reflected a symbiotic but hierarchical relationship between English and Irish. Although Irish migrants were not ostracized and locked in an urban ghetto, most were relegated to the side streets and back alleys of their neighborhoods. They lived close to the English, but they remained apart. Ethnicity, operating within constraints posed by London's economic and residential geography, shaped patterns of Irish settlement. The result was a chain of Irish buildings and enclaves located within English working-class territory. Although neighborhoods were shared, neither geographic nor social assimilation took place. In the tiny world of a London street, the social distance between a court and a corner house was vast.

15. Charles Booth, *Life and Labour*, ser. 3, *Religious Influences*, vol. 7, p. 243.
16. Robert Park, *Human Communities* (Glencoe, Ill., 1952), p. 177.

Irish newcomers flocked to London's back streets, to the haunts of the nearly destitute. Indeed, contemporaries identified Irish London with the city's slums.[17] But the slums were not of their making. In areas of high density or rapid growth, every scrap of land could become a building site; plots next to factories or in backyards were regularly covered with tiny cottages or two-story brick dwellings. Tucked behind row houses, railway viaducts, and gasworks, the homes of the Irish were separated by the pattern of land use from more desirable housing. These places were the residues of the housing supply in districts where there was a demand for and a supply of casual labor.[18] Typical was the maze of streets in the St. Giles Rookery. Tenements enclosed certain courts on all four sides, leaving only a tunnel-like passage for escape. These areas could have been visible to outsiders only from the air. Automatic physical segregation resulted from the rental of quarters in such places. Irish London was a network of similar abominations stretched across the metropolis. While the poorest ended up in the centers of these areas, those slightly better off could pull themselves up and out to the fringes. Circles of lessening Irish density are traceable around these cores of particularly heavy settlement, although some streets even within the core areas always remained noticeably free of Celtic inhabitants.

I have investigated in detail five Irish neighborhoods in London, three in central areas of relatively heavy Irish concentration and two in the outer ring of suburban parishes where the proportion of Irish was much smaller. (See Map 3.) While these districts cannot be shown statistically to be representative of the entire London Irish population, they typify conditions in other Irish neighborhoods I have studied and have characteristics that mark them out for special attention. (Additional information on the selection of parishes in the sample is provided in Appendix A.) The Irish colonies in St. Giles, Whitechapel, and Southwark were the oldest and largest districts of Irish settlement in London;

17. John Hollingshead, *Ragged London in 1861* (London, 1861), pp. 44–46, 88–89, 107, 147; Thomas Archer, *The Pauper, the Thief, and the Convict: Sketches of Some of Their Homes, Haunts, and Habits* (London, 1865), pp. 92, 94.
18. H. J. Dyos, "The Slums of Victorian London," *Victorian Studies* 11, no. 1 (September 1967):25–27, 30.

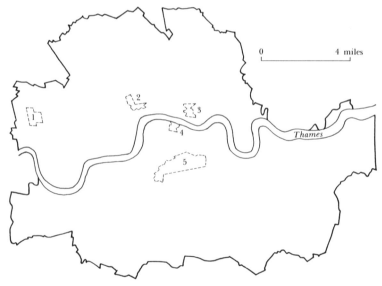

0   4 miles

Thames

1. St. John, Notting Hill, Kensington
2. St. Giles in the Fields
3. Aldgate, Whitechapel
4. St. Olave, Southwark
5. St. George, Camberwell

3. Sampled London census districts

in addition, they were districts of first reception for newcomers, making them particularly interesting to a researcher seeking the patterns of adaptation to the city chosen by Irish immigrants. The movement of the Irish over time into suburban parishes of the West End and South (see Map 2) suggested that Irish neighborhoods in these areas should also be examined. In order to discover whether the suburban Irish behaved differently from their compatriots in central London, I selected two parishes having substantially different social and economic profiles from my earlier choices, ones into which the Irish moved when they left central London. Few differences emerged in either 1851 or 1861, the years most intensively studied. Their districts of residence had little effect on the way Irish migrants lived in the capital.

The oldest and most notorious of the Irish districts lay in the middle and southern sections of St. Giles in the Fields. Although the northern part of the parish, which borders the British Museum and Russell Square, remained as elegant as the Bloomsbury section of the Bedford estate, the southern half of St. Giles deteriorated during the eighteenth century into one of the foulest places in London. During the seventeenth century, parish authorities attempted periodically to clear out all newcomers, pregnant women, and cellar dwellers by directing the beadles to remove such undesirables, but to no avail. These efforts to exclude the Irish and other poor tenants failed completely when large seventeenth-century houses built by wealthy parishioners were given up by their owners. As a result, Jacobean mansions were replaced by gin shops and narrow courts — the homes of ragamuffins and ruffians, "rendezvous and nursery for lewd women" — portrayed so vividly by Hogarth in many of his pictures of lower-class London.[19] The area around Church Lane was known to outsiders as the Rookery or the Holy Land, even Little Dublin, because of its Celtic population.

It was one dense mass of houses, through which curved narrow tortuous lanes, from which again diverged close courts — one great mass, as if the houses had originally been one block of stone eaten by slugs into numberless small chambers and connecting passages. The lanes were thronged with loiterers; and stagnant gutters, and piles of garbage and filth infested the air. In the windows, wisps of straw, old hats, and lumps of bed tick or brown paper alternated with shivered panes of broken glass; the walls were the colour of bleached scot, and doors fell from their hinges and worm-eaten posts.[20]

Various attempts to rid St. Giles of this blot upon the urban landscape finally succeeded in 1878–1879, when the area was pulled down. In its heyday as the center of the St. Giles Irish colony, Church Lane and the adjoining courts were almost solidly Irish, while streets on the border of the Rookery had many English residents.

Streets to the north, in the area around Bedford Square, were quite respectable. A few Irish professionals and one Irish M.P. settled there, and a few Irish artisans moved into the mews behind the fashionable squares and crescents of upper-middle-class

19. John Parton, *Some Account of the Hospital and Parish of St. Giles in the Fields, Middlesex* (London, 1822), pp. 124–132, 153, 299–302.
20. John Timbs, *Curiosities of London* (London, 1876), p. 379.

Bloomsbury. But most of the Irish residents north of Great Russell Street lived in English households as domestic servants. Elsewhere in the district a third pattern prevailed. South of High Holborn and on both sides of Drury Lane, Irish families were more evenly distributed than in the Rookery and much more numerous than in northern St. Giles. In 1851, Irish households accounted for over 35 percent of the population in the back alleys between Drury Lane and Great Wild Street, and they occupied most of the houses on Wild Court and Queens Place. In the remainder of the parish east of Seven Dials, they represented from 12 percent to 18 percent of the households. In general, ethnic segregation in the southern part of St. Giles was far less pronounced than in the northern section.[21]

This difference in ethnic distribution within the parish is linked to the economic geography of St. Giles. In few other districts were the measurable distinctions between rich and poor so great. North of High Holborn and New Oxford streets, high property values went along with low birth and death rates and low densities per acre, while south of those streets exactly the reverse situation existed. The streets in St. Giles where large numbers of Irish families lived were the poorest in the parish; 97 percent of the houses in the Rookery were taxed less than £30 per year in 1830, and in the other principal Irish areas, the courts off Drury Lane and Wild Street, over 75 percent of the houses fitted into this category. (In contrast, only 2 percent of the houses between Bedford Square and Alfred Place in the northern section were assessed less than £30.)[22] The pattern of ethnic segregation in St. Giles paralleled that of social segregation, which gave the northern section of the parish to an overwhelmingly English middle class and the southern section to the English and Irish poor.

The Irish in St. Mary, Whitechapel, lived in the area closest to the river. Although they were scattered throughout the entire census district, the center of Irish settlement was between Rosemary Lane (Royal Mint Street) and East Smithfield. North of this section, in Goodman's Fields, the major streets had an Irish-born

21. Enumerators' Books, Censuses of 1851 and 1861, H.O. 107:1508, 1509; R.G. 9:168-172, Public Record Office, London.
22. St. Giles in the Fields and St. George, Bloomsbury, "An Abstract of Assessments Divided into Neighborhoods" (London, 1830).

population of only 2 to 4 percent, but in cul-de-sacs and yards, between 10 and 15 percent were Irish-born. Then along the border of Aldgate and Goodman's Fields, the Irish population jumped to 30 percent, reaching a high of 60 percent on the south side of Rosemary Lane, and finally 74 percent in the alleys around Glass House Yard and Crown Court; East Smithfield was English territory again. Very few streets were entirely English or Irish, and a regular minority of Europeans — Germans, Belgians, and a few Russians and Poles — were mixed among the Celts and Anglo-Saxons.[23] Shopkeepers, artisans, and the few merchants and professionals lived on the major streets, while journeymen and laborers inhabited the less desirable houses in back courts. The Irish, therefore, were segregated by both their ethnicity and their economic position.

South of the river too the Irish settled amid the buildings of industrial London. The Irish-born living in St. Olave, Southwark, and St. John Horsleydown in 1851 were concentrated in the block between Vine Street, the river, London Bridge, and Tooley Street. Although the Irish-born constituted only 15 percent of the total St. Olave population, over two-thirds of the families in the eastern half of this block had Irish-born members, while over half did in the western section. The most heavily Irish streets in the parish were the alleys nestled among the warehouses, the varnish factory, the brewery, and the distillery. The main streets of St. Olave had English tenants almost exclusively, mostly artisans and shopkeepers. The few Irish who escaped the back courts were servants who lived with their employers.[24] Fine gradations of social and economic status were therefore mirrored in the residential patterns of working-class London.

The influence of social status on the geography of Irish settlement in the suburbs was even more marked than in the central area. London's transportation system imposed geographic and financial limits on those moving out of the urban center. While technological advances periodically extended the area from which one could easily reach Westminster and the City, until

23. Enumerators' books, Census of 1851, H.O. 107:1546, Public Record Office, London.
24. Ibid., H.O. 107:1559. See also the Ordnance Survey maps of 1870 and 1871.

industry moved into the suburbs and trams and railroads offered cheap fares for workers, whole areas of greater London were closed to all but the most prosperous artisans.[25] Under these circumstances, Irish settlements beyond the circle formed by the Regent's Canal, Marylebone, Westminster, and the southern riverbank from Lambeth through Greenwich were of a specialized sort. Celtic enclaves consisting of laundresses and laborers grew up in areas where they were needed to build and maintain the homes of the affluent. The few first-generation migrants who had risen into the middle class or had been born into it were concentrated in suburban territory, but they were outnumbered by compatriots who worked as domestic servants for English families.

In 1851 the percentage of Irish-born in the outer ring of London census districts was consistently lower than in the center. (See Map 2a.) South of the Thames, Camberwell, with 2.9 percent of its population Irish-born, had the highest concentration of Celtic residents among the districts outside the inner ring, while Kensington, whose percentage of Irish was only 3.6, held this position in the north and west. The limited penetration of these outer areas by Irish migrants at mid-century represented, first of all, an increase in the suburban labor force, and only secondarily the upward and consequently outward mobility of individuals.

The triangular district of Camberwell housed many different social groups in 1851. Those closest to central London were generally the poorest. From north to south, density decreased while social exclusiveness increased. Dulwich, in the south, remained a sparsely populated preserve of the affluent. Since the parish lacked industrial employment, the cost of daily travel into central London effectively insulated it from the ever expanding circle of workers' households. But in the north of Camberwell lay the parish of St. George, from which workers could still walk to jobs in Southwark or the City. And as industry moved into the parish, so did a labor supply. In consequence, residential density rose from 25 persons per acre in 1841 to 148 per acre in 1901.[26] The

25. Harold Pollins, "Transport Lines and Social Divisions," in Centre for Urban Studies, *London: Aspects of Change* (London, 1964).
26. H. J. Dyos, *Victorian Suburb: A Study of the Growth of Camberwell* (Leicester, 1961), pp. 35–38, 53–57, 190.

Camberwell Irish comprised both lower-middle-class families and workers' households, the former more scattered throughout St. George than the latter. Between Albany Road, the Surrey Canal, and Old Kent Road lived a sprinkling of Irish families and servants. Although most had laboring jobs, a few had risen into the lower middle class as clerks, law reporters, or teachers. No Irish colony was established in this section of the parish; the Irish-born population stayed within 3 percent and rarely rose above 1 percent in any of the enumerators' districts. But to the east and west of central St. George, two heavily Irish settlements grew up around Lovegrove Street and around the meadow north of Wyndham Road. The Irish colony near Wyndham Road became one of the worst slums in London. The infamous Sultan Street slowly developed out of a mass of two-story cottages enclosed by a railroad and terraced housing to which were added piggeries, a glue factory, a linoleum factory, a haddock-smoking yard, a brewery, and several cow sheds. The cutting of Sultan Street through the meadow in front of the linoleum factory merely provided more undesirable space to house the local labor force. As might have been expected, Irish migrants moved into some of the newly built houses. Despite much turnover among inhabitants, this sorry spot remained remarkably the same for over half a century. Booth called it one of the vilest slums in London when he investigated it around 1900.[27]

In the West End, in Kensington, there were similar links between an Irish population and notorious streets, although many lived in rather ordinary working-class corners of the districts. Irish residents can be separated into two groups: middle- or lower-middle-class families who with a few artisans lived in predominantly English areas and families of domestics and laborers who chose to settle near other Irish in the poorer parts of Kensington, Paddington, and Hammersmith. There were several such centers of Irish residence in the West End: all lay near the few industries of the area and shared either noxiousness or noise. In particular, neighborhoods along railway tracks drew groups of Irish families. "Soapsuds Island" in Kensal New Town was

27. Dyos, "Slums," p. 31; Booth, *Life and Labour*, ser. 3, *Religious Influences*, vol. 6, pp. 15–16.

defined by its proximity to local laundries, but the major barriers isolating the heavily Roman Catholic population were the gasworks, the Grand Junction Canal, and the railroad. The streets of concentrated Irish settlement in the West End resembled those in the East End. As the Irish scattered throughout London in the second half of the nineteenth century, most moved from one crowded street to another, from one cluster of dilapidated housing to its twin in a slightly different setting.

The Habitat of the Slumdweller

Penetrating the courts and rooms of the Victorian poor was and remains a difficult task. Then fevers and resentment awaited the curious; now historians find time has altered irrevocably those outer signs of the social life they seek to understand. Trying like the archaeologist to reconstruct a culture from its artifacts, we find only the bare outlines of our subject: a few buildings long since mended and sanitized beyond recognition by renewers and medical men. The misery and rags overflowing into the streets, the stinks, and the bugs have vanished, remembered only in the indignant prose of Victorian social reporters. Their trips down "melancholy [avenues] of vermin-haunted furniture"[28] take us as close to the daily life of the poor as we are likely to come, and we must use them as our guides.

Entering the cul-de-sacs favored by the Irish required thick boots and a strong stomach. "Rookeries are bad, but what are they to Irish rookeries?" wrote Montague Gore, a social reformer who visited London slums.[29] "In some cases, these courts are choked up with every variety of filth; their approaches wind round by the worst kind of slaughter-houses . . . they are crowded with pigs, with fowls, and with dogs; they are strewn with oyster shells and fish refuse . . . their drainage lies in pools wherever it may be thrown."[30] Everywhere, defects of age combined with builders' mistakes to produce a familiar catalog of environmental disasters. The courts were badly drained and lit and had too many people and too little water. Falling plaster, broken windows, and decay-

28. Hollingshead, *Ragged London*, pp. 15–16.
29. Montague Gore, *On the Dwellings of the Poor*, 2d ed. (London, 1851), p. xiv.
30. Hollingshead, *Ragged London*, p. 88.

ing wood testified to neglect by both tenants and owners. Water
was a scarce commodity. The better provided places had a tank or
perhaps only a water barrel for common use in the yard or under
the stairs. Even in areas judged well cleansed, private companies
supplied water just three times a week, and not all houses in the
1850s had their own taps.[31] Sanitary facilities were even less
adequate. In the general absence of water closets, the juxtaposi-
tion of water supply, privy, and dust heap was virtually ubiqui-
tous.

Descriptions of such buildings are depressingly similar and
repeat a familiar litany of structural defects:

Calmell buildings . . . is a narrow court, being about 22 feet in breadth;
the houses are three stories high, surrounded and overtopped by adjacent
buildings; the drainage is carried on by a common sewer running down
the center of the court, the receptacle for slops etc. from the houses on
both sides; the lower apartments, especially the kitchens, which are
under ground are damp and badly ventilated, light and air being
admitted through a grating on a level with the court. At all times, but
especially so in warm weather, a most offensive effluvia is perceptible
everywhere.[32]

Another such series of three-story tenements lay in the heart of St.
Giles on Church Lane. They too were dirty, dark, and dank.
Local amenities consisted of three gaslights and a few water
pumps. Overcrowding compounded builders' sins of omission.
The shopkeepers and dealers who rented the houses sublet to
undertenants, generally one family per room, and these families
often sub-sublet, bringing lodgers into every spare corner. Although most of the Church Lane cellars were untenanted in 1848,
the dank underground dwellings in the parish had provided
homes for the poor since the days of Charles I. Not until 1858 did

31. Committee of the Council of the Statistical Society, "Report of an Investigation into the State of the Poorer Classes of St. George in the East," *Journal of the
[Royal] Statistical Society* 11 (1848):196–197; *Builder* 12, no. 615 (November 18,
1854):589; Committee of the Council of the Statistical Society, "Report . . . to
Investigate the State of the Inhabitants and Their Dwellings in Church Lane, St.
Giles," *Journal of the [Royal] Statistical Society* 11 (1848):1–2.
32. Great Britain, *Parliamentary Papers* (Commons), "Supplementary Report
on the Practice of Interment in Towns; Report on the Sanitary Condition of the
Labouring Population," 1843, 12:257.

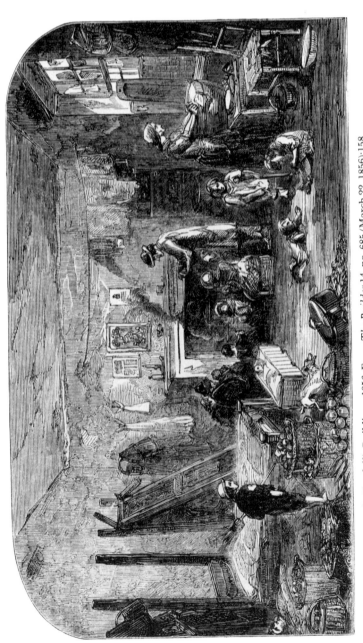

1 A room in Tyndall's Buildings, 1856. From *The Builder* 14, no. 685 (March 22, 1856):158.

2 Dudley Street, Seven Dials, c. 1870. By Gustave Doré, from Gustave Doré and Blanchard Jerrold, *London: A Pilgrimage* (London, 1872), p. 158.

the local Board of Works force landlords to empty them completely.[33]

Another haunt of the Irish, Wild Court near Drury Lane, was taken over by Lord Shaftesbury's Society for Improving the Condition of the Labouring Classes in 1854. They found thirteen rickety ten-room houses that together held more than a thousand people. The gutters, which flowed uncovered through garret rooms, were used as sewers; in the mornings backyards flowed six inches deep in filth. Shaftesbury's group cleaned up the houses, increased the supply of water, and added privies and dust shafts on every floor before they rented the rooms, one to a family. Although the movement to provide decent housing for the London poor generally passed by the Irish, most of whom could not afford the rents charged in model buildings, they continued to inhabit Wild Court after its partial transformation. The presence of "a good many low Irish" was said in 1858 to "keep decent respectable English from living there."[34]

Not all Irish enclaves contained buildings as large as those of Church Lane or Wild Court. Houses were smaller in the riverside alleys of Wapping, Southwark, and Bermondsey, areas "thickly inhabited, chiefly by Irish." Dwarf two-story houses with one window per room looked out upon blank walls or upon mirror images of themselves. Here too defects of both site and building practices had produced unsanitary houses. In Southwark, much of which consisted of low-lying land, a tidal river in the 1850s regularly flooded cellars and overflowed the open ditches used by local tanneries and mills. High tides periodically brought backed-up sewage and refuse into the streets. At Jacob's Island, dubbed "the Venice of Drains" by Henry Mayhew, a putrid mill stream served as sewer, bathing spot, and well for a group of wooden houses it surrounded on four sides. Irish squatters had moved into some of the ancient buildings, which in the late 1840s still had galleries running along the sides. Pigs, ducks, and chickens

33. Committee of the Council of the Statistical Society, "Report . . . [on] Church Lane," pp. 1–2; Board of Works of St. Giles in the Fields, *Annual Report for 1855* (London, 1859), p. 27.
    34. *Builder* 12, no. 615 (November 18, 1854):589–590; Board of Works of St. Giles in the Fields, *Annual Report for 1858*, p. 39; see also A. S. Wohl, "The Housing of the Working Classes in London, 1815–1914," in *The History of Working-Class Housing*, ed. Stanley D. Chapman (London, 1971), p. 41.

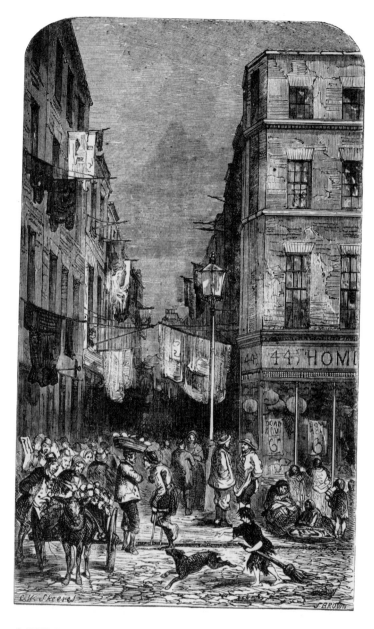

3 Wild Court and Great Wild Street, 1854. From *The Builder* 12, no. 615
(November 12, 1854):595.

4 House no. 2, Wild Court, 1854. From *The Builder* 12, no. 615 (November 12, 1854):595.

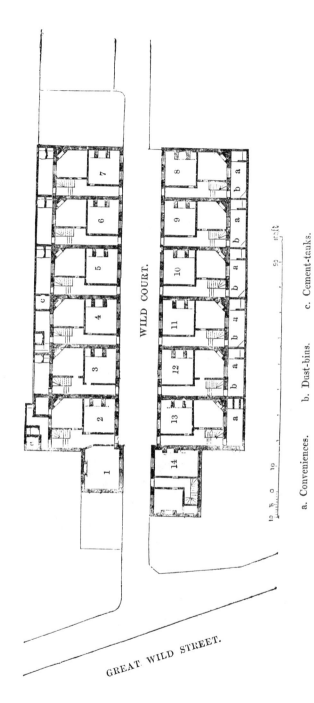

5 Floor plan of Wild Court, 1854. From *The Builder* 12, no. 615 (November 12, 1854):589.

a. Conveniences.   b. Dust-bins.   c. Cement-tanks.

shared the territory, no doubt flourishing more than the human inhabitants, who died regularly of scarlet fever, typhus, and cholera. The Board of Health forced landlords to fill the ditch after the cholera epidemic of 1848 raged in the neighborhood, but the tumbledown houses and refuse-filled yards remained.[35]

The dilapidated appearance of London workers' housing was not limited to the facades. Inside, shaky narrow staircases led into dim, overcrowded apartments. George Godwin, editor of *The Builder*, visited and sketched in the mid-1850s a series of very poor workers' dwellings, some with Irish inhabitants. Fireplaces dominated the interiors, which were sometimes devoid of all furniture. Cupboards and shelves held only a few bits of crockery, and other household furnishings were in similarly short supply. The poverty of such places was almost unrelieved. Still, these rooms teemed with life:

One room contained two large bedsteads, put up against the wall, and a bed on the floor, which was occupied. There was a very old woman close to the fire surrounded by a group such as is often to be met with in these places smoking their pipes and watching the pot upon the fire: a number of pictures were over the fireplace, and not far from them two large slices of dried fish. Before the fire a young child lay in a cradle manufactured out of an orange chest: in other parts of the room were baskets of oranges, fruits, onions and other things forming their stock in trade. This room is much larger and better furnished than the majority.[36]

In St. George in the East, where about 10 percent of the population was Irish and most were English artisans, the majority of families lived in "ill" or "scantly furnished" rooms. Half the households possessed only a few chairs, a table, a bed, a few cooking utensils, and cheap prints for decoration. The comfortable added good furniture, a clock, a carpet, and perhaps a piano, but only 32 percent of the families had reached this state of affluence. Still, investigators for the Statistical Society who toured the area in 1848 reported a general "struggle for neatness": only 16 percent of the families lived in dirty rooms.[37]

35. George Godwin, *London Shadows: A Glance at the "Homes" of the Thousands* (London, 1854), p. 79; *Builder* 13, no. 647 (1855):183–184; Henry Mayhew, "Home Is Home, Be It Never So Homely," in *Meliora: or, Better Times to Come*, ed. C. J. Talbot, Viscount Ingestre (London, 1852), pp. 276–278.

36. *Builder* 14, no. 685 (1856):157; see also Godwin, *London Shadows*.

37. Committee of the Council of the Statistical Society, "Report . . . [on] St. George in the East," pp. 214–215.

Although social reporters usually were preoccupied with the dismal quarters of the nearly destitute, not all Irish migrants lived in such places. Henry Mayhew's investigations of the street Irish in the East End led him to a labyrinth of Irish courts near Rosemary Lane where the inhabitants had turned their rooms into homes:

In all the houses that I entered were traces of household care and neatness that I had little expected to have seen. The cupboard fastened in the corner of the room, and stocked with mugs and cups, the mantelpiece with its images, and the walls covered with showy coloured prints of saints and martyrs, gave an air of comfort. . . .[38]

In another house the floors "were strewn with red sand, and the front apartment had three beds in it, with the curtains drawn closely round." The family's second room was "crowded to excess with chairs and table, the very staircase having pictures fastened against the wooden partition." Beds with cotton hangings were used to provide privacy, and prints, perhaps from illustrated magazines, brought touches of color and comfort. "If there was one picture, there must have been thirty — all of 'holy men' with yellow glories round their heads." Two-thirds of the workers' rooms in St. George in the East in 1848 had such pictures, "paper prints tricked out in glaring colours." The poor prized these tiny treasures, carefully transporting them from house to house to provide some continuity and color in otherwise dreary surroundings.[39]

There were ways, then, to cover and compensate for their houses' structural defects. Yet fundamental constraints remained. The luxuries of space and privacy were far beyond the reach of the London poor, English and Irish. Rents were too high and housing was too hard to find. Almost half the laborers' families in St. George in the East lived in one room in 1848, and only 27 percent had more than two rooms. The workers of Westminster were even more crowded: 75 percent of the families in St. Margaret's and St. John's parishes had only one room in 1840. Moreover, most of these dwellings were small; 85 percent were 12 feet

38. Henry Mayhew, *London Labour and the London Poor*, 4 vols. (London, 1861–1862), vol. 1, p. 110.
39. Ibid.; Committee of the Council of the Statistical Society, "Report . . . [on] St. George in the East," p. 219.

by 14 feet or less. Living in one room or less was the prevailing pattern for the Irish in Church Lane and other parts of St. Giles. Their practice of subletting exacerbated their situation: over 30 percent of the Church Lane rooms held more than one family in 1848.[40]

Not only were workers' families crammed into tiny spaces, but their buildings in central London held several households. Only one Irish family in eight sampled in 1851 had a house all to itself, while one in three lived in buildings that contained five or more separate households and more than twenty persons. Most lived surrounded by other families, with only a few thin walls separating them. The most intense crowding in 1851 stemmed from recent migration, which decreased markedly by 1861. Newcomers at first lived with friends or went into lodging houses before setting up their own households. The proportion of Irish households living in buildings with more than thirty persons fell by 50 percent by 1861, but almost two-thirds of the Irish households still lived in dwellings holding between ten and twenty-nine persons.

Crowding varied directly according to a family's social and economic status. The lower down the ladder, the more neighbors one had. While 55 percent of Irish households whose heads held professional or other white-collar jobs lived in one-family houses, only 10 percent of the unskilled household heads could afford to rent their own dwellings without subletting to others. In contrast, 48 percent of the unskilled lived in buildings sheltering four or more households; only 15 percent of the white-collar workers had so many neighbors. Irish laborers' families were markedly more crowded than those of skilled or semiskilled migrants, far more of whom rented entire houses. For most Irish families, moreover, the omnipresence of others using the same stairways and halls was a new experience. Although their housing in Ireland had been abysmal, they had been less densely packed together. There, moderately sized nuclear or stem families inhabited one- or two-roomed cabins. Overcrowded housing was an unavoidable exper-

40. Ibid., p. 211; Committee of the Council of the Statistical Society, "Report . . . [on] Church Lane," pp. 2–18, and "Report . . . [on] the State of the Working-Classes in the Parishes of St. Margaret and St. John Westminster," *Journal of the [Royal] Statistical Society* 3 (1840):17, 23.

ience for virtually all low-paid workers in London because the available stock of housing was badly distributed among areas and income groups. Acceptable homes existed, particularly in suburban areas, for those who could pay regularly, but the poor had to make do with low-quality dwellings, many designed for subdivision in order to maximize rents. The efforts of early public health enthusiasts merely increased overcrowding, as they were more interested in demolition than in rebuilding. When their projects were added to the clearances for railways and streets, the result was a large decrease in the stock of cheap housing within walking distance of jobs in central London. Enid Gauldie argues, in fact, that conditions deteriorated throughout the century despite growing awareness of the problem, for every move for improvement of workers' housing led directly to increased pressure on the available housing supply. Certainly, as Anthony Wohl has shown, medical officers had little success in dealing with the problem. The more astute were reduced to neglecting to report cases of overcrowding in order to avoid hounding the poor from place to place and increasing the population density of adjacent, similarly overcrowded buildings.[41]

Like slum dwellings today, the homes of the London Irish were limited functionally as well as spatially. They provided shelter from weather and a place to eat and sleep but little more. Not only was privacy impossible, but the wealth of goods and special rooms now used in leisure time were absent. Small wonder that denizens of such places regularly fled their rooms in favor of the street outside. As Mayhew and others looked into the nests of the Irish, they glimpsed an important dimension of their semiprivate lives. "It is the custom with the inhabitants of these courts and alleys to assemble at the entrance with their baskets, and chat and smoke away the morning." Streets served as extensions of cramped interiors, playgrounds for children, drying areas for laundry, and meeting places for neighbors. They provided a framework, intimate yet limited, within which information could

41. Enid Gauldie, *Cruel Habitations: A History of Working-Class Housing, 1780–1918* (New York, 1974), pp. 87, 90; Anthony S. Wohl, "Unfit for Human Habitation," in *The Victorian City: Images and Realities*, 2 vols., ed. H. J. Dyos and Michael Wolff (London and Boston, 1973), vol. 2, pp. 606–615.

be exchanged and a local social life maintained without the burdens and dangers of inviting outsiders into one's home.[42]

Groups apparently graded by age and sex used the streets for their own purposes. All outsiders noticed the children, ragged urchins running barefoot through the puddles, who virtually lived in the streets. John Hollingshead found them eating and playing outside, their toys the refuse littering the ground.[43] Women sat on the curbstones or leaned on the walls near their homes. "Every court entrance has its little groups of girls and women, lolling listlessly against the sides, with their heads uncovered, and their luxurious hair as fuzzy as oakum." Men tossed for pennies, smoked, and talked in groups. They were seen "lounging about in remnants of shooting jackets, leaning on the window frames . . . with young boys gathered round them."[44] Much more evidence is needed before it can be shown that this segregation by age and sex was the norm in Irish street life. Yet it was a useful way to organize social contacts in a crowded urban environment. Today one finds this same use of the street for social life by groups segregated by age and sex who reproduce outside the home the male and female worlds found within.[45]

Migrants were helped substantially by the presence of other Irish nearby. Irish neighbors contributed money for funeral expenses, if the dead person's kin could not raise enough. Neighbors loaned money and kitchen utensils, helped orphans to find jobs and lodging, attended wakes and weddings. Newcomers were given a corner of a room in which to sleep and helped in their search for work. It is impossible to reconstruct from the meager observations of outsiders the extent of these services, but it is clear that migrants offered aid to those who lived nearby and maintained some social contacts with neighbors.[46]

42. Mayhew, *London Labour*, vol. 1, p. 109.
43. Hollingshead, *Ragged London*, pp. 41–42.
44. Mayhew, *London Labour*, vol. 1, p. 109; Gore, *On the Dwellings of the Poor*, p. viii.
45. Gerald D. Suttles, *The Social Order of the Slum: Ethnicity and Territory in the Inner City* (Chicago, 1968), pp. 73–83.
46. Tom Barclay, *Memoirs and Medleys: The Autobiography of a Bottle-washer* (Leicester, 1934), pp. 11–12; Mayhew, *London Labour*, pp. 21, 115, 136, 466; John O'Neill, "Fifty Years' Experience as an Irish Shoemaker in London," *St. Crispin* 2

The courts and alleys of the poor were their territory, places where their carts, children, and animals could run freely and where outsiders were immediately noticed. But it was a small territory; beyond their cul-de-sacs stood larger streets with shops, factories, and middle-class residences. Because of their scattered pattern of settlement, the Irish had to live within areas of mixed functions and mixed ethnicity. Although some services could be found inside Irish territory, others required a trip outside. "Neighborhood" for the Irish must have had a complex meaning, reflecting the varying and irregularly demarcated areas they inhabited and frequented.

The social geography of St. Giles in the Fields shows us the shape of one Irish social world in central London. The southern half of St. Giles, south of Oxford Street and east of the Soho boundary, was an area of sixty-eight acres inhabited in 1851 by more than 19,000 people at a density of more than 300 per acre. Although the larger streets had some middle-class residents (11 percent of the people in the area as opposed to 21 percent of the total London population), the back streets and interior courts were packed with the families of the poor. Despite and to some extent because of the persistent slumminess of the area, local people used and joined a network of outside institutions and organizations in South St. Giles. Within this territory we find in 1871 a post office, a hotel, a music hall, a workhouse, an almshouse, a hospital, public baths and a washhouse, a boys' refuge, six schools, eight churches and chapels, a foundry, a cooperage, and forty-three pubs, not to mention the many lodging houses and small shops. Just across the parish boundary to the south lay a police station, several theaters, and the Covent Garden markets and opera house.[47]

These institutions served differing clienteles, some living in the area and others coming in from outside. A building's site and size helped to signal which social groups it served. Major thoroughfares housed the large public and commercial buildings — the hotels, theaters, and post offices — while those serving workers

(1869):87; Great Britain, *Parliamentary Papers* (Commons), "Supplementary Report on the Practice of Interment in Towns," 1834, 12:32.

47. Ordnance Survey of London, 1870 and 1871, for St. Giles and St. George, Bloomsbury, Greater London Council Map Room.

nestled on back streets or near the gateways to interior courts. Pubs lay virtually everywhere, occupying choice corner lots. Workers' residential areas also harbored a multitude of small shops and street dealers. Seven Dials, just south of the Rookery, was a shopping emporium for the poor:

... shops for the purchase of rags, bones, old iron and kitchen-stuff vie in cleanliness with the bird-fanciers and rabbit-dealers. ... Brokers' shops, which would seem to have been established by humane individuals as refuges for destitute bugs, interspersed with announcements of day-schools, penny theaters, petition-writers, mangles, and music for balls or routs, complete the 'still life' of the subject.[48]

Residents could buy food, drink, and clothes without leaving working-class territory. And the poor had a vested interest in patronizing local merchants: only where they were known could they receive credit. Limited in any case to establishments within walking distance of their homes, they were bound even more closely to their neighborhoods by the exigencies of time and "buying on tick." The world of nonworking women and children must have been small indeed.

Those who wished contact with the poor had to come to them. Ragged schools, intended for young "street arabs" and the poorest of the poor, were located on seedy back streets where their clientele felt comfortable. In St. Giles, one lay at the end of Brewer's Court, enclosed on three and one-half sides by pubs and other buildings. Many other local "social services" were also to be found in close proximity to migrants' homes. The St. Giles workhouse, infirmary, baths, washhouses, and lying-in hospital occupied a block off Endell Street just southeast of the Rookery.[49] Churches intentionally located chapels, missions, and schools where workers would be tempted to enter. Finding the area infiltrated with Protestant missions, Roman Catholics opened a school in south St. Giles. Priests recognized that keeping the Irish within the Catholic fold required the multiplication of facilities. One priest who worked in central London complained in 1853 that "several of the poor children do not come to Mass or attend to their duties, merely because they are ashamed to be seen going to

48. Charles Dickens, *Sketches by Boz* (London, 1892), p. 66.
49. Ordnance Survey of London, 1870 and 1871.

the chapel through the 'big streets' without shoes on their feet or any sort of covering on their heads. They all say, however, that there will be no excuse for them when the new chapel is built, as it will be at their very doors.''[50] Even the children had a sense of territory and knew the areas where they could not stray without being considered out of place. London for them may well have been a chain of Irish islands. Within each, one moved freely; among them only limited excursions were made.

Not all working-class streets in St. Giles were Irish territory. Migrants had to learn to function within an ethnically and socially mixed neighborhood. Most of those with jobs had to leave their alleys and enter English areas, accommodating themselves to English employers. Even the St. Giles street traders had to purchase stock at the large markets outside the parish, and domestic craftsmen walked to and from employers' shops with the goods they were to finish. Organizations that migrants joined were located near but not in solidly Irish territory. The local Roman Catholic church lay two and one-half blocks west of the Rookery. Those active in Irish Repeal or Confederate clubs met at various temperance halls or pubs along major streets bordering St. Giles. These areas had to be shared with English inhabitants.[51]

Despite their residence in mixed neighborhoods, migrants could remain within an Irish social network by patronizing local Irish businesses. Although parish institutions were led and to a large extent staffed by middle-class English, private enterprises serving the Irish were often run by other Irish. Irish lodging house keepers in the East End regularly met the Cork steamer to offer new arrivals a bed, and some of the Church Lane lodging houses had Irish landlords or landladies.[52] As early as 1808 there were Irish pubs in London where newcomers could get information and trace kin. A bootmaker from Carrick ran the Black Lion on Berwick Street, and in the 1830s John Savage's pub in St. Pancras functioned as a center for both Irish songfests and radical

50. *Catholic Standard* 9, no. 212 (October 29, 1853).

51. *Poor Man's Guardian*, no. 40 (March 17, 1832); *Northern Star* (November 3, 1844).

52. Mayhew, *London Labour*, vol. 1, p. 117; Committee of the Council of the Statistical Society, "Report . . . [on] Church Lane," pp. 2–8.

political meetings.[53] Some Irish pubs served particular buildings
rather than trades; the migrant costermongers and laborers of
Charlotte's Court near Grey's Inn Lane used a "low public
house" run by another Irishman located at the entrance to their
court.[54] Only 4 percent of the Irish household heads sampled in
1851 were shopkeepers, but this figure excludes most second- and
third-generation adults and the street traders. Without more
information it is impossible to estimate the extent to which
migrants remained within their ethnic community when they
drank or bought food and clothing, but in heavily Irish areas they
could keep many social and commercial contacts within the
group.

In London, however, networks of Irish businesses, homes, and
services were not sufficiently compact to constitute distinct
geographic neighborhoods. The Irish shared St. Giles with too
many others. Herbert Gans has shown that in Boston's West End
an ethnically and socially mixed population lived within a small
area without conflict because each segment had its own reference
groups. What outsiders saw as an undifferentiated slum was in
fact a series of communities organized on social rather than
spatial lines. Each group largely ignored the others, confining its
interests to its kin, its friends, its street, and the stores it frequented.[55] Moreover, ethnic groups had their own institutions.
What Gans calls an "urban village" was in fact more a cultural
than a physical community. So too with the London Irish, whose
social world consisted of a multitude of Irish networks that
crisscrossed the working-class territory they inhabited. A study of
the London Irish community therefore requires us to move
beyond geography to the economic, social, and cultural organization of the group.

53. O'Neill, "Fifty Years' Experience," St. Crispin 2:183; James Williamson
Brooke, The Democrats of Marylebone (London, 1839), p. 47.
54. Metpol. 2, no. 48 (July 2, 1859), Public Record Office, London.
55. Herbert J. Gans, The Urban Villagers: Group and Class in the Life of
Italian-Americans (New York, 1962), pp. 4, 11, 15, 104–105.

CHAPTER 4

Economic Roles

The social and economic position of the Irish in London was determined to a large extent by the jobs they found. Their work influenced not only the area where they would live but the way they would live and the people with whom they would associate. The level of wages and the timing and extent of unemployment shaped their patterns of expenditure and consumption as well as their ability to save, to educate, and to place their children. Their work marked out the rhythm of their days and helped set a pattern of interaction with English Londoners. Since most Irish could find only low-skilled, low-paying jobs in nineteenth-century London, they were channeled into the bottom ranks of the capital's social and economic hierarchy, a position that forced a constant scramble for survival and severely limited their prospects for improvement. Yet their labor provided a major resource for employers in the metropolis; the existence of the Irish helped to keep alive the vast pool of casual labor upon which such industries as transportation, construction, and food distribution depended. The Irish quickly became a functioning part of the complex London economy.

The London Labor Market

The Irish who came to London in the nineteenth century entered a labor market where the Industrial Revolution had far different effects than in the manufacturing towns of the north. London had no one dominant industry. In 1861, 61 percent of those employed worked in the service sector of the economy, while those engaged in manufacturing had jobs in a wide variety of trades ranging from the production of ships and machinery to the making of artificial flowers. London's position as capital, port, and world city gave this variety a special shape and bent it to the needs of Britain's largest and wealthiest market. Long before the Industrial Revolution, London had been a center for artisans, and the presence of court and government encouraged the production of luxury goods. Then too, the port attracted a continuing stream of imported goods and raw materials for processing and transshipment. Although there was virtually no primary industry in London, the presence of a highly skilled labor force made it possible for engineering works, tanneries, refineries, and other workshops producing capital and semifinished goods to prosper in an inner industrial district. While the amount of heavy industry in the capital was limited, foundries and workshops that made everything from machinery to precision instruments employed over 8 percent of the male labor force in 1851. Yet the average size of firms remained small, since there were few large factories. In 1851 only 3 percent of London's industrial labor force worked in firms employing more than 100 workers; 95 percent of all industrial employers had fewer than 20 employees. Skilled artisans working in small shops dominated the labor force in 1851, as they had for centuries.[1]

Industrialization did not destroy this economic pattern, but it altered London's industrial geography decisively. Entrepreneurs in the capital found it increasingly difficult to compete against northern manufacturing towns, particularly in the production of semifinished goods and textiles. And in all branches of heavy industry, London's inner industrial district became unsuitable for large-scale production: rents were too high and coal was too expensive. As the city grew and the central business district expanded, rents and land values rose dramatically throughout inner London. Even more serious was the cost of power and materials; coal and iron cost much more in London than they did

1. Peter Hall, *The Industries of London since 1861* (London, 1962), pp. 21–27; François Bedarida, "Londres au milieu du XIXe siècle: Un analyse de structure sociale," *Annales: Economies, Sociétés, Civilisations* 23, no. 2 (March–April 1968): 273, 277; Charles Booth, *Life and Labour of the People in London*, ser. 2, *Industry*, 5 vols. (London, 1904), vol. 5, pp. 83–84.

in districts close to the mines. Therefore, where technology dictated the use of factories and steam engines, where space was needed for production on a large scale, London could no longer compete. The solution for industries where these conditions prevailed was to move either into the provinces or to the periphery of the metropolis and to close their inner-city workshops. Spitalfields silk weavers felt the effects of provincial and foreign competition strongly after 1824, and master shoemakers sent goods to Northampton to be finished after the strike of 1812. The collapse of traditional London trades was most intense in the second half of the century, however, accelerated by the conjunctural crisis of the 1870s and 1880s. Shipbuilding workshops closed in the East End, as did Southwark's engineering firms. The tanyards left Bermondsey, and there was a gradual exodus by book printing establishments, chemical works, hat factories, and many other industries. Although some relocated in outer districts such as West Ham or parts of Lambeth, many firms abandoned London altogether. Gareth Stedman Jones has characterized this movement as the "crisis of the inner industrial perimeter," which produced a steady economic decline in riverside districts and central London between 1870 and 1914.[2]

The vulnerability of metropolitan industry was overcome only in the long run after much relocation took place and after electricity supplanted coal fires as the major source of power. The nineteenth century was therefore a period of transition for London's economy. The older manufacturing areas had to shift their economic base to produce goods of high value and low bulk, items requiring much specialized labor. London had in fact a comparative advantage in the finishing of consumption goods and in labor-intensive processes of production in which a complex mixture of skills and materials was needed, trades where artisans could not be replaced by machines. Thus, as Gareth Stedman Jones has argued, London's economy remained preindustrial as industrialization progressed. Home and workshop

2. Eileen Yeo and E. P. Thompson, *The Unknown Mayhew* (New York, 1971), pp. 107, 111–112, 238–239, 244–245; Booth, *Life and Labour*, ser. 2, *Industry*, vol. 5, pp. 90–92; Gareth Stedman Jones, *Outcast London* (Oxford, 1971), pp. 152–153.

production of consumer goods by skilled artisans continued to hold a dominant position in the inner industrial district.[3]

But the complexity and subdivision of the London labor market made it difficult for newcomers to find a place within it. Not only were there hundreds of firms located in the capital, but the manufacture of any one product was often subdivided into several operations, each of which might be carried out separately. Information about jobs circulated largely by word of mouth. Some workers' societies acted as labor exchanges for members, but Irish newcomers were outside this network. Although employers seeking skilled artisans might place press advertisements, few Irishmen had the kinds of scarce qualifications that could make this avenue of job hunting a practical alternative. In general, the unemployed had to fend for themselves, using informal channels in which rumors, tips, and personal contacts assumed major importance. Local reputation, recognition by masters, or the recommendation of someone already employed counted for much, particularly when work was scarce. But the help that could be obtained from friends usually operated only within a limited geographic area. Since workers in mid-nineteenth-century London were relatively immobile in the short run, their knowledge of job opportunities outside their own area was correspondingly limited. They were unlikely to travel far within the city in search of work or to hear of job opportunities at some distance. The unskilled were most bound by these circumstances; for them, as Eric Hobsbawm has said, "all that lay beyond a tiny circle of personal acquaintance or walking distance was darkness."[4]

In such circumstances, Irish migrants depended on the help of kin and friends to locate work. John O'Neill, a shoemaker from Waterford, found a job soon after his arrival in London through the help of kin and other shoemakers from his town. O'Neill was part of a chain migration of Munster shoemakers to the capital. Each new link in the chain received aid from those who preceded him and performed similar services for migrants who came after.

3. Booth, *Life and Labour*, ser. 2, *Industry*, vol. 5, pp. 92–94; Jones, *Outcast London*, p. 26.

4. E. J. Hobsbawm, "The Nineteenth-Century London Labour Market," in Centre for Urban Studies, *London: Aspects of Change* (London, 1964), p. 8.

Several of the Irish interviewed by Henry Mayhew told of the role played by relatives and friends in helping them to find work. Mayhew once interviewed an Irish tanner who came to London around 1840 with his wife and child. He did odd jobs for three weeks, earning only a few pence a day, until a friend helped him to find work in a Bermondsey tanning yard.[5]

Those without such assistance could find themselves in difficult circumstances. Mayhew tells of a young journeyman tailor from Limerick who went to London because it "has such a name among the tailors in Ireland." Upon arrival he found that his one contact there had died, but an acquaintance directed him to the East End, where supposedly he would "do best." Once there he met a sweater who expected him to work seven days a week, fifteen hours a day, for 3s. 6d. plus a few meager meals and lodging. The tailor said he accepted because "I had no friends and thought I had better take it."[6]

But even with the aid of compatriots, the prospects for Irish newcomers were bleak. Since Irish migrants before 1880 settled predominantly in the central industrial area, its economic problems became their own. The immobility of the unskilled trapped them in a region where their employment opportunites were increasingly limited to casual or sweated jobs and declining trades. The economic position of the Irish must be seen against this background of economic transition and decline.

The Occupations of the Irish in 1851

Although some Irish-born worked in almost every London industry, the distribution of Irish migrants among London trades differed sharply from that of all London workers and from that of the employed population in the districts from which the Irish sample was drawn. Instead of being distributed proportionately among metropolitan industries, the Irish were heavily concentrated in a few trades, in occupations that placed most of them among the lowest social and economic groups. (See Table 4.1.) In general, fewer Irish than English worked in almost every special-

5. John O'Neill, "Fifty Years' Experience as an Irish Shoemaker in London," *St. Crispin* 1 (1869):241, 254, 307, 314; 2:27; Yeo and Thompson, *Unknown Mayhew*, pp. 456–457.

6. Yeo and Thompson, *Unknown Mayhew*, p. 225.

Table 4.1. Distribution of occupations by sex, London, 1851

Industrial group	Total population M	Total population F	Registrar general's districts from which sample is drawn[a] M (N=84,022)	Registrar general's districts from which sample is drawn[a] F (N=52,253)	Irish sample M (N=1,260)	Irish sample F (N=750)
Agriculture	3.1%	0.4%	4.5%	1.0%	1.7%	0.9%
Construction	9.5	—	10.2	—	12.8	0.4
Metalworking	4.8	0.2	3.5	0.1	1.1	0.1
Machinery	3.6	0.1	3.0	0.1	1.4	0.1
Shipbuilding	0.7	—	0.2	—	—	—
Gas and fuel	0.8	0.1	0.8	0.1	0.2	0.3
Glass	0.9	0.2	0.7	0.1	0.5	—
Textiles	3.2	4.0	3.0	3.5	0.8	0.9
Clothing	9.0	25.6	9.0	20.4	7.2	17.2
Leather	1.8	0.3	1.7	0.2	0.6	0.7
Wood	4.8	0.8	3.6	0.6	1.1	0.5
Paper	2.0	1.2	1.2	0.9	1.9	2.0
Printing	2.9	0.7	1.4	0.2	0.5	0.7
Food	9.6	3.6	10.5	4.0	7.3	15.1
Transport	12.3	0.1	11.2	0.1	20.8	0.4
Service	5.5	50.7	6.0	55.7	1.8	42.7
General labor	7.3	2.8	10.1	3.3	30.8	0.9
Administration	1.8	0.2	1.9	0.2	0.3	—
Commerce and finance	6.3	1.6	7.9	2.4	3.8	8.1
Military and police	3.4	—	2.3	—	0.5	—
Professions	3.2	—	0.4	—	0.5	—
Art, education, entertainment	1.5	3.2	2.0	3.8	0.5	0.1
Other and unknown	1.9	4.2	4.9	2.9	3.5	8.8

[a] Kensington, St. Giles, Whitechapel, St. Olave, Camberwell.

ized industrial occupation with the notable exception of the construction, paper, and food industries. In the highly skilled jobs of metalworking, machinery making, and printing, the Irish were notably absent, and very few were to be found in leather processing, textile production, or shipbuilding.

Although there were Irish craftsmen in London, they formed a minority of the employed migrant population. Mayhew interviewed some in 1849. While most were in the clothing trades, he found a few Irish tanners and coopers. But it is noteworthy that migrants in these two industries worked in the less skilled jobs and were not members of craft unions. The Irish tanners were yard men who merely placed the prepared hides in the tanning pits and checked their progress intermittently. The Irish coopers he found worked in the "slop" part of the trade, producing simple kegs and pails at home after regular working hours and when they could not get casual work as journeymen coopers at the docks.[7]

It was only in industries offering a high proportion of low-skilled jobs or artisan trades having large numbers of sweated workers that more than a small number of Irish were employed. Among skilled trades, the Irish were concentrated in shoemaking and tailoring, both depressed industries where conditions were slowly deteriorating with the influx of child and female labor. Foreign immigrants — the Irish in the first two-thirds of the century and Eastern European Jews in the last third — moved heavily into these sectors, even though the wages paid were barely adequate to maintain a worker's family. But access to these trades was easy, the centers of employment were located within the inner industrial district, and such trades permitted women to work at home. Moreover, English poor law authorities reinforced the movement of migrants into these industries. London Guardians of the Poor bound workhouse children to local craftsmen who were willing to take on apprentices for very small sums of money, not to men under whom apprenticeship was a coveted position. The register of apprentices for St. Giles in the Fields for the years 1823 to 1912 listed the names of many Irish children sent to shoemakers and boot closers for terms averaging eight years. No wages were paid, but the children received food, clothes, and lodging at a rate to be set by the master. Apparently many apprentices were used to replace adult workmen, for some masters took in several boys and set up what were in effect tiny shoe factories run by slave labor. One apprentice whom Mayhew interviewed claimed that he and six others worked sixteen hours a day turning out goods worth several pounds a week.[8] By far the largest group of Irish males in

7. Ibid., pp. 426–427, 456.

8. St. Giles in the Fields, "Register Of Apprentices," vol. 3 (1823–1912), Greater London Council Archive; Henry Mayhew, London Labour and the London Poor, 4 vols. (London, 1861–1862; reprinted New York, 1968), vol. 2 pp. 352–354.

1851 worked simply as general laborers, joining the army of underemployed that haunted the streets. Others had laboring jobs on the docks or on construction projects.

Irish women were drawn into occupations dominated by females. Irish as well as English women in London worked primarily in domestic service and the clothing trades. (See Table 4.1.) Domestic service heads the list. Irish servants abounded in London. Allegedly saucy and incompetent, they seem to have taken up the less desirable posts in the metropolis. And many more Irish women wanted such jobs than could find them. London priests often published warnings in the *Catholic Standard* of the dangers to body and soul of hunting such jobs in London. One said in 1853 that positions were almost impossible to find. Girls had usually to accept work either in a pub or with an East End Jewish family, where they were paid only one or two shillings a week plus board. In any case, the priest claimed that they usually quit or were fired, their final recourse being prostitution or begging.[9]

Needlework was the principal "skilled" occupation open to women in London, but it was a sweated trade, paying low wages for long hours. Mayhew interviewed many almost destitute needlewomen earning less than five shillings a week for fifteen hours or more of work a day. But even this wage declined in the slack season, when there was less work to be had. Over 15 percent of the needlewomen who attended a meeting in the East End in 1849 had been in the workhouse, and most had recently gone without food or had been forced to pawn household goods. Mayhew estimated that there were 28,577 females employed in needlework and the slop sewing trades, most of them under twenty years of age.[10] The number increased later in the century, when the invention of the sewing machine made London's reservoir of unskilled female labor even more profitable for sweaters. The trade of needlewoman in London was less a skilled occupation that brought pride in craftsmanship than oppressive labor at subsubsistence wages. Staffed by foreigners and women, the industry maintained itself in London before the First World War at the expense of its workers.

9. Henry Mayhew, *The Greatest Plague in Life* (London, 1857), pp. 67–83; *Catholic Standard* 7 (September 17, 1853):208; 9 (November 5, 1853):213.

10. Yeo and Thompson, *Unknown Mayhew*, pp. 163, 179–180.

Many semiskilled occupations in London were women's jobs in which wages were substantially below the level earned even by unskilled male laborers. Unorganized and largely untrained, women provided a huge pool of labor that could be cheaply hired and used for simple operations in the manufacture of goods. The making of embroidery or artificial flowers, the scraping of lint, the pulling of fur, in addition to many finishing operations on accessories and clothing, were London-based industries whose labor force was predominantly female.[11] Many in these trades could be seen in the mornings near London Bridge:

One meets them at every step; young women carrying large bundles of umbrella-frames home to be covered; young women carrying wooden cages full of hats, which yet want the silk and binding . . . and above all, female sackmakers. These last are peculiar to London Bridge, for they all live in Bermondsey and fetch their work from the warehouses somewhere near Billingsgate. These girls have a yellow oily look and are many of them slight and delicate; but they carry immense loads of sacking on their heads.[12]

Irish women worked in some of these trades, doing subsidiary tasks in the leather, clothing, and paper industries.

Despite the complexity of the metropolitan economy and the growing impact of industrial change during the nineteenth century, women's urban economic roles differed little from what they had been in preindustrial times. Most made clothing or did domestic work. Very few had middle-class occupations; instead females dominated certain semiskilled or unskilled trades where wages were abysmally low.

One major occupation of both Irish men and women was street selling. Mayhew estimated that around 1850 at least 10,000 Irish made their living by hawking in various parts of London. Over three-quarters sold only fruit, but some of the men branched out into fish and vegetables, thereby competing with English coster-mongers. Irish women and children took over the fruit trade around the coaching stations during the late 1830s and dominated

---

11. Clive Day, "The Distribution of Industrial Occupations in England, 1841–61," *Transactions of the Connecticut Academy of Arts and Sciences* 28 (1927):126, 231; Clara Collet, "Women's Work," in Booth, *Life and Labour*, ser. 1, *Poverty*, vol. 4, pp. 266–280; ser. 2, *Industry*, vol. 3, pp. 59–63.

12. Derek Hudson, *Munby: Man of Two Worlds* (London, 1972), p. 99.

it from then on. While some could make a decent living as street vendors, the majority seemed to have drifted into the trade for lack of an alternative and used it as an occupation of last resort. Unemployed construction laborers and farm workers became hawkers temporarily whenever no other jobs were available, and Mayhew claimed that Irish women took up street selling because of their inability to sew and to keep house. Even the minimal qualifications of the needlewoman or domestic servant were beyond them. A certain number of Irish street traders became sellers of refuse, damaged fruit and vegetables that the coster-mongers removed from their regular stock. Elderly Irish women kept stalls in the poorest neighborhoods selling these castoffs in halfpenny lots to those who could afford nothing else. Since two of the best locations for such sales were Saffron Hill and Rose-mary Lane, at least part of the clientele was Irish. In general, Irish street traders concentrated on the simplest and least rewarding kinds of hawking and carried the heaviest goods.[13]

The distribution of the Irish sample among London industries gives only an approximate notion of the extent to which migrants had moved into low-skilled jobs. A much clearer picture of their position in London's socioeconomic hierarchy can be obtained by dividing the Irish sample among the five social groups outlined by the English registrar general in 1911 and comparing the results with a similar tabulation for the entire London population. (See Figure 4.1.) Group I represents the upper class and the top ranks of the middle class — the professionals, employers of more than twenty-five workers, top-level managers and administrators — while group II is reserved for intermediate-level white-collar workers — teachers or owners of small firms, shopkeepers, some managers, and subordinates in administration or in the profes-sions. Workers and the lowest level of white-collar employees are divided among the remaining three groups: III represents arti-sans, other skilled workers, clerks, and a few other white-collar workers; IV comprises a wide variety of semiskilled workers; and V is composed solely of unskilled workers.

About 20 percent of the total London employed population had middle-class occupations in 1851. In comparison, the size of

13. Mayhew, *London Labour,* vol. 1, pp. 104, 118; vol. 2, p. 352.

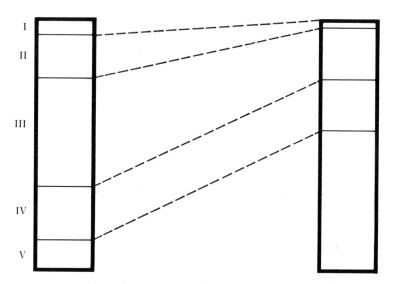

London Employed Population   Sampled Irish Employed Population

Registrar general's social groups:

   I. Professionals, large employers, top-ranking administrators
  II. Shopkeepers, clerks, teachers, lower ranking administrators, small business
      people
 III. Skilled workers
 IV. Semiskilled workers
  V. Unskilled workers

Figure 4.1. Proportions of London and sampled Irish employed populations in various occupational groups, 1851

the Irish middle class in the five parishes sampled in 1851 was small, less than 4 percent of the working population. When the socioeconomic distribution of Irish workers is compared with that of the total London population, major differences can be seen. Although a majority of employed Londoners held skilled jobs and only 11 percent belonged to the lowly ranks of the unskilled, among the Irish these proportions were reversed. Over 50 percent of the employed Irish held unskilled jobs in the five parishes sampled and only 20 percent had skilled occupations. Moreover, most of this latter group worked as sweated tailors or shoemakers, having only nominal status as artisans. This extraordinary difference between English and Irish workers does not disappear if we compare the Irish and the English residing in a poor workers' district, south St. Giles. Only one-quarter of the employed English but one-half of the Irish workers sampled in this area held unskilled jobs. Even within the slums of central London, many more of the Irish occupied the lowest rungs of the social ladder.

This concentration of the Irish in low-skilled occupations held true for all ages and stages of the life cycle: a majority of male adolescents, adults, and the old belonged to social group V. Yet if the socioeconomic distribution of male Irish workers in 1851 is assumed to reflect changes that would occur over the lifetimes of individuals, a small shift into more highly skilled jobs can be identified. Those who entered the labor market before the age of fifteen took unskilled jobs almost exclusively. As the proportion of those working climbed, so did the proportion of craftsmen and clerks. Middle-class Irish entered the labor force later, and their proportion of the total employed Irish population increased over the life cycle. While only 4 percent of twenty-five- to twenty-nine-year-olds belonged to social groups I and II, among those aged fifty-five to fifty-nine, 13 percent had occupations that could be classified as middle-class. Those who moved into higher ranking occupations did so after working for many years in positions of lower status, perhaps as clerks or lower level white-collar employees. For nonmanual workers, middle age was a time of limited upward mobility. The occupational distribution of the Irish also varied according to stage in the cycle of family development. The few Irish who became shopkeepers and who had moved into the upper and medium ranks of white-collar jobs were almost exclusively household heads, and more household heads had skilled jobs in 1851 than did either sons or lodgers. (See Table A.2, Appendix B.) Over 4 percent worked in retail trading as shopkeepers. Moreover, they were less likely to be either semiskilled laborers or hawkers than were less well-established sections of the Irish community. Though occupational mobility was slight for migrants as a whole, the chance of moving into a higher social group varied with the stage in a man's working life. Sons and lodgers, often young and unmarried, were virtually excluded from white-collar occupations and from shopkeeping;

in contrast, household heads, particularly those over thirty-five years old, could be found in these positions with increasing frequency. With seniority, experience, and perhaps capital saved from the wages of wives and children, older men could move up in the working class or even out of it. But they also could slip downward. Many of the unskilled jobs in which the Irish were concentrated were jobs of last resort into which workers shifted when they were forced out of other trades.

The Dimensions of Irish Poverty

The occupations followed by the Irish meant that poverty was a virtual certainty for most during some part of their lives. Neither in female-headed households nor in those of casual or sweated workers with several young children did the wages of the household head begin to cover minimum consumption needs. Even households headed by males in better paid occupations found their economic health made precarious by the risk of unemployment. Not all Irish families were below the poverty line, to be sure, and not all below it remained there always, but the dimensions of poverty among Irish workers were wide, deep, and for most inescapable.

Although data on the wages and expenditures of the sampled Irish families were not recorded or have not survived, this information can be approximated by use of average London wages, rents, and prices around 1850. Some sample budgets for workers' families in the mid-nineteenth century are available, as are data on workers' consumption patterns and diets. With this evidence Irish workers' incomes can be estimated and then compared with living costs.

Since most Irish males were laborers, wages in this category provide a good starting point. The average weekly wage of more than 350 laborers who headed households in St. George in the East in 1848 was 15s. 7d.; the best paid of the laborers employed at the London docks in the late 1840s averaged 16s. 6d. per week.[14] But only men who were regularly employed could count on

14. Committee of the Council of the Statistical Society, "Report of an Investigation into the State of the Poorer Classes of St. George in the East," *Journal of the [Royal] Statistical Society* 11 (1848):200–201; Mayhew, *London Labour*, vol. 3, p. 303.

earning this much. The amount of dock employment varied considerably according to wind and weather. In addition, more men were in the trade than could be employed on an average day. Mayhew estimated that the most industrious and well known of the casual dock laborers earned 13s. a week during a good summer, but that the lowest grades averaged only 5s. a week.[15] Casual laborers in other industries could anticipate a similarly wide spread of average wages. In the parish of St. Giles in the Fields, casual laborers, many of whom were Irish, were paid 2s. or 2s. 4d. a day during the late 1820s and 3s. a day in the late 1860s. During the summers, men worked six days a week, giving them an income at best of between 12s. and 14s. in 1828 and 18s. in 1868.[16] These figures do not allow for unemployment or under-employment, however; average weekly wages would have been several shillings lower. A reasonable estimate of laborers' wages, therefore, would require two categories, one for the regularly employed and another for those with only irregular earnings. Around 1850, men in the former category made about 15s. per week, while men in the latter could earn perhaps 8s. to 10s. per week.

Skilled Irish workers could make more. Since most Irish artisans were in the clothing trades, shoemakers and tailors' wages will be used to stand for the earnings of skilled migrants. In 1848 in St. George in the East, shoemakers and tailors earned respectively 17s. 5d. and 21s. 6d.[17] But both of these averages neglect the factor of unemployment. Moreover, a large proportion of both tailors and shoemakers worked for sweaters at lower rates. Not only did tailors' incomes vary according to the season, but their piecework wages fluctuated according to the type of garment they made and the nature of the employer. Of the tailors interviewed by Henry Mayhew, those working in the honorable part of the trade earned about 15s. 5d. a week, while those working for sweaters in the East End averaged only 8s. Shoemakers' wages also fluctuated widely. East End society men — boot

15. Mayhew, *London Labour*, vol. 3, p. 309.

16. St. Giles in the Fields and St. George, Bloomsbury, "Wages Book" (1821-1831) and "Casual Labour Book" (1860-1900), Holborn Public Library.

17. Committee of the Council of the Statistical Society, "Report . . . [on] the Poorer Classes of St. George in the East," pp. 200–201.

closers and bootmen, for example — could make between £1 and £1.10 in 1847 and 1848, but those in the slop trade even when fully employed made only 12s. or 13s. In the late 1840s, in any case, many were only partially employed for much of the year; men in this situation reported to Mayhew weekly incomes of between 3s. and 10s.[18]

Hawkers' earnings were at the lower end of the scale of Irish incomes. For many it was an occupation of last resort, used either permanently or temporarily when one could find no employment elsewhere. While those with stalls and a good reputation could earn more, Mayhew thought that a costermonger averaged about 10s. a week throughout the year. But many Irish street sellers were women and children who had only a tray of oranges, onions, or flowers to sell. They took in far less — 1s. or 1s. 6d. a day; 5s. per week would be a reasonable estimate for their incomes.[19]

Women's wages were less than those of men in all trades. (Since domestic servants were given room and board, their standard of living fluctuated with the decisions of employers; I have excluded them from these calculations.) Needlewomen and female shoe binders claimed weekly earnings of between 2s. 6d. and 6s. 4d. per week in the late 1840s. Women in a variety of semiskilled trades, even when fully employed, could rarely earn more than 5s. or 6s. per week. The self-supporting single women and widows living in St. George in the East in 1848 reported average earnings of 6s. 10d. Most were needlewomen who earned about 5s. 9d. a week. Only by working as a prostitute, a dressmaker, or a laundress could a woman earn a few shillings more. The only women who earned as much as a regularly employed male laborer were a maker of straw bonnets and a shirtmaker.[20] Irish workers earned, therefore, anywhere from 3s. or 4s. a week to slightly over £1, depending on their trade, their sex, and the extent of underemployment.

Now let us look at what they spent. Rents in London were comparatively high. The Irish living in Church Lane in 1848

18. Yeo and Thompson, *Unknown Mayhew*, pp. 206, 248, 276.
19. Mayhew, *London Labour*, vol. 1, pp. 56, 88, 94, 172.
20. Yeo and Thompson, *Unknown Mayhew*, pp. 120, 123, 147, 164, 166, 259; Committee of the Council of the Statistical Society, "Report . . . [on] the Poorer Classes of St. George in the East," p. 206.

paid 3s. a week for an unfurnished, ramshackle room; laborers' families in St. George in the East at this time averaged 3s. 3d. a week for rent, and the average rent for workers' households in St. James, Westminister, was 2s. 11¼d. a week.[21] A rent of 4s. was the level of respectability, for this sum paid for a year totaled slightly more than £10; this rate entitled one's family to a Poor Law settlement, although local Guardians of the Poor were reluctant to recognize such a claim by those who had occupied only one or two rooms. A 4s. rent was not an impossible sum for unskilled workers to raise. Indeed, 42 percent of the St. Giles Irish who asked for relief during the late 1830s and had spent several years in the parish had at some point paid a rent of this amount, but they had done so only intermittently, when their chief earner was a regularly employed male.[22] Rents for those down on their luck were much lower. A single person or a small family could lodge with another for 1s. or 1s. 6d. a week, and single rooms could be had in central London for 2s. or 2s. 6d. around 1850.[23] Although rents varied with family size and with the amount of crowding and dirt one was prepared to endure, an average of 3s. for an Irish household seems a reasonable estimate.

The total cost of living for an Irish family depended on its size, diet, and level of expenditure for such items as fuel, candles, clothes, beer, and liquor. Benjamin Seebohm Rowntree calculated a budget for a family of five in York in 1901 which represented a late-nineteenth-century judgment of life at the poverty line. (See Table 4.2, budget D.)[24] Before this budget can be accepted as a standard for 1850, however, certain differences in prices and levels of consumption between the middle and the end

21. Committee of the Council of the Statistical Society, "Report . . . to Investigate the State of the Inhabitants and Their Dwellings in Church Lane, St. Giles," *Journal of the [Royal] Statistical Society* 11 (1848):2; "Report . . . on the State of the Working Classes in the Parishes of St. Margaret and St. John, Westminister," ibid. 3 (1840):17; "Report . . . [on] the Poorer Classes of St. George in the East," p. 208.

22. Board of Guardians, Holborn Union, St. Giles, "Examinations of Paupers" (1830–1840), London County Council.

23. Committee of the Council of the Statistical Society, "Report . . . [on] the Inhabitants . . . in Church Lane," pp. 3, 4, 7, 8, 9; Board of Guardians, "Examinations of Paupers."

24. Benjamin Seebohm Rowntree, *Poverty: A Study of Town Life* (London, 1901), p. 110.

Table 4.2. Estimated workers' family budgets for two adults and three children, England, 1849, 1860, and 1901

Budget items	A. 1849	B. 1860	C. 1860	D. 1901
Food	11s. 6d.	10s. 4¼d.	13s. 9d.	12s. 9d.
Rent	2s. 0d.	2s. 6d.	3s. 0d.	4s. 0d.
Fuel, clothing, miscellaneous	2s. 0d.	2s. 7¾d.	3s. 9d.	4s. 11d.
Total	15s. 6d.	15s. 6d.	20s. 6d.	21s. 8d.

A. An Irish street seller's budget, adapted to the needs of a family of five (Henry Mayhew, *London Labour and the London Poor*, 4 vols. [London, 1861-1862; reprinted New York, 1968], vol. 1, p. 113).

B. Budget for the bottom ranks of the unskilled, those whose incomes were in the lower quartile of all incomes (W. A. Mackenzie, "Changes in the Standard of Living in the United Kingdom, 1860-1914," *Economica* 1, no. 3 [1921]:228-229).

C. Budget for the top ranks of English unskilled workers, those who earned a median income (ibid.).

D. Subsistence-level budget for York (Benjamin Seebohm Rowntree, *Poverty: A Study of Town Life* [London, 1901], p. 110).

of the century must be noted.[25] London workers in 1850 bought and consumed less than York workers in 1900, partly because they earned less, partly because things cost more. The 1901 poverty-level budget corresponds to the expenditures of a worker with a median income in 1860. Budgets for mid-nineteenth-century unskilled laborers' households set a standard of consumption lower than that of Rowntree's poverty line. Budgets B and C, which apply respectively to the bottom and top ranks of unskilled workers in England, were compiled by W. A. Mackenzie from retail prices, consumption data, and estimates of adult male earnings.[26] She allotted families of five a tiny allowance for fuel, clothing, and miscellaneous expenses and then calculated the cost

25. The consumption of commodities had increased markedly during the second half of the century. According to George Wood's index, per capita consumption of commodities rose by 61 percent between 1860-1864 and 1900-1920. At the same time, prices decreased. Indeed, indices of London prices of food, fuel, clothing, and household goods were about 20 percent higher in 1850 than in 1900. See George H. Wood, "Real Wages and the Standards of Comfort since 1850," *Journal of the Royal Statistical Society* 72 (1909):101; Rufus S. Tucker, "Real Wages of Artisans in London, 1729-1935," *Journal of the American Statistical Association* 31 (1936):79-80.

26. W. A. Mackenzie, "Changes in the Standard of Living in the United Kingdom, 1860-1914," *Economica* 1, no. 3 (1921):216-217, 226, 228-229.

of a diet based primarily on potatoes, bread, and tea supplemented by small amounts of milk, butter, sugar, and bacon. Budget C provided an adult male with 3,200 calories a day; under budget B, adult males got only 2,900 calories a day. These consumption levels were set to correspond to her estimates of the average incomes of various grades of worker.

An Irish street seller, who lived approximately on the scale proposed by budget A or B for a family of five, told Henry Mayhew how he spent his weekly earnings of 5s. A bed in a lodging house cost 1s.; 2s. 2d. went for washing, one shave, material to mend his clothes, a donation to his church, and a Sunday half pint of beer. The remaining 2s. 10d. was spent for food. His breakfast was bread and coffee; dinner consisted of three herrings and two or three pounds of potatoes; he made his supper from tea and leftover bread from breakfast. On Sundays he added a little butter and meat.[27] The cost of even this dull and inadequate diet rose to around 11s. per week for a family of five. (See Table 4.2, budgets A and B.)

The only Irish families with one wage earner and several children who could have afforded to live at the level proposed by Rowntree as the poverty line would have been headed by steadily employed male artisans. Unskilled laborers could reach that standard only by adding several shillings' weekly income from other family members. While couples without children could consume at the level proposed by budget A for about 8s. per week, the cost of feeding three children (estimated to eat about 75 percent of an adult diet) and renting a single room for even 2s. would almost double their cost of living.

Several conclusions are suggested. Most Irish families of three or more would regularly require the earnings of wives and children in order to feed themselves and certainly to reach the standard of consumption suggested by Rowntree's subsistence-level budget D. During those years when children were too young to work, a high proportion of Irish families could not have afforded to live even at the level proposed for unskilled laborers in budgets A and B, unless the husband was fully employed. Any unemployment for a male laborer with four dependents would reduce income below the restricted levels of budgets A and B. Most female-headed households must have normally lived well below Rowntree's poverty line, since virtually no female occupation paid wages equal to those of a regularly employed laborer. John Foster has calculated from wage and price data that in Oldham, 41 percent of all workers' families lived in poverty during a bad year, and that fully 15 percent remained in poverty when prosperity returned. Over the course of a family's developmental cycle, 89 percent of all laborers' families in Oldham lived through at least one period when their income fell below the subsistence level.[28] No doubt Irish laborers in London were at least as unfortunate. Poverty was a normal part of the social and economic order within which they lived. It came with unemployment and underemployment, with illness or the death of a husband and father. It came with old age and with the birth of children. It came with the inescapable events of the human life cycle.

The Transformation of the Irish Family Economy

Irish wage earners in London ought not to be considered only as individuals; they formed family economies in which all contributed earnings and services in order to maintain the family unit. The extent of underemployment and the low levels of unskilled workers' wages made it necessary for all to earn during some part of their lives. This pattern of earning by all members of a family as needs and opportunities arose also existed in rural Ireland, but migration into a city altered the familial division of labor, the types of work done, and the amount of contact individuals had with the marketplace.

In Ireland, the basis of the peasant economy was the family farm or plot of potato ground, usually rented from an absentee landlord or a middleman. The farms were run as family enterprises, children working alongside parents as unpaid laborers and receiving a share of the land on their marriage or the death of

28. John Foster, *Class Struggle and the Industrial Revolution: Early Industrial Capitalism in Three English Towns* (London, 1974), pp. 96–98; see also Michael Anderson, *Family Structure in Nineteenth-Century Lancashire* (Cambridge, 1971), p. 30.

their father.[29] Women joined in the routine of the fields when necessary and took care of the cottage garden and animals in addition to their household chores. As economic pressures mounted, rents rose, and holdings were subdivided, the rural Irish devised supplementary ways of maintaining themselves on the land. The rural tenantry was drawn into a market economy. Both Arthur Young in the 1770s and the royal commissioners investigating the Irish poor in 1835 and 1836 tell of the precarious economic equilibrium of cottiers' and laborers' households that depended for part of their income on the raising and sale of animals and animal produce. These households survived by "converting every pig, fowl, and even egg into cash."[30] Women's role in this process was crucial, for they made the butter, spun the wool, cared for the pigs and poultry, and sold the eggs, diverting food away from the family in order to maximize income. Both landholders and laborers continued to depend on such earnings through the 1830s and 1840s. The royal commission, reporting on laborers' families in Munster, discovered that between 18 and 31 percent of a family's income came from the sale of eggs, poultry, and pigs.[31] Families also earned money from nonagricultural pursuits. In the late eighteenth century, the proceeds from domestic industry formed an important part of rural incomes. "Spinning is the general business of women [in Cork]," reported Arthur Young. "Flax is sown by everybody for their own use, which they spin, and get woven into linen for themselves, and what they have to spare sell in yarn." Investigating the poor in the area around Westport, Young found "they reckon that the men feed the family with their labor in the field, and the women pay the rent by spinning."[32] Unfortunately, competition from English and Ulster spinning factories slowly destroyed the by-

29. Great Britain, *Parliamentary Papers* (Commons), "First Report of the Commissioners for Inquiring into the Condition of the Poorer Classes in Ireland," 1835, 32:355–427, app. A; K. H. Connell, *The Population of Ireland, 1750–1845* (Oxford, 1950), p. 15; see also Anderson, *Family Structure*, pp. 80–81.
30. Arthur Young, *A Tour in Ireland . . . in 1776, 1777, and 1778*, 2 vols. (London, 1780), vol. 2, p. 103.
31. Great Britain, *Parliamentary Papers* (Commons), "First Report . . . [on] the Condition of the Poorer Classes in Ireland," Appendix D, pp. 89–90, 108–111.
32. Young, *Tour in Ireland*, vol. 1, pp. 312, 369, 372.

occupations of women. By the mid-1830s laborers' wives in Munster could earn little by spinning or weaving, although some continued to spin thread for their own use.[33]

By the time of the potato famine, the family economy in rural Ireland had been reshaped by changing circumstances. As farms were subdivided, more and more men had to leave their own plots temporarily to work elsewhere, leaving women and children to tend the land. Both seasonal and permanent migration increased, while underemployed day laborers paid their rents by working for local farmers. The unity of home and workplace had broken down for these men and their unmarried children, many of whom migrated or took jobs as servants. Although married women continued to earn money, the amount they brought in was decreasing. Families that did not hold enough land to support themselves became less units of production than economic partnerships to which each member contributed wages earned elsewhere and the meager profits of odd jobs and by-occupations. This growing proletarianization of the Irish peasantry undermined the operation of the rural family economy and threatened its continuance.

Migration permitted familial economic cooperation to continue but channeled it into new forms. Louise Tilly and Joan Scott have shown that both peasants and urban workers' families throughout nineteenth-century Europe behaved according to a customary code by which each member contributed his or her work and earnings to the household. Strategies for ensuring the survival of the family which had been developed in the countryside were adapted to the changed circumstances of the city, not abandoned. Even in the city, where the market employed migrants as individuals, their response to their economic world was a familistic one, with all working for the common good.[34]

The form of these Irish family economies in London differed in two important ways from the ideal type of a preindustrial family enterprise. Home and workplace were no longer identical; neither

33. Great Britain, *Parliamentary Papers* (Commons), "First Report . . . [on] the Condition of the Poorer Classes in Ireland," Appendix D, pp. 84–90.

34. Joan W. Scott and Louise A. Tilly, "Women's Work and the Family Economy in Nineteenth-Century Europe," in *The Family in History*, ed. Charles E. Rosenberg (Philadelphia, 1975), pp. 18–21. See also Daniel Thorner et al., eds., *A. V. Chayanov on the Theory of the Peasant Economy* (Homewood, Ill., 1966).

did families commonly share tasks of production. Only in a few tailoring and shoemaking households did an Irish family work together at home. In fact, only 4 percent of wives and 4.2 percent of all employed sons shared their husbands' or fathers' occupations in 1851. Husbands, wives, and children commonly took up different trades, which varied according to age and sex. The household became a unit of consumption rather than of production, a place from which adult males and most adolescents were absent during the day. Migration into the city pushed to completion this process that had begun earlier in rural Ireland.

Irish families in the city could adopt several strategies to ensure that earnings covered their minimum consumption needs. The irregularity of a male laborer's income meant that supplemental sources had to be sought. Money from children, wives, and lodgers provided the margin that permitted survival. Indeed, tabulations of laborers' budgets for the parish of St. George in the East during the late 1840s indicated a gap of 18.4 percent between husbands' wages and total family income.[35] Households apportioned both tasks and the obligation to earn among all their members. While we have no window into Irish homes to allow us to witness the decision-making process, it seems likely that children and wives were pressed into service as needed, their role being essentially dependent on the level and regularity of the male head's income. If he had only unskilled, casual work, the pressure on all to earn would be great. Writing in 1853, a priest in central London described a family in which such pressure was especially severe:

Timothy — wife, and four children — Nano, 11 years old; Patrick, 9; Teddy, 5; and Ellen, 3; Timothy, the father, has been ill for the last three months, is better now; sells onions in the streets; his wife sells onions also; Nano sells apples during the day, and goes to school in the evening; Patrick minds the house and his little brother and sister, while father and mother and Nano are out selling.[36]

Sending children into the labor force at a very early age was a common decision of Irish migrants, one that signaled a change

---

35. Committee of the Council of the Statistical Society, "Report . . . [on] the Poorer Classes of St. George in the East," pp. 200–201.
36. *Catholic Standard* 9 (October 29, 1853):212.

from rural habits. Among laborers' families in Ireland before the famine, the surplus of unemployed adults left little work for children except on a family's own land. Some adolescents went into service or joined other farming families as live-in laborers, but most who did not migrate stayed at home until they married, working alongside their parents.[37] But in London it was far easier for unmarried sons and daughters to earn money. The help of children at home was less useful than the few pence they could bring in, for after migration families had to buy all their food and clothing. This increased involvement in a money economy put a premium on paid employment. In consequence, parents sent children out to work at an early age. A Roman Catholic priest surveying the working children in his parish found some who sold on the streets before they were ten years old. He thought that between 400 and 500 children living in Clerkenwell made their living by selling wood. "Great numbers" of boys swept crossings; others sang on the streets with their families or scoured the gutters for rags and bones. In one court he visited, about one-third of the children between the ages of seven and twenty hawked either firewood or food. Some of the rest took odd jobs as they could find them.[38] The nature of the London economy shaped this pattern of employment. Unlike Lancashire textile towns, the capital supplied few factory jobs for adolescents but did offer them casual laboring jobs.

In the 1851 sample of Irish families, 57 percent of coresiding sons and 41 percent of coresiding daughters aged ten and over listed occupations for the census taker; because of the nature of the work these children did and its episodic character, however, it is likely that these figures underestimate the extent of child labor among the Irish. The proportion of young people who worked rose rapidly with age, a majority of both sexes listing occupations by age fifteen. Young women were somewhat less likely to have occupations than young men, but because of the high demand for female servants who would live with their employers, women left home at an earlier age. (See Tables 4.3 and 4.4.)

After the age of fifteen, children began to move out of the home,

---

37. Great Britain, *Parliamentary Papers* (Commons), "First Report . . . [on] the Condition of the Poorer Classes in Ireland," Appendix D, pp. 80–81.
38. *Catholic Standard* 9 (November 26, 1853):216; 9 (December 10, 1853):218.

Table 4.3. Age of entry of Irish into London labor force, by sex, 1851

Age group	Percentage listing occupations in census	
	Males	Females
5–9 (N=421)	3.3%	2.5%
10–14 (N=437)	22.6	22.8
15–19 (N=377)	77.6	64.0
20–24 (N=402)	92.9	71.2
25–29 (N=324)	96.6	48.3

most disappearing by age twenty, even though the average marriage age among Irish migrants was twenty-six for women and twenty-eight for men. (See Table A.8, Appendix B.) Their destinations, therefore, were not homes of their own but those of other families, where they boarded or worked as servants. (See Table 4.4.) Some of these young lodgers were themselves migrants, having left their nuclear families in Ireland, but 18 percent were London-born and had chosen or were forced to live apart from their parents. This assertion of independence, linked no doubt to their ability to support themselves in a city that employed much child labor, shows the family economy at its point of disintegration. The young contributed their labor and earnings to their families of origin for a time, then distanced themselves for a few years of limited independence before marriage. Since marriage and the establishment of an independent household were almost universal among the London Irish, families could not count on economic help from children for more than a few years during their adolescence.

Since children contributed money to their households of origin for only a limited time in a family's developmental cycle, Irish wives periodically entered the labor market. They followed a pattern of participation that varied according to the numbers and ages of their children and the economic needs of their families. When first married, most Irish wives left the labor force. Although 66 percent of the sampled single Irish-born women over the age of ten listed occupations for the census taker, only 20 percent of the childless married women under age forty-five claimed they followed a trade. This proportion dropped to 13 percent among married women with children not yet in the labor

Table 4.4. Residential status of young Irish, sampled London parishes, 1851

	Age group							
	10–14		15–19		20–24		25–29	
Residential status	M (N=226)	F (N=211)	M (N=183)	F (N=194)	M (N=170)	F (N=232)	M (N=149)	F (N=175)
Living with parents	77.9%	77.3%	66.7%	54.6%	25.9%	24.6%	13.4%	6.9%
Living with other kin	3.1	1.9	6.6	5.7	7.6	4.7	6.0	6.3
In lodgings	18.6	17.5	20.2	22.7	47.1	32.3	34.9	27.4
In service	0.0	2.8	1.1	14.4	1.2	18.5	0.7	7.4
Living alone	0.0	0.0	1.1	0.0	2.9	0.4	4.0	3.4
Married and in own household	0.0	0.0	0.0	0.5	11.2	17.2	39.6	46.9
Unknown	0.4	0.5	4.4	2.1	4.1	2.2	1.3	1.7
	100.0%	100.0%	100.1%	100.0%	100.0%	99.9%	99.9%	100.0%

Source: Enumerators' books, Census of England, 1851.

force. Only when at least half of their children found jobs did married women begin to reenter the labor market. As children became more self-sufficient and moved out of the home, more and more Irish wives worked. The only Irish wives who listed occupations for themselves while several small children were at home were married to unskilled laborers, those whose incomes were the most irregular and insecure. Working wives with young children were women on whom the economic pressure to supplement their husbands' wages was especially severe. (See Figure 4.2.)

The employment pattern of widows and deserted wives, however, was the opposite of that of married women. Although only 22 percent of all married women worked, 75 percent of the Irish widows and married women living apart from their husbands had occupations. Virtually all female family heads took jobs when they had young children at home. Only as children became employed did they retreat from the labor market. Decisions about women's participation in the labor force thus varied according to a family's developmental cycle and the intensity of its need for cash. Married women's work moved to different rhythms from that of men, single children, or widows.

This different rhythm helps to account for married women's officially low rate of employment. Indeed, the census almost certainly understates wives' participation in the labor force, for women found part-time and seasonal alternatives to full-time jobs outside the home, repeating in the city the rural practice of taking on by-occupations in odd hours. Hawking food intermittently could bring in needed pence, but if one took to the streets to sell only a few days a month, why mention it to the census taker? It is therefore in the realm of the part-time or casual job that an unknown amount of married women's employment was located. Intermittent or seasonal work could supplement income or compensate for sudden losses of husbands' or children's wages. Irish laborers' wives in some areas worked seasonally when demand existed for their services. The wives of Roman Catholic garden laborers in Deptford would take their older children out of school to care for younger ones during the spring and fall, when they could get a few days' work in the fields, and many Irish families left town each year to pick hops in Kent.[39]

39. Ibid. 2 (March 30, 1850):25; 2 (September 21, 1850):50.

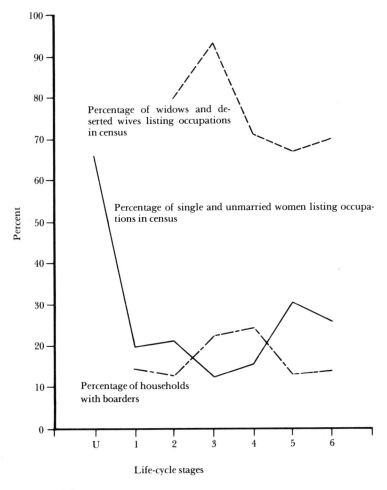

Percentage of widows and deserted wives listing occupations in census

Percentage of single and unmarried women listing occupations in census

Percentage of households with boarders

Life-cycle stages

U=unmarried
1=wife under 45, no children
2=wife under 45, one child under age 1
3=wife under 45, children at home, none working
4=children at home, fewer than half working
5=children at home, half or more working
6=wife 45 or older, no children or only one over 20 at home

Source: Census of 1851, London, five sample parishes only.

Figure 4.2. Employment patterns of Irish women, by life-cycle stage, London, 1851

Parliamentary investigators in 1895 reported a regular pattern of women's work during the slack season in men's trades. Wives took on sweated jobs at home when husbands were unemployed. Battersea laundries were staffed by gasworkers' wives in the summer and builders' wives in winter. Jobs for women as fur pullers and hat workers brought in extra income seasonally to the families of unemployed dock and leather workers in Bermondsey and Southwark.[40] The entry of these women into the labor market was not an independent activity but an expedient to maintain family income during periods of distress.

The home itself offered a means of earning. About one-fifth of all sampled Irish households in London took in boarders, who sometimes contracted for services from the female head of the household — the doing of laundry, mending, the provision of tea or breakfast. But a family's willingness to take in lodgers changed greatly over the life cycle, varying inversely with wives' regular participation in the labor force. The taking in of boarders was an alternative to women's work outside the home during the stages of a family's developmental cycle when children had to be fed and cared for but were too young to earn. When expenses were highest but earning power and available space lowest (life-cycle stages 3 and 4), Irish families permitted outsiders to share their cramped quarters. Far fewer households accepted lodgers when a majority of the children or their mothers entered the labor force. (See Figure 4.2.)

Irish women participated in several ways, therefore, in their urban family economies. During adolescence they entered the labor force and contributed wages to their families of origin. Sometime during their late teens, however, girls left their parents and boarded with other families, either as servants or as lodgers. Then after marriage, most left the labor force and worked at home to maintain their newly formed households. For the next several years, most Irish wives held only part-time or seasonal jobs. But they sometimes took in lodgers or contracted with a small-scale manufacturer to finish items at home to ease an increasing need for cash as family size increased. Their work was contingent upon the dual household needs for both money and labor services.

40. Jones, *Outcast London*, pp. 40–41, 48; see also Great Britain, *Parliamentary Papers* (Commons), "Select Committee on Distress from Want of Employment," 1895, 9:Q. 90, 137.

The urban Irish family economy therefore depended on women's and children's work as well as on that of the father. Despite the large proportion of married Irish women who declared to the census taker that they had no occupation, Irish wives regularly contributed small amounts of cash to their families. They took in lodgers and held part-time or seasonal jobs. Children earned a few pennies as opportunities arose, and supplemented parental income during their adolescence. This pattern of family labor resembled the family economy of the rural Irish, although in London the types of jobs available and the conditions under which work was done represented a major change from the Irish countryside.

A Tale of Stability and Modest Successes

Irish peasants and laborers had dreams of social mobility; yet they seem to have been modest dreams, not of the pot of gold at the end of the rainbow but of a few coins jingling in the pocket. The achievements of Irish heroes and heroines and the wishes proclaimed in London street ballads are small ones. Biddy the Basket Woman was happy with her hod-carrying husband, who was a ten-pound householder. Patrick Fagan, who proposed to his sweetheart Kitty, thought himself fortunate because:

> Of sov'reigns I had twinty, and says she I've seventeen,
> Faith, we'll join ourselves and them together, and live like king and queen.
> So we both set sail for Liverpool and packed our kits together,
> And married got so nate and cool, in spite of wind and weather;
> With our money we open'd a shop, in business not amiss.
> We sold oysters, haddocks, mac'rel, mussels, praties and fried fish.[41]

Emigrants' hopes were limited: "They say there's bread by working for, while the sun shines always there."[42] A job and higher wages sufficed. A Liverpool builder's laborer, who had been a cottier in Wexford, told his boss in the early 1840s that "there was a general impression among his countrymen that if they came to England their fortunes would be made, wages are so much higher here."[43]

41. Crampton collection, 8 vols., British Library, vol. 3, p. 56.
42. Baring-Gould collection, 7 vols., British Library, vol. 2, p. 5.
43. Great Britain, *Parliamentary Papers* (Commons), "Report on the State of the Irish Poor in Great Britain," 1836, 34:vi.

Whether even these modest dreams were realized is another matter. At first glance it would seem that the hopes of the Irish in England had been disappointed. In the 1830s, witnesses before the Royal Commission on the Irish Poor painted a rather dark picture of Irish chances for upward social mobility. Those in Manchester "seldom rise." An observer said of migrants in Liverpool:

Any of the Irish that get forward learn to live like the English, in the very same style, so that you could not distinguish their houses, furniture, wives, or children. Not many of them get forward in this way; but a few do: there are several hundred in Liverpool of this kind. All these persons had some money or a friend to start them; I know of no instance among the Irish of a common labourer getting into business, nor of a mechanic getting on by his trade to any great extent. . . . They are kept down by large families and small wages.[44]

Very little changes if one moves from descriptions of Irish workers in London at mid-century to the investigations of Charles Booth in the 1880s and 1890s. The cast of characters seems to duplicate itself. The laborer, the hawker, and the laundress reappear, many living on the same streets as their predecessors of fifty years earlier. In south St. Giles around Seven Dials and Drury Lane, Booth found Irish street sellers and market porters living in a "dirty, violent" area where poverty turned imperceptibly into criminality. Dotted throughout the East End, but particularly around Commercial Road and East India docks, were colonies of Irish dock laborers, "generally poor and thriftless." The Bermondsey Roman Catholic population consisted of "men and lads getting casual employment at the wharves or elsewhere, whilst the women and girls obtain work at the jam factories or in similar trades, or are engaged in sack-making."[45] For Booth, the Irish were the Irish poor, a rather shiftless, improvident lot living at best in want and at worst in a semisavage, nomadic state. Yet one must remember that Booth's aim was to quantify the extent of poverty in London, and clusters of Irish families in the poorest areas were bound to attract attention. Although Booth establishes the fact of continued Irish membership in the lowest socioeconomic groups, his evidence does not imply the lack of social

44. Ibid., p. xv. American evidence confirms this lack of mobility; see n. 46.
45. Booth, *Life and Labour*, ser. 1, *Poverty*, vol. 2, app. 1, pp. 20, 30; ser. 3, *Religious Influences*, vol. 5, Table 1, pp. 126–127.

mobility for individuals. The Irish he observed were different people from the migrants of Mayhew's acquaintance.

The measurement of vertical mobility is a complex matter. Ideally, an investigator would collect data on income, wealth, property holdings, occupational changes, and geographic movement both for individuals and for successive generations. The most common sources of these data — the census, tax records, wills, and city directories — could then be linked together to provide a running record of changes. Several such studies of urban populations in the United States have been done or are now in progress.[46] Unfortunately, local tax records and London city directories largely exclude the Irish poor because as unskilled laborers and tenants who sublet only part of a house, they neither operated their own businesses nor paid taxes directly. It has proved equally impossible to trace their property holdings through centrally recorded wills. Only the census remains as a source, and since the Irish were highly mobile and my sample covered only five small districts within the metropolitan area, the tracing of individuals at ten-year intervals was impractical. I have therefore used the London census in a different way, charting the changes in group occupational distribution that occurred between 1851 and 1861 and examining the relationship between social status and family status, between vertical mobility and the life cycle.

The changes that took place between 1851 and 1861 in the occupational distribution of the Irish-born and their children were small and statistically insignificant, for the most part. While the amount of change was minor, its direction was toward the occupational distribution of the London population as a whole. Increases occurred in the proportion of Irish men holding white-collar jobs. A few more professionals, administrators, teachers,

46. Clyde Griffen, "Workers Divided: The Effect of Craft and Ethnic Differences in Poughkeepsie, New York, 1850-1880"; Herbert G. Gutman, "The Reality of the Rags-to-Riches Myth: The Case of the Paterson, New Jersey, Locomotive, Iron, and Machinery Manufacturers, 1830-1880"; Stephan Thernstrom, "Immigrants and Wasps: Ethnic Differences in Occupational Mobility in Boston, 1890-1940"; Stuart Blumin, "Mobility and Change in Ante Bellum Philadelphia"; all in *Nineteenth-Century Cities*, ed. Stephan Thernstrom and Richard Sennett (New Haven, 1969); Stephan Thernstrom, *The Other Bostonians: Poverty and Progress in the American Metropolis, 1880-1970* (Cambridge, Mass., 1973).

and merchants were recorded, and the proportion in several specialized industries, such as printing and metalwork, rose also. (See Table 4.5.) At the same time, the proportion employed in construction work and general labor fell. The group identified with no specific industry, men who shifted jobs with the season and demand, decreased from 20.0 percent to 9.7 percent of the employed male population. Nevertheless, the chance that a man in the sampled Irish population would be a general laborer was still twice as high as the chance for the average London male.

Similar shifts took place in the occupational profile of employed Irish women. By 1861, more women had teaching or other white-collar jobs than a decade earlier, and the numbers in the paper, printing, and service industries increased. Slightly fewer worked in the most depressed trades, in street hawking and sewing. These changes, which took place in a period when

Table 4.5. Distribution of occupations in Irish sample, by sex, 1861

Occupational group	Males (N=1,050)	Females (N=697)	Percentage change from 1851	
Agriculture	0.5%	1.1%	− 0.5	+0.2
Construction	11.5	0.6	− 1.3	+0.2
Metalworking	2.3	0.3	+ 1.2	+0.2
Machinery	0.4	—	− 1.0	−0.1
Shipbuilding	—	0.1	0.0	+0.1
Gas and fuel	0.5	0.1	+ 0.3	−0.2
Glass	0.5	—	0.0	0.0
Textiles	—	1.7	− 0.8	+0.8
Clothing	4.9	13.6	− 2.3	−3.6
Leather	1.1	3.2	+ 0.5	+2.5
Wood	1.0	—	− 0.1	0.5
Paper	1.7	4.7	− 0.2	+2.7
Printing	1.8	1.3	+ 1.3	+0.6
Food	9.0	13.0	+ 1.7	−2.1
Transport	32.1	0.9	+12.7	+0.5
Service	3.9	44.8	+ 2.1	+2.1
General labor	17.8	0.6	−22.9	−0.3
Administration	0.6	0.1	+ 0.3	+0.1
Commerce and finance	5.1	7.2	+ 1.3	−0.9
Military and police	1.2	—	+ 0.7	0.0
Professions	1.0	0.3	+ 0.5	+0.3
Art, education, entertainment	1.3	1.1	+ 0.8	+1.0
Other and unknown	1.7	5.2	− 1.6	−3.6

migration decreased sharply, denote no striking improvement in the economic position of Irish migrants as a whole. But they do show that a process of differentiation had begun among a formerly agricultural population, separating it into more varied occupational groups and leading it toward economic assimilation with the English population.

These changes in the occupational composition of the sampled Irish population cannot be explained by changes in the London labor market. Although fewer Irish were unskilled laborers in 1861 than a decade earlier, the role of unskilled labor in the London economy was increasing rather than decreasing at this time. Between 1861 and 1891, the proportion of males over ten years of age working in unskilled jobs increased by 1.5 percent and of females by 1.0 percent. The Irish shift from skilled into semiskilled jobs, however, can be seen as a reflection of larger structural changes in the London economy, where mechanization transformed more and more industries, decreasing the importance of skilled jobs.[47]

This relative lack of change in the occupations of the group sampled says nothing about changes in incomes or property accumulation, both of which would affect a family's social status.[48] Vertical mobility ought not, therefore, to be measured purely in terms of occupational changes. The London Irish could improve their position in many small ways: by saving, by joining workers' organizations, by remaining at one job and establishing a local reputation for honesty and dependability. Small successes perhaps, but not negligible gains for an unskilled laborer and his family. William Pollard-Urquhart, who investigated Irish laborers in the East End in the early 1860s, reported on the kinds of social mobility he found among those working on the docks. Some had lifted themselves entirely out of the ranks of the manual laborers. Those who had been able to save some money and had not sent it back to Ireland chose two major forms of investment: they became either landlords who rented houses and then sublet rooms or small shopkeepers who set up grocery stores for a local clientele. Although Pollard-Urquhart thought that very few

47. Jones, *Outcast London*, Tables 13 and 14, p. 387.
48. See Stephan Thernstrom, *Poverty and Progress: Social Mobility in a Nineteenth-Century City* (Cambridge, Mass., 1964), pp. 117, 120.

laborers used the post office savings banks, there were similar Roman Catholic institutions and much church encouragement to use them. The accumulation of property and its investment in a small business was therefore a path taken by some workers' families.[49]

Another possible mode of Irish achievement was the exchange of casual employment for a regular job. Pollard-Urquhart found that by the early 1860s a fair percentage of Irish dock laborers in the East End had moved from casual labor to the permanent staff and that some had become superintendents. By mid-century the Irish dominated the better paid lines of dock work, and they passed their positions on from father to son. Later the system of preferential hiring, which was introduced in the 1890s, marked out a clear path by which those not permanently employed could work their way into positions of greater security.[50]

The signposts of success for laborers ought not to be measured in middle-class terms. While an Irish actor could aspire to fame on the London stage, a migrant selling oranges in Whitechapel saw his future in less exalted terms. "Getting ahead" signified not the duplication of Andrew Carnegie's rise to fortune but small achievements that brought a measure of security and help for one's children. Such hopes could be shared even by the poorest of the poor. A Liverpool builder reported to the Royal Commission on the Irish Poor in Great Britain a conversation with an Irish laborer who after migration earned more in a week than he had in a month back in Wexford:

He told me that he could get his clothing as cheap here as at home and generally all the things he wanted. . . . He said likewise that it was a great inducement to them to come here that they can get situations for their children, which they could not do at home. He told me likewise that he could more easily get his children educated here than in Ireland. This man lives in a cellar. He will never return to Ireland; he has no wish to go back.[51]

49. William Pollard-Urquhart, "Condition of the Irish Labourers in the East of London," *Transactions of the National Association for the Promotion of the Social Sciences*, 1862, p. 747.

50. Ibid., pp. 746–747; Booth, *Life and Labour*, ser. 2, *Industry*, vol. 3, pp. 409–427; John Lovell, *Stevedores and Dockers: A Study of Trade Unionism in the Port of London, 1870–1914* (New York, 1969), pp. 61, 64.

51. Great Britain, *Parliamentary Papers* (Commons), "Report on the State of the Irish Poor in Great Britain," p. vi.

Evidently even a Liverpool cellar with its fringe benefits was preferable to an Irish cabin when a man had little or no land. As Charles Booth recognized when he tried to gauge the response of the poor to the desolation of their surroundings, it was less the realities of the present than the contrast between present and past that mattered: "What is true of the individual is no less true of the class. To interpret aright the life of either we need to lay open its memories and understand its hopes."[52] To those fleeing unemployment and famine, any job signified improvement in their situation. And reminded by their priests that poverty was holy and that the needs of the soul far outranked those of the body, Irish migrants were isolated from the sternest taunts of the Calvinist and later of the social Darwinist. For Celtic newcomers, the model to follow was less that of Horatio Alger than that of Biddy the Basket Woman and her husband, Pat, who created a reasonably comfortable life even though both were unskilled laborers.

52. Booth, *Life and Labour,* ser. 1, *Poverty,* vol. 1, p. 173.

CHAPTER 5

Families and Households

Irish families both in rural Ireland and in urban England conformed to common Western European patterns in their demographic and social behavior. People married late, and a relatively large proportion did not marry at all. After a wedding, a couple normally formed a separate household built around a conjugal family, rather than join the household of either set of parents or of other kin. One did not find in nineteenth-century Ireland the large complex households common in Eastern Europe that included agnatically related kin or hired laborers' families.[1] Irish households resembled the relatively small, simple English ones far more than their rural counterparts east of the Elbe. But within demographic and structural patterns prevalent among Western European families, there is much scope for variation. Urbanization produced several changes in the demographic decisions of the migrating Irish.

Rural-to-urban migration altered the size and timing of the formation of Irish families. Migrants in London married earlier than the rural Irish and had fewer children. The pattern of Irish demographic adaptation in London was similar to that occurring

1. John Hajnal, "European Marriage Patterns in Perspective," in *Population in History: Essays in Historical Demography,* ed. D. V. Glass and D. E. C. Eversley (London, 1964); Joel M. Halpern, "Town and Countryside in Serbia in the Nineteenth Century. Social and Household Structure as Reflected in the Census of 1863," in *Household and Family in Past Time,* ed. Peter Laslett and Richard Wall (Cambridge, 1972), pp. 401–428; Andrejs Plakans, "Peasant Farmsteads and Households in the Baltic Littoral, 1797," *Comparative Studies in Society and History* 17 (1975):2–35.

simultaneously in Dublin, Liverpool, and Manchester, and dis-
similar to the postfamine demographic changes among the rural
Irish. The Irish seem to have made two different sets of demographic decisions, one for the countryside and another for the city.
The *composition* of Irish families and households, however,
changed little as a result of rural-to-urban migration. Most Irish
families were nuclear both in the city and in the countryside,
although a substantial minority of families in both localities
included relatives beyond the nuclear unit at some points in
their developmental cycle. The extended family therefore did
not disappear with long-distance migration. It persisted both
as a residential unit and as a group with shared activities. Kin
not only helped to introduce newly arrived migrants to urban
life but provided services and support during times of crisis.
Migration thus destroyed neither the claims of kinship nor recognition of those claims. Irish households were flexible structures. They expanded as other kin, lodgers, visitors, or servants
came to join them, and they contracted as these additional residents died, formed their own households, or went elsewhere.
In London, boarding and the coresidence of kin beyond the
nuclear family were creative adaptations to urban life, which
increased the economic security and the social solidarity of the
Irish community. Relatives and lodgers brought needed cash
and services to low-income families, who in return provided
newcomers with food, shelter, information, and a familiar cultural milieu. The urban Irish household therefore helped migrants
to adapt to urban life. Both the changes and the continuities in
Irish families and households can be seen clearly when the
prefamine rural Irish are compared with migrants in London in
1851.

Family and Household in Prefamine Ireland

Very little is known of prefamine Irish family structures and
demographic decisions, in part because few vital records exist for
the period before 1850 and in part because scholars are only now
analyzing those records that have survived.[2] The paucity of

2. Only a small number of Roman Catholic parish registers survive for years
before 1800, and few of the early sets are complete. Civil registration of the

adequate data has too often led historians to substitute descriptions written by anthropologists in the twentieth century for quantitative studies of prefamine families. In particular, the work of Conrad Arensberg and Solon Kimball has led historians back to the hypotheses of Le Play, to a vision of traditional Irish society dominated by patriarchal extended families. Their beautifully written study of communities in county Clare during the 1930s analyzes farming households that normally spanned three generations. When the heir to a farm married, his parents retired to the "west room" of the farmhouse and lived there until their deaths. Broken families, they imply, brought in relatives from the outside to take the place of deceased kin. Brothers, sisters, nephews, and cousins moved in to work the land or to help raise orphaned children.[3] Arensberg and Kimball clearly demonstrate the social and economic importance of the extended family in Ireland, but they present no statistics on the incidence of extended families as residential units. And even if they had collected such information, so many changes have taken place over the last 200 years in Irish inheritance patterns, land distribution, standards of living, and life expectancies that it is illegitimate to apply their evidence retroactively to the prefamine population. The pattern of family decisions seen by Arensberg and Kimball, which combined late marriage with high marital fertility, impartible inheritance, and emigration of the noninheritors, became common only in the second half of the nineteenth century. Before 1850, the Irish married earlier and more frequently than they did in the 1930s.[4] Moreover, parents died earlier and subdivided farms among their children, each of whom would live within a nuclear family. To interpret the demographic decisions and family structures of the prefamine Irish, we must turn to sources other than the descriptions of contemporary anthropologists.

As information on the demography of the Irish in the last 150 years slowly becomes available, we find that the vast majority of rural Irish families in the period 1821 to 1845 were nuclear.

Catholic population began in 1864. In any case, virtually all of the nineteenth-century manuscript census schedules were destroyed by fire in 1922.

3. Conrad M. Arensberg and Solon T. Kimball, *Family and Community in Ireland*, 2d ed. (Cambridge, Mass., 1968), pp. 66–67, 76, 129.

4. Robert E. Kennedy, Jr., *The Irish: Emigration, Marriage, and Fertility* (Berkeley, 1973), pp. 176, 179, 215.

Tabulations done by F. J. Carney on a sample of households in five counties of Leinster, Ulster, and Connaught in 1821 show that approximately 70 percent of the households were simple nuclear families.[5] They were very similar in composition, therefore, to preindustrial households in England, where only about one in ten included relatives beyond the nuclear family. They conform to a Western European pattern in which the nuclear family normally predominates. This finding could have been predicted, for demographers have recently shown that a majority of households in a society tend to be simple in structure, whatever the prevailing ideals of family composition or rates of fertility and mortality. Particularly if death rates are high, it is rare for parents or siblings to survive long enough to form extended families. Extended families are therefore usually temporary phenomena within a minority of households.[6]

Yet such households were not unimportant in prefamine Ireland. In central and western counties in 1821, 17.2 percent of the families sampled by F. J. Carney were extended and 5.1 percent included two or more conjugal units. These proportions shifted during the life cycle of the head, reaching their peaks when the head was sixty-five or older. The Cambridge Group for the History of Population and Social Structure has discovered even higher rates of extension in two southern Irish villages near Waterford in 1821. Among the Cork households tallied in 1841, at least 17 percent had had additional relatives living with them at some point in the preceding decade, and if a complete record of residence in these households were available, the total proportion of residential units that had been extended at some point would doubtless be higher. Since the census measures household composition as it exists on only one day every ten years, much of the regular expansion and contraction that residential units undergo is missed.[7]

5. F. J. Carney, "An Introduction to Irish Household Size and Structure, 1821," unpublished paper, Trinity College, Dublin (1976), p. 18.

6. Marion J. Levy, "Aspects of the Analysis of Family Structure," in Ansley J. Coale et al., *Aspects of the Analysis of Family Structure* (Princeton, 1965); Thomas K. Burch, "Some Demographic Determinants of Average Household Size: An Analytic Approach," in *Household and Family*, ed. Laslett and Wall, p. 100.

7. Carney, "Introduction to Irish Household Size," p. 18; manuscript census schedules for 1841; Peter Laslett, personal communication, February 8, 1978.

Irish households before the famine also included a variety of people not related to the household head. In 1841 over one-third of Cork households included servants, visitors, or apprentices. About one-half of farmers' households included at least one person between the ages of ten and twenty-two identified as a servant. The males would have helped work the land, while the females tended animals or gardens and helped in the dairy. In the area for which census documents have survived, there were no single-member households. Adolescents lived with parents or a farmer's or craftsman's family; the old lived with their children or sought shelter as visitors within other households. Figures for Ireland in 1821 confirm the relative unimportance of households not based on family units. Only 3.7 percent of the total sample consisted of solitary individuals; an additional 4.3 percent were made up of unrelated individuals.[8] Prefamine Ireland was a family-centered society. Children had a moral obligation to support parents in their old age and commonly did so. Orphans were placed by their parishes in foster homes or were taken in by neighbors. Homeless women in Connemara during the 1840s would be taken in by local householders even in bad times and traded board and lodging for knitted garments.[9] People commonly lived with a family, that of an employer or a benefactor if not their own.

Preindustrial Irish households were relatively large. Although the mean size of English preindustrial households in the communities investigated by Peter Laslett was only 4.75, the number of inhabitants per household in sampled Irish areas in 1821 was 5.45.[10] The Irish census for 1841 shows even larger sizes: the twenty-nine Cork households whose records survive held an average of 6.3 persons. In the three decades before the famine, therefore, Irish households were substantially larger than those

8. Carney, "Introduction to Irish Household Size," p. 18; manuscript census schedules for 1841. See also Great Britain, *Parliamentary Papers* (Commons), "First Report of Her Majesty's Commissioners for Inquiring into the Condition of the Poorer Classes in Ireland," 1835, 32:Appendix A, 100–427.

9. Ibid., pp. 200–355; Mr. and Mrs. S. C. Hall, *Ireland, Its Scenery, Character, etc.*, 3 vols. (London, 1841), vol. 3, p. 472; T. Crofton Croker, *Researches in the South of Ireland* (London, 1824), p. 227.

10. I use in this chapter the definitions and conventions outlined by Peter Laslett in *Household and Family*, ed. Laslett and Wall, pp. 23–44; see also F. J. Carney, "Aspects of Pre-Famine Irish Household Size: Composition and Differentials," unpublished paper, Trinity College, Dublin (1976), p. 10.

found in France and England during the late eighteenth and early nineteenth centuries, although they did not reach the average sizes of almost 7 persons found in Massachusetts communities in the 1790s.[11]

When the servants, visitors, and other inmates of Irish households are subtracted, a smaller conjugal unit remains. The mean family size found in the sampled Irish counties in 1821 was 5.05, while families in the Cork census of 1841 included 5.40 members. Both of these averages, however, exceed the mean sizes of English and French preindustrial families, largely because there were more children in Irish prefamine households. Although English preindustrial households numbered on the average only 2.03 children, the households of the Cork 1841 census included 3.30 children. In St. Michael, Blackrock, Cork, in 1843, the average family had 2.04 children under the age of fourteen and an unknown number above that age.[12] Evidence on the fertility of the prefamine Irish is still fragmentary, but what is available shows that Irish fertility was probably higher than English fertility in the decade before the famine. The ratio of children under five to married women of childbearing age was 21 percent higher in Ireland than in England in 1841, and average crude birth rates that can be calculated from Irish parish registers of the 1830s were higher than comparable figures for England.[13]

11. Laslett and Wall, eds., *Household and Family*, Table 20.1, p. 550; Table 9.1, p. 255; Table 1.13, p. 83; Census of Ireland, 1841, manuscript returns, Public Record Office, Dublin. Other figures for prefamine Ireland confirm the larger size of the Irish household. In Knockainy, county Cork, a parish of 4,300 people, an average of 6.4 persons resided in each house in 1821 and 6.6 persons in 1841 (Domhnall MacCarthaigh, "Marriage and Birth-Rates for Knockainy Parish, 1822–1941," *Journal of the Cork Historical and Archeological Society* 47 [1942]: 4). The mean household size among the almost 5,000 tenants who rented lands in Munster from Trinity College, Dublin, in 1843 was 5.6 (Trinity College, Dublin, Muniments 5, ser. 78, p. 61).

12. Carney, "Introduction to Irish Household Size," p. 8; manuscript census schedules for 1841; Laslett and Wall, eds., *Household and Family*, pp. 1, 13, 83; North Ludlow Beamish, "Statistical Report on the Physical and Moral Condition of the Working Classes of St. Michael, Blackrock, near Cork," *Journal of the Statistical Society of London* 7 (1884):251–254.

13. G. S. L. Tucker, "Irish Fertility Ratios before the Famine," *Economic History Review* 23, no. 2 (August 1970):280; MacCarthaigh, "Marriage and Birth-Rates," p. 6; Registrar General of England and Wales, *Twenty-fourth Annual Report, 1861* (London, 1863), p. ii.

Virtually all of the data presented thus far describe rural Irish households. If comparisons are made between the demography of rural and urban Irish populations, clear differences emerge. The family patterns of the urban and the rural Irish had diverged by the mid–nineteenth century. In the 1840s, Irish townsmen married on the average two years earlier than their country cousins, but they had fewer children, although the houses they lived in held many more people. Households in Dublin, the largest Irish city, averaged 4.5 persons at a time when those in rural areas averaged 5.5 persons. (See Table 5.1.) And because of either lower fertility or much higher mortality rates, the ratio of children to married women in the capital was far lower than in rural Ireland.[14] As we shall see, urban Irish families in England share these demographic characteristics. Whether the Irish migrated to a foreign city or lived in an Irish urban area, their households were smaller, they had fewer children, and in most cases they married earlier than their country cousins.

Table 5.1. Characteristics of urban and rural Irish households, 1851

Household characteristics	Dublin	All towns	Rural areas
Persons per household	4.5	5.1	5.5
Persons per house	11.6	8.1	6.0
Children per married woman	2.9	3.6	5.1
Percentage of males married, ages 25–34	—	56.0%	39.0%

Whether the composition of urban families and households in Ireland differed from that of rural households is still an open question. Printed census returns offer no information on this point, and most of the available primary sources describe rural households only. I suspect, however, that rural and urban families were structurally similar. Not only do demographic conditions limit the range of variation, but the Irish who migrated to foreign cities formed families whose structure differed little from that of the prefamine rural Irish. Urban residence in other societies did not cause Irish migrants to shift from patriarchal extended families to nuclear ones, as Le Play predicted, for the

14. Census of Ireland, 1851.

nuclear family seems to have been the most common form of organization among the Irish residing in both urban and rural areas.

Family and Household among the London Irish

If we follow Irish migrants to the English capital, we find that their households were structured much like prefamine rural households. Most were built around a unit of parents and unmarried children. Some included other relatives, lodgers, or visitors, but these were temporary additions undertaken to help both the host family and its dependents withstand the economic and social pressures of urban life. Irish households were flexible and adaptable to the needs of their environment. Most complex Irish families were merely temporary extensions of nuclear families and did not differ from them functionally.

On census day in 1851, three-quarters of the Irish households sampled in London were headed by married men.[15] Less than 10 percent were headed by either a single person or a married woman. (See Table A.4, Appendix B.) Whatever the pressures produced by high unemployment rates or by the temptation of work in another area, men who had families in London stayed with them. The combination of poverty and easy migration elsewhere produced few households headed by women or single individuals. Most female-headed households, only 17 percent of the total, resulted from death, not desertion or the temporary absence of a husband. High death rates ravaged workers' families in English urban areas in the early nineteenth century, and Irish migrants belonged to social groups with the lowest life expectancies.[16] At least 17 percent of the sampled families in 1851 had been broken by death, and almost four times as many households were headed by widows as by widowers. (See Table A.4, Appendix B.) Higher male mortality rates and the excess of females in most age groups increased the chances both that a woman would outlive her

15. These and all other figures in the chapter on the London Irish are drawn from a five-parish sample of Irish households. For details of the sample, see Appendix A.

16. Great Britain, *Parliamentary Papers* (Commons), "Supplementary Report on the Practice of Interment in Towns; Report on the Sanitary Condition of the Labouring Population," 1843, 12:256–265; Registrar General of England and Wales, *Fifth Annual Report, 1841* (London, 1843), p. 35.

husband and that she would not find another spouse if she were widowed. Since three-quarters of the widows lived with unmarried children, potential husbands might have been deterred by the cost of supporting a widow's family. Conversely, widowers had a larger pool of eligible mates from which to choose, and they could offer a woman a level of financial support higher than she was capable of earning for herself. As a result of these demographic and economic pressures, Irish widowers remarried with greater frequency than did widows.

Whether an Irish household was headed by a man or a woman, it was usually organized as a nuclear family. Few young married couples lived with parents, and only 13 percent of households contained other relatives or a second conjugal family of kin. (See Table A.7, Appendix B.)

The Irish nuclear family was not a static form, however. The London Irish adjusted their household compositions to fit family and communal needs. When John O'Neill, the Irish shoemaker from Waterford, came to London, he and a friend moved into the home of another Irish shoemaker, to whom they paid two shillings a week for board and a bed in his attic. As soon as O'Neill had saved enough money, he brought his wife and children from Ireland and formed a separate household. For most of his life in London, O'Neill headed a nuclear family. Yet the structure within which he lived underwent periodic changes. On at least one occasion, other relatives from Ireland moved in with him until they became established in the capital; when his first wife died in childbirth, kin and friends cared for his children temporarily. Finally he remarried and established a new nuclear family.[17] Many other migrants followed a similar pattern. Just as in rural Ireland, at any point in time only a minority of Irish households would include kin beyond the nuclear unit, but over the family developmental cycle many would at some point include additional kin. The nuclear family was the norm from which families deviated for a time and to which they then returned.

The times at which kin joined a nuclear family came most

17. John O'Neill, "Fifty Years' Experience as an Irish Shoemaker in London," *St. Crispin* 1 and 2 (1869).

often at the beginning and end of its developmental cycle. (See Table A.7, Appendix B.) Young couples without children and couples over age forty-five whose children had left the household took in other relatives with the greatest frequency. At these two stages of a family's evolution, available space would be at a maximum and economic claims at a minimum. Families with young children were far less likely to make room for relatives. If they took in outsiders it was a financial arrangement, an exchange of space for cash to pay the rent. Irish urban extended families therefore were temporary, unstable structures. Rather than being based on joint ownership of property or joint production, which gave all concerned an interest in the maintenance of the household, they were short-term expedients designed to offer care to the old and widowed or aid to siblings and their children who had come to the city. Almost 60 percent of the coresiding kin sampled in 1851 were of the same generation as the household head or one generation younger. Most of these relatives were single, and half were between the ages of fifteen and forty, typically migrants who had not yet established their own households. They were drawn from both the husbands' and wives' families — an indication that bilateral kinship obligations were recognized.

John O'Neill took in his brother, his sister-in-law, and their children after they came to London. Even though he and his brother did not get along well, he regarded the expansion of his household as an obligation.[18] Kin regularly took in children or the old in time of need. Widowed parents or grandchildren commonly joined Irish nuclear families for both short and extended periods. Pauper examinations of those applying for relief show that, even among the poorest, relatives could be relied upon to give shelter. When Margaret Hearn, age twenty-five, a second-generation migrant, was deserted by her husband in the winter of 1862, she and her five children moved in with her mother-in-law until Poor Law authorities decided to send the family back to Bristol, where the husband had been born. Similarly, Mary Connor, a first-generation migrant, sent her oldest daughter to a sister after the death of her husband in 1864, while

18. Ibid., 1:307, 314.

she and her ten-year-old son entered the workhouse. Families also provided aid in time of illness. Dennis Burke, a twenty-nine-year-old migrant who came to London in 1842, moved in with relatives in 1854 when he became ill and needed relief.[19]

Few Irish born in London lived by themselves or with other unrelated individuals in 1851. Over 85 percent resided with at least one relative in 1851. Widows commonly lived with their children, and only 17 percent did not have at least one kinsman in the same household. The elderly, for the most part, shared a dwelling with children or other relatives: only about one-quarter of those over sixty-five lived alone or with an unrelated person. Not only did the Irish provide for their kin, but the ethnic community provided homes for newcomers, for the single, and for those without the means to set up their own households. Those without families regularly boarded within other Irish households, either as lodgers or as visitors, instead of setting up on their own.[20] With the exception of female servants, very few Irish-born individuals lived within non-Irish households. (See Table A.3, Appendix B.) The Irish segregated themselves or were segregated from the English population in London.

The composition of Irish households depended on the socioeconomic status of the head. The Irish middle class had servants; workers took in lodgers and visitors. While only 2 percent of the unskilled laborers had servants, 55 percent of the Irish migrant middle class did. Conversely, in 1851 only 10 percent of Irish middle-class families took in boarders, but 21 percent of the households of unskilled laborers included one or more lodgers. In addition, more visitors, kin, and friends of the host family were to be found in workers' households. All workers' households were roughly similar in composition. A clear dividing line separated them from households headed by professionals, civil servants, and

19. Guardians of the Poor, Holborn Union, Liberty of Saffron Hill, *Pauper's Examinations,* vol. 4 (October 1862–May 1864), p. 131 (January 29, 1863); vol. 6 (August 1865–March, 1866), p. 147 (November 29, 1865); St. Olave's Union, Bermondsey, *Minutes of the Guardians of the Poor,* vol. 9 (1853–1855), October 5, 1854.

20. Little is known of the identity of visitors, and up to this time family studies have largely ignored the group. Although 16 percent of Irish households sampled in 1851 had at least one visitor, this proportion shrank as migration declined over the next decade. I suspect that visitors in Irish households were friends and distant kin who were taken in for varying lengths of time when they first came to London.

entrepreneurs. Workers took in outsiders to increase their incomes and to help them adjust to the city; the more affluent expanded their households to provide services and increase their own leisure. Much more rarely than among the less affluent did they use their homes to aid or to socialize unrelated newcomers to London. Middle-class Irish families therefore had less intimate relationships with incoming migrants of similar social status than did workers' families.

In 1851 the residential patterns of the London Irish community diverged in four major ways from those of English urban populations. First, a higher percentage of English households consisted of solitary individuals or of unrelated persons. In London these two groups made up 11 percent of all households, while they comprised only 8 percent of the Irish sample.[21] Second, English households were much more likely to include servants. Fully 29 percent of London households employed at least one servant, while 10 percent of Preston households and 20 percent of York households did so.[22] But among London Irish families in 1851, only 6 percent could afford to keep a servant. If an English household in London included a nonrelated individual, it was most likely to be a servant; in an Irish household, the additional member was usually a lodger or a visitor.

The third major difference in English and Irish household composition concerns the incidence of extended families. The proportion of Irish households in London that included kin beyond the nuclear unit in 1851 (13 percent) was substantially less than that of Ireland in 1821 (22 percent) but was roughly equal to the proportion found among English communities in the seventeenth and eighteenth centuries. By the middle of the nineteenth century, the proportion of extended families in English urban populations had risen substantially. Michael Anderson has found that 23 percent of Preston families at mid-century included relatives beyond the nuclear unit, a figure much higher

21. David Chaplin, "The Structure of London Households in 1851," unpublished paper, Western Michigan University, 1975, p. 16.
22. Ibid., Table 4a; Michael Anderson, *Family Structure in Nineteenth-Century Lancashire* (Cambridge, 1971), p. 85; Alan Armstrong, *Stability and Change in an English County Town: A Social Study of York, 1801–1851* (Cambridge, 1974), p. 179.

than that among the Irish sample. In York in 1851 the proportion
was 22 percent, in London 19 percent.[23] It seems likely therefore
that the coresidence of kin became more common in English
towns during the early stages of the Industrial Revolution.
Housing shortages together with the wish and the obligation to
help new arrivals and older relatives swelled the number of
extended and multiple families during the decades of rapid
movement into cities. The highest rise in this proportion took
place in Preston, where 70 percent of all migrants came from
thirty miles away or less. Long-distance migration apparently
slowed this increase, for there were fewer relatives nearby to move
in with kinsmen.

A final difference between Irish and English populations
concerns the frequency with which each group accepted lodgers.
The taking in of lodgers was partly a function of socioeconomic
status, but it also varied among types of towns and regions. In
Preston, which drew thousands of migrants into the cotton
industry, 23 percent of all households took in lodgers. Households headed by women and by lower paid workers were the most
likely to expand in this way. A similar pattern can be found in
York. In London, however, far fewer residents took in lodgers.[24]
In the capital, only the Irish commonly added a boarder to their
numbers. Although only 4.8 percent of all London households
included lodgers, among Irish households in the metropolis the
proportion rose to 18.5 percent, and in Irish unskilled workers'
households it reached 21 percent. Irish households in London
therefore had a rather different composition from those of the
total London population. More lodgers but fewer servants and
kin distinguished Irish from English.

Irish Family and Household Size in London

A stereotype of improvident Irish who married early to produce
children and little else shaped English misconceptions of the
Irish. Nourished by popular resentment of Celtic migrants, the
example of population increase in Ireland, and Malthusian

23. Anderson, *Family Structure*, pp. 37, 44; Armstrong, *Stability and
Change*, p. 185; Chaplin, "Structure of London Households," p. 16.
24. Anderson, *Family Structure*, p. 46; Armstrong, *Stability and Change*, p.
182; Chaplin, "Structure of London Households," Table 6.

theory, an image of the dissolute and fertile Irish appears in a variety of works of the 1830s and 1840s, from the poetry of Ebenezer Elliott, the "Corn Law Rhymer," to the descriptions of Manchester workers by James P. Kay.[25] Elliott's "Malthus and Paddy" tells the tale:

> Why dost thou toil, poor dwindled lad,
>   Twelve hours for pennies three?
> 'My father married, when a boy,
>   My mother young as he;
> And times are hard, for work is scarce;
>   We're eight, sir . . . five and three.'[26]

Behind accounts of the mid-nineteenth-century migrant Irish that stressed the crowdedness of their homes and the hordes of children in the streets lay the assumption of high fertility and population increase. But as we shall see, this assumption was inaccurate in several ways. The mean family size of the London Irish was relatively small, and their demographic behavior differed little from that of English workers.

If we compare the mean family size of the London Irish sample with that of several English urban populations, we discover that most of these groups had nuclear families of very similar dimensions, between 3.5 and 3.8 persons. The mean family size of the London Irish in 1851 (3.7) was close to that of the York population and varied only slightly from the mean of 3.8 persons per family calculated by Peter Laslett for English preindustrial communities. But both in London and in Preston, a cotton town where the demand for female and child labor in factories was high and where children regularly remained at home until they married, mean family sizes were higher (4.0 and 4.6).[27] Not only did the London Irish have smaller families in 1851 than the total London population, they also had substantially smaller families than those of the rural Irish in the prefamine period. The urban Irish quickly adjusted their demographic behavior to the urban environment. Soon after migration, the demographic behavior of

25. J. P. Kay, *The Moral and Physical Condition of the Working Classes Employed in the Cotton Manufacture in Manchester*, 2d ed. (London, 1832), pp. 21, 80–81.

26. *The Poetical Works of Ebenezer Elliott* (Edinburgh, 1840), p. 152.

27. Laslett and Wall, eds., *Household and Family*, pp. 214, 233.

the Irish community resembled that of their host population more than that of rural Irish society.

Hidden behind the averages are many different combinations of fertility and mortality and wide variations in the economic structures and age and sex compositions of the populations. Nevertheless, the net effect of these variations is small. As Thomas Burch has shown, mean family sizes remain relatively small under almost any conditions of fertility or mortality as long as the units are organized around nuclear or stem families. Indeed, the range of possible variation in nuclear family size for a stable population under conditions of high mortality and fertility is limited.[28] Mean family size therefore tells us little about the nature of a group's demographic choices. But by looking at the distribution of family sizes and recalculating these mean sizes for different sections of the sample, we can explore some of these differences.

Family size varies according to the age of the family head, revealing a regular pattern of growth and decline. Mean Irish family size rose slowly during the young adulthood of the head (under age forty) and reached its peak (4.4) when he or she was between the ages of forty-five and forty-nine. The mean size then declined slowly until the age of fifty-five and more rapidly thereafter. Yet after migrants married and had children, they usually spent the rest of their lives with one or more of them. At no point in the life cycle did mean family sizes dip as low as two.

Despite the rather small mean family size, actual family sizes extended over a wide range; 30 percent of the sample in 1851 and 32 percent in 1861 had families that numbered five or more persons. Also, 33 percent of the families in 1851 consisted of only one or two people. (See Table A.6, Appendix B.) This size distribution varied considerably, moreover, according to the socioeconomic status of the household head. Craftsmen and semiskilled laborers had the smallest families while those of higher social status — shopkeepers, professionals, and employers — had the highest proportion of families of more than five persons. The distribution of Irish household sizes was also wide. One-fifth of migrants' households

28. Thomas K. Burch, "Some Demographic Determinants of Average Household Size: An Analytical Approach," in *Household and Family*, ed. Laslett and Wall, pp. 96, 100.

comprised only two people or less, while another fifth numbered seven or more persons. Just as in the English preindustrial communities tallied by Laslett and in York in 1851, the higher the social status of an Irish family, the larger the household. Mean household size for middle-class Irish was 5.6 in 1851 and 6.0 in 1861, but only 5.0 and 4.7 for unskilled laborers in those years. Among professionals and employers, 36 percent of the households numbered seven or more persons in 1851, but only 25 percent of the unskilled had such large households.

The sizes of Irish migrant families and households varied, therefore, in accordance with the age of the household head and socioeconomic status. Yet the mean sizes of both families and households were smaller than those of the prefamine Irish population. Just as Dublin households were smaller than their rural counterparts, so were those of the London Irish. A pattern of demographic adaptation to the constraints of an urban environment existed among Irish migrants. This meant that their demographic behavior slowly became like that of the host population. In Liverpool between 1851 and 1871, the mean sizes of Irish nuclear families and households decreased until they were slightly smaller than those of the non-Irish population. A similar decrease in Irish household size took place in Manchester, until by 1871 it reached a level virtually identical to that of the non-Irish residents.[29] The mean family size of the London Irish was closer to that of the London population than it was to the mean family size of the prefamine Irish. And as we shall see in Chapter 6, the London Irish in 1851 and 1861 chose to marry at ages virtually identical to those of the total London population but rather earlier than in Ireland. Robert Kennedy has shown that in the twentieth century married Irish migrants in England and the United States adjusted their fertility to the levels obtaining in the native population and did not duplicate abroad the high levels of the Irish in the Republic. The migrant Irish, who resided for the most part in urban environments, adopted a pattern of much smaller family sizes than did the Irish who remained at home.[30]

29. William James Lowe, "The Irish in Lancashire, 1846–1871: A Social History," Ph.D. thesis, Trinity College, Dublin, 1975, pp. 81, 84.

30. Robert E. Kennedy, Jr., "The Persistence of Social Norms: Marriage and Fertility among the Overseas Irish," in Social Demography: The State of the Art, ed. William Petersen and Lincoln H. Day (Cambridge, Mass., forthcoming).

These demographic adaptations of the migrant Irish were coupled, however, with certain continuities of family behavior. The composition of Irish families and households was very similar in London in 1851 and prefamine Ireland, and kinship obligations and the duty of caring for parents and for the elderly continued to be honored. Irish families did not separate themselves from kin, although fewer, more closely related kin were probably included in the circle for whom services were performed. And the nature of those services changed as well when migrants entered an urban environment with different work patterns and communal organization. Common family obligations became the provision of jobs or housing and attendance at the rituals of marriage and death rather than help with the harvest or seasonal celebrations. At a time when the state provided minimal social services for the Irish, families were an alternative system of support. Whatever the emotional climate within the nuclear family and its close kin, individuals relied on relatives to help them cope with the practical problems of migration and the uncertainties of life as low-skilled urban workers.

CHAPTER 6

Marriage and Migration

Celebrated with feast and piper, the rural Irish marriage ceremony signaled the transition to adulthood, a woman's departure from her family of origin, and often the transfer of land from parent to child. How did migration affect these peasant unions? Were Irish marriages any different when consecrated in London rather than a Munster farming community? Many social scientists would predict so. There is a growing literature on the relation between family life and the economic development of European societies, which links affectivity, patterns of authority, and roles within the family to the social and economic organization of society.[1] Scholars dispute, however, the nature of changes and their timing. The transformation of migrant Irish family life that took place between 1750 and 1900 conforms best to the analyses of the British sociologists Peter Willmott and Michael Young.[2] They have constructed three ideal types of workers' families, each fostered by a specific stage of European economic development. In stage 1, the family was the unit of production in a preindustrial economy and was held together by the need for mutual economic cooperation. In stage 2, industrialization disrupted work patterns and therefore family relations. Patterns of author-

1. Philippe Ariès, *Centuries of Childhood: A Social History of Family Life* (New York, 1962); Edward Shorter, *The Making of the Modern Family* (New York, 1975); Lawrence Stone, "The Rise of the Nuclear Family in Early Modern England," in *The Family in History,* ed. Charles E. Rosenberg (Philadelphia, 1975), pp. 13–57.

2. Michael Young and Peter Willmott, *The Symmetrical Family: A Study of Work and Leisure in the London Region* (London, 1973), pp. 23–30.

ity changed as wives and children were forced out of the labor market and became economically dependent on a man's wages. Roles within the family became more highly segregated by sex and age. Willmott and Young view these changes as disruption and link them to such consequences as an increase in male brutality toward wives and children and husbands' control over income distribution, which forced wives and children to bear the burden of increased expenses. When the state ordered children out of work and into school and when factories took over jobs that married women had formerly done at home, Willmott and Young argue, husbands began to view their families less as helpers than as parasites and tended to treat them harshly. Only when fertility declined and married women reentered the labor force in large numbers was the way paved for the reestablishment of equality within the marriage bond. At a later stage of economic development, when consumption became the major focus of joint family activity, internal balance within the family was restored. Movement into stage 3, the "symmetrical family," took place as a pattern of decreasing segregation of sex roles emerged. More tasks were shared, and authority became much more equally divided. Willmott and Young argue that these stages finally diffused throughout Western Europe, although they succeeded each other among different social groups at different times.

Their models of stage 1 and stage 2 describe Irish families well before and immediately after migration. Moving into London removed the Irish from an essentially preindustrial economy and placed them in an urban industrializing one where manufacturing and the division of labor were far advanced. They therefore experienced acute pressures for economic change. As we have seen, adaptation occurred quickly in Irish demographic behavior and in female work roles, and it lessened parental control over children. It probably also changed male attitudes toward female roles within the family. In the city, the economic functions of the family decreased; few produced goods jointly. The young chose their own marriage partners, apparently on the basis of affection and personal preference. The ideal of romantic love was clearly present in urban popular culture, as it had been a part of rural folklore. Yet Irish urban marriages were not sagas of companionate, romantic bliss and privatized domesticity. Sex roles remained moderately segregated; men and women seem to have had different values and expectations of ideal spouses' behavior, ideals that were in conflict at several points. Moreover, it is not clear that husbands and wives spent much time together. Neither the label "traditional" nor "modern" fits these families; they correspond most closely to Willmott and Young's stage 2 families, those struggling to cope with the consequences of the separation of home and workplace and with differences in urban and rural sex roles, employment opportunities, and recreational patterns.

Rural Irish Marriage Patterns

We know relatively little about the functioning of marriages among the European lower classes in preindustrial settings. That economic cooperation was the foundation of such unions seems fairly clear: men, women, and children shared in tasks of production, although the most prestigious jobs were done by men. But what besides economic need held these units together? A second generally accepted characteristic of such families is their patriarchal organization. Adult male heads had both legal and customary authority over women and children. They represented the family in the outside world, and their wishes were supposedly obeyed within the family circle. But legal and practical authority are two different matters. Did all power rest in male hands? Was a wife's subordinate status compatible with much authority within the private sphere of the household? To what extent were children subject to fathers' wishes when they wanted to court and to marry? The answers to such questions are not easy to find, but the information available on the rural Irish in the early nineteenth century suggests that peasant marriages were not affectionless, nor were wives passively obedient to their husbands or children to their parents. Romantic love spurred the marriages of the laboring poor. It seems clear that a range of emotional commitments to family life underlay economic considerations.

Economic pressures and opportunities encouraged people to marry in rural Ireland before the potato famine. In the early 1840s the Irish married earlier than they do today, and fewer of them failed to marry. F. J. Carney has recently shown that the estimated singulate mean marriage age for males was 28.5 in 1821 and 28.9 in

1841; the figure for women was 25.9 in both of those years.[3] In comparison with the contemporary Irish pattern, few people in prefamine Ireland remained single. Only 10 percent of all men and 12 percent of all women aged forty-five to fifty-four were still single in 1841, whereas in 1961, 30 percent of the men and 23 percent of the women in this age group had not married.[4] Celibacy was then far less common than it became in the twentieth century. Witnesses before the 1836 Poor Inquiry reported almost universal marriage among those with farms. The running of a farm required the labor of a woman and of children; since farms were small and profits low, the hiring of servants to do the work would have been an impractical solution. The landless also discovered economic benefits in marriage: in Coshlea the poor married even when their choice of partners was limited. "They find the convenience of a wife in preparing their meals, and they look forward to the assistance which their children will afford them when old."[5]

The economic benefits and relatively low costs of marriage in an economy where a family's food could be easily grown on a bit of potato land, however, tell only part of the story. Marriage was an accepted social institution, part of the life cycle that each person ought to experience. Irish proverbs, however cynical the attitude expressed toward women, generally assert that people should marry. "Three things a man ought not to be without; a cat, a chimney, and housewife."[6] Nineteenth-century Irish folk songs speak of marriage as the expected fulfillment of love:

3. F. J. Carney, "Pre-Famine Irish Households: Formation, Size, and Structure," unpublished paper, Trinity College, Dublin, 1976, pp. 43–44; see also K. H. Connell, *The Population of Ireland, 1740–1845* (Oxford, 1950); Michael Drake, "Marriage and Population Growth in Ireland, 1750–1845," *Economic History Review* 16 (2d ser.), no. 2 (1963):301, 307, 309, 311–312; Joseph Lee, "Marriage and Population in Pre-famine Ireland," *Economic History Review* 21 (2d ser.), no. 2 (1968):283, 285.

4. Robert E. Kennedy, Jr., *The Irish: Emigration, Marriage, and Fertility* (Berkeley, 1973), pp. 139, 215.

5. Great Britain, *Parliamentary Papers* (Commons), "Report of Her Majesty's Commissioners for Inquiring into the Condition of the Poorer Classes in Ireland," 1836, 33:Appendix F, 36, 39, 66.

6. Sean Gaffney and Seamus Cashman, *Proverbs and Sayings of Ireland* (Dublin, 1974), p. 107.

> If thou art mine, be mine, white love of my heart;
> If thou art mine, be mine by day and by night;
> If thou art mine, be mine every inch in thy heart,
> And my misfortune and misery that thou art not with me in the
>   evening for wife.[7]

This and other songs written in Irish by anonymous balladeers combine respect for marriage and fidelity with expressions of romantic love. The relationships they described differed markedly from parent-imposed "matches" arranged for the economic gain of the family.

Courtship patterns differed among the propertied and the nonpropertied. The amount of parental control exercised varied directly with the wealth of the family. Amateur ethnographers who toured southern Ireland in the late 1830s and 1840s reported two sets of practices, one when a family could provide a marriage portion and one when it could not. If neither set of parents had property to bestow, children were apparently left free to make their own matches. Courtship began after the young reached their teens and included casual visits by the young man to the young woman's home. "If two young people form an attachment for each other, and have hardly enough between them to pay the priest his dues, the only parental observation is "Wee, sure! We did the same thing ourselves. Its asy to halve the potato when there's love. Its an ould saying marriages are made in heaven."[8] A Connaught priest complained to the Poor Inquiry of recklessness in the local marriage market: "He that is destitute hardly hesitates at all."[9] And the poor themselves sang of their disregard for material circumstances:

> I have no silver, I have no gold, have no coat, have no shirt;
> Have no penny in my pocket — and may the Son of God relieve
>   me. . . .
> My sweet heart, my affection, be faithful and be firm,

7. "The Soosheen Bawn," in Douglas Hyde, *The Love Songs of Connaught*, 4th ed. (London and Dublin, 1905), p.75.

8. Mr. and Mrs. S. C. Hall, *Ireland: Its Scenery, Character, etc.*, 3 vols. (London, 1841), vol. 1, p. 169; see also T. Crofton Croker, *Researches in the South of Ireland Illustrative of the Scenery, Architectural Remains, and the Manners and Superstitions of the Peasantry* (London, 1824).

9. Great Britain, *Parliamentary Papers*, "Report . . . [on] the Poorer Classes in Ireland," 1836, 33:Appendix F, 38.

And do not forsake the secret love of your inner heart on
    account of him to be poor;
I would take the Bible (as oath) or any other thing on earth,
That the Son of God will give us our nights' portion to eat.[10]

When there was property to bestow, however, parents remained in
control and would not agree to a marriage unless a suitable
financial bargain could be struck. Children's wishes might be
considered, but property and family gain remained primary. The
cows of the dowry had to be balanced with grants of land or
animals from the groom's family. When the parents' choice was
not that of the child, the young allegedly were persuaded to place
family wishes ahead of their own.[11]

Whatever the degree of parental control or the amount of
property transferred, local communities openly supported the
marriages of their people. Weddings were times of communal
celebration. The landlord, the gentry, all the neighbors, and any
beggars in the area were invited. The ceremony was not held in a
church but was performed by the priest in a local barn or cabin.
All assembled for as splendid a feast as could be afforded. Guests
ate, witnessed the ceremony, took some of the bridecake, and then
helped to pay for the festivities by donating money for the piper
and priest. Sometimes a group of local men disguised in costumes
of straw visited these parties to bring luck to the newlyweds and
wish them good health and prosperity. Once admitted to the
celebration, they would dance or sing for the guests. A night of
jigs, reels, and drinking followed; the final dances paired off the
unmarried guests.[12]

After the ceremony, how did couples behave toward one
another? The evidence available is meager, but a few generaliza-
tions can be made. On one level, a familiar picture of male
dominance reappears. Male authority was supposedly strong in
rural Ireland throughout the nineteenth century, and sex roles
were carefully differentiated. In form, at least, women were
subservient. In Clare as late as the 1930s conventional peasant
women walked several paces behind their husbands. Husbands

---

10. "The Coolun," in Hyde, *Love Songs of Connaught*, p. 73.

11. Hall, *Ireland*, vol. 1, pp. 169–170.

12. Ibid., pp. 165–166; Croker, *Researches*, pp. 234–235; Alan Gailey, *Irish Folk
Drama* (Cork, 1969), p. 91.

customarily ate first, and women denied themselves food when there were shortages.[13] Edward Wakefield noted in 1808 that a man "considers his wife his slave." Irish husbands, he said, assumed more authority than was either "claimed or submitted to in England" and treated their wives as "beasts of burden."[14] Yet public rituals of obedience do not preclude the exercise of much domestic power and influence. If a peasant marriage was arranged by parents who traded a dowry for land and animals, a wife entered the union as an equal contributor. She had brought to it as much property as had her husband. This circumstance should have conferred upon her status and respect. Commentators of the 1830s noted the frequency of intergenerational domestic conflict when wives challenged mothers- and fathers-in-law for power within the household. Husbands either were unable to keep the peace or sided with their wives. And in Irish nuclear families, wives were never placed at the bottom of the domestic hierarchy, outranked by mothers-in-law and other members of the husband's family. They automatically took control of house, garden, animals, and later children.[15]

Irish proverbs that speak of women certainly do not portray them as docile and obedient. "The three [things] most difficult to teach: a mule, a pig, and a woman." "Three things that leave the shortest traces: a bird on a branch, a ship on the sea, and a man on a woman." A woman is supposedly one of "the three most bothersome things in the world." The scolding wife, the shrewish wife, the "woman unruly as a hen" are stock characters in the world of proverb and folktale.[16] As early as the third century, a would-be Irish groom was told by his father, when asking how he could recognize a good woman, that there was "no sort fit for a man to trust to if he wishes to live in peace."[17] The image of wives

13. Conrad M. Arensberg and Solon T. Kimball, *Family and Community in Ireland*, 2d ed. (Cambridge, Mass., 1968), p. 196; Padraic Colum, ed., *A Treasury of Irish Folklore*, 2d rev. ed. (New York, 1967), p. 412; Kennedy, *The Irish*, p. 52.

14. Edward Wakefield, *An Account of Ireland Statistical and Political*, 2 vols. (London, 1812), vol. 2, p. 801.

15. Great Britain, *Parliamentary Papers* (Commons), "First Report from Her Majesty's Commissioners for Inquiring into the Condition of the Poorer Classes in Ireland," 1835, 32:Appendix A, 206.

16. Gaffney and Cashman, *Proverbs and Sayings*, pp. 103, 106.

17. James Hardiman, *Irish Minstrelsy; or Bardic Remains of Ireland*, 2 vols. (New York, 1971), vol. 2, p. 369.

that circulated in Irish peasant society therefore portrayed them as having wills of their own and the ability to challenge male authority. This image is not incompatible with the exclusion of women from public spheres of activity. All societies differentiate male and female roles and place lower value on female ones. Michele Rosaldo argues that although "women everywhere lack generally recognized and culturally valued authority," they exercise many kinds of power and influence, particularly in the domestic sphere.[18] Whatever their postures of public deference, Irish rural wives had considerable opportunity for independent action within the household, and they acquired power through their control of certain activities. As we have seen, in laborers' families they earned a substantial fraction of the family's income. They took care of its animals and marketed butter and eggs. Particularly if husbands were seasonal migrants, women had a major responsibility for a family's own land. Under conditions of poverty, male underemployment, and seasonal migration, a family's survival depended on the strength and resilience of the wife and mother.

The preceding description of rural families should be applied to Ireland only in the period before 1850. After the famine the demographic and social behavior of the rural Irish began to change. People married later and later, and more remained permanently single; marriage and birth rates declined. On the eve of World War II, when this tendency was at its height, one-third of Irish men and one-fourth of Irish women aged forty-five to fifty-four were single; in 1945, the average Irish groom was thirty-three, while the mean age of marriage for Irish farmers was thirty-eight. This pattern of demographic choice resulted in part from the economic restructuring of rural society after the potato famine. The poorest families, whose demographic behavior differed from that of people who had property, were removed from the community by death and the lure of American and British wages. Then changes in land law during the late nineteenth century converted the countryside into a land of peasant proprietors. As a result of these changes and shifts in farming

18. Michelle Zimbalist Rosaldo, "Woman, Culture, and Society: A Theoretical Overview," in *Women, Culture, and Society,* ed. Michelle Zimbalist Rosaldo and Louise Lamphere (Stanford, 1974), p. 17.

technology, which increased the size of a farm that could be worked by one family, the pattern of impartible inheritance and late marriage spread throughout the community. A farm was left to one child, and the noninheritors, if they could not be given a fortune and married into other farming families, had to migrate. Their choice, in the words of Joseph Lee, was either "the emigrant ship or the shelf." For those who remained, an economic calculus of "the match" replaced the carefree marriage customs of the laboring poor.[19]

Irish Marriages in the City

If industrial or urban environments directly influence marriage customs, we should find specific changes from the rural Irish pattern appearing among migrants in London. And changes did occur. In the city, the Irish married more frequently and at different ages. Courting customs became more varied, and the rate of illegitimacy seems to have been higher in London than it was in Irish rural parishes for which data have been collected. It is not clear, however, whether this increase in illegitimate births resulted from an increase in premarital intercourse or from changes in the composition of the population and in community supervision, which meant that there were more single people living under conditions that made men less likely to marry their pregnant girl friends.

There was also much continuity of rural mores in London. The young married when and whom they pleased. Parents had little control over the choice of spouse. The ideals of romantic love were held by at least the unmarried, and men continued to assert or attempted to assert control over wives and children. Almost all of the information used in this analysis dates from between 1840 and 1870; it therefore covers both first- and second-generation Irish. When we meet our subjects in census, church, and local government records, some have just arrived in London; others have been there for many years.

19. Joseph Lee, *The Modernization of Irish Society, 1848-1918* (Dublin, 1973), pp. 3-6; Kennedy, *The Irish*, pp. 139-143, 213, 215; K. H. Connell, "Peasant Marriage in Ireland: Its Structure and Development since the Famine," *Economic History Review* 14 (2d ser.), no. 4 (1962):502.

> Oh the English girls are beautiful, their love I don't decline,
> But the eating and the drinking is beautiful and fine;
> But in the corner of the heart where nobody can see,
> Lie two eyes of Irish blue always looking out on me;
> But never mind, Molly darling, I am still your faithful boy,
> For Ireland is my country, and your name shall be Molloy.[20]

Migrants' dreams of courtship were often set in rural Ireland. Exiled laborers sang of Ballymornach and Nora M'Shane and "pretty Susan, the pride of Kildare."[21] In ballads, migrants swore they would return to marry the girl with the cheeks like roses and the eyes like stars who waited for them. City women were sometimes dangerous, as ballads detailing adventures with prostitutes who robbed and mugged the unwary testified.

Still, London offered a host of places for meeting members of the opposite sex and opportunities for courting. Since most migrants lived in Irish enclaves that offered an active street life, Celtic neighbors of appropriate ages were near at hand, and the young could frequent the pubs, music halls, and "penny gaffs" at low cost. While an unknown number brought over their Irish sweethearts, available Londoners became the pool from which many spouses were chosen.

The Roman Catholic church attempted to regulate stringently the social lives and courting practices of its flock and to keep a watchful eye on their offspring, forbidding their entry into "bad dancing and singing houses, . . . gambling houses and theaters." The normal settings of most working-class social life — pubs, gin shops, races, fairs, music halls, gambling houses, theaters, the streets at night — were viewed with strong disapproval. Parents were not to let children "play about the streets with anyone or keep dangerous company with persons of the other sex."[22] The church tried valiantly to enforce unisexual recreation. Parish church activities were usually segregated by sex unless entire families were invited. Catholic women were told not to drink in the company of men, and even engaged women were always to be

---

20. Crampton Collection, 8 vols., British Library, vol. 5, p. 51.
21. Ibid., vol. 4, p. 18; vol. 5, p. 188.
22. Father John Furniss, *What Every Christian Must Know* (London and Derby, 1856), pp. 8, 16, 25.

chaperoned. Whether these instructions were followed closely is questionable. Yet Henry Mayhew concluded from his conversations with London Irish peddlers in 1849 that they attempted to supervise closely at least their daughters. Girls were not allowed to go unaccompanied to dances or to penny theaters, and he concluded that the Irish generally stayed away from many urban amusements, preferring dancing parties at one another's houses.[23]

But even if parents enforced the standards recommended by the church, by the age of twenty most adolescents had left home to board with other families or were migrants themselves far from direct parental supervision. For several years before marriage, therefore, most Irish adolescents were in control of their own social lives. And since no transfer of property was associated with the marriage of Irish urban workers, parents had no real leverage over the choice of spouse. Children's responsibility, according to the Roman Catholic church, was only to ask their parents' consent. Parents were told that it was a sin to force children to marry against their will or to forbid a child's marriage without just cause.[24]

In Irish ballads of courtship, relations between the sexes were simple and idealized. Boy met beautiful girl, fell in love, proposed, and got married unless emigration or hostile parents intervened. The scenario was short, sweet, and chaste.

> When first I beheld her from love I was free,
> But now stand a captive as plain as you may see;
> So grant me your favor, and don't me deny,
> Or won't you relent for a poor wounded boy.
>   . . .
> She says lovely William your love it is true,
> And for to go with you its more than I'll do
> Get me from my parents and if they comply,
> I have plenty in store for a poor wounded boy.[25]

"The first time that I saw my love she struck me in a trance," sighs a young man whose yellow-haired, red-cheeked sweetheart

23. Henry Mayhew, *London Labour and the London Poor*, 4 vols. (London, 1861–1862; reprinted New York, 1968), vol. 1, p. 109.

24. Furniss, *What Every Christian Must Know*, pp. 22, 31.

25. "The Poor Wounded Boy," in Robert L. Wright, *Irish Emigrant Ballads and Songs* (Bowling Green, Ohio), p. 413.

appeared to him to be fairer than the lily.[26] He sighed for her and wished to set her on his knee but suggested nothing bolder. Marriage and/or emigration to America was the common resolution of such encounters.

Relationships in the real world were no doubt less idyllic and physically freer than in the romanticized land of ballad lovers. We know very little about premarital sexual behavior among the urban Irish; the young were probably less closely supervised by the local community, but the Catholic church attempted to take on that role. Catholics were expected to confess sins of sexual behavior, and the church was concerned enough about the chastity of the young to give specific warnings. Girls were cautioned against letting any male "take liberties" with them, even if he were a fiancé. All "keeping company" between individuals of opposite sexes was "dangerous," particularly if they were alone. Women working in factories were warned against the male clerks, masters, and foremen, who were "the means of bringing many girls to ruin," and London priests worried that young women who lost their jobs would soon end up as prostitutes.[27]

Whether premarital intercourse was more common among the London Irish than among their country cousins is impossible to say, but the incidence of illegitimacy in London, as computed from the baptismal registers of five London Roman Catholic parishes, seems to have been somewhat higher than in rural Ireland. Catholic clergy in Ireland before the famine claimed that illegitimate births were rare, and travelers came to the same conclusion. K. H. Connell has calculated illegitimacy ratios for parishes where statistics were given to the Poor Inquiry in 1835; in a group of 49 parishes, fewer than 2 percent of all births were illegitimate in 29; the ratio was between 2 and 4 percent in 9 and between 4 and 6 percent in 11 of them. In any case, illegitimacy ratios were very low by late in the century, being only 1.63 percent of total births between 1871 and 1880, the first decade of civil registration.[28] In mid-nineteenth-century London, however, Cath-

26. Wright, *Irish Emigrant Ballads*, p. 384.
27. Furniss, *What Every Christian Must Know*, pp. 24–25, and *Books for Children for First Communions, Missions, Retreats, etc.* (Dublin, 1860–1861), pp. 9, 27; *Catholic Standard* 9, no. 213 (November 5, 1853).
28. K. H. Connell, *Irish Peasant Society: Four Historical Essays* (Oxford, 1968), pp. 79, 82.

olic baptismal registers show higher ratios of illegitimacy. In several central London parishes an average of 4 percent of all baptized children were illegitimate between 1850 and 1870, and the level rose as more second-generation Irish had children. And in the parish of St. Patrick's, Soho, which included the notorious St. Giles slums, the ratio of illegitimate to total births exceeded 10 percent in 1850. In any case, these figures must be regarded as minima, for parents had no legal obligation to baptize their children. The illegitimate offspring of Irish who were Protestant or who feared priestly disapproval more than the possible consequences of failure to baptize their infants would not appear in parish registers.[29]

Examinations of Irish requesting entry into the poorhouse during the mid–nineteenth century reveal a steady but small sprinkling of illegitimate children. Most were the offspring of illiterate servants who themselves were second-generation Irish. Ann Sullivan, one of six children of Irish migrants to London, bore an illegitimate child at the age of twenty-two to the son of a Southwark pub owner. She applied to enter the workhouse after father and lover both died of the fever in 1838.[30] Ellen Collins, the London-born widow of an Irish Catholic who married her in London in 1820, became a servant after his death and then had an illegitimate child by Dennis Callaghan, who worked near the pub where she was employed.[31] In several cases the bearing of illegitimate children was part of a pattern of stable consensual unions. Sara Sullivan lived with John Sullivan in south London for fifteen years and bore him three children before they were married by a priest two weeks before John's death in 1838.[32] The reluctance of this couple to tie the knot might have been increased by the fact that until 1837, Roman Catholic marriage ceremonies were not legally recognized in England. Although priests conducted marriage services in London before that date, the couple also had to have a Protestant or civil service.

29. Baptismal registers for the churches of St. Anne, Underwood Road; St. Mary of the Angels, Bayswater; Holy Trinity, Dockhead; St. Patrick, Soho, 1850–1870.
30. Guardians of the Poor, St. John Horsleydown, Southwark, *Poor Law Examinations,* June 9, 1838, Greater London Council Archive.
31. Ibid., September 17, 1835.
32. Ibid., April 9, 1838.

Irish men residing in five London parishes in 1851 married at an average age of twenty-eight and women at an average age of twenty-six. (See Table A.8, Appendix B.) These figures probably reflect a general postponement of marriage by migrants during the famine years. Thousands of Irish moved to London in the half decade preceding the census and brought little with them. Hit hard by events in Ireland, they found themselves attacked by cholera and other diseases in London. Under these circumstances, reluctance to marry seems plausible. As economic circumstances in England brightened in the mid-1850s, more Irish migrants married, and at earlier ages. While marriage ages in Ireland rose to approach thirty, those among London migrants fell to the mid-twenties. By 1861 the London Irish had lower ages of marriage than those of the total English, Irish, and London population, and their rate of celibacy was lower. (See Table A.8, Appendix B.)

Young men and women chose partners of approximately the same age as their own. If we look only at marriages in which the groom was under forty years old in order to eliminate most second marriages, we find that 48 percent of all unions in 1851 took place between people whose ages differed by less than two years. When the sample as a whole is examined, however, large age gaps appear with increasing frequency as couples aged. An age gap of ten years or more occurred among only 6 percent of couples headed by a man under forty, but in 23 percent of all cases when the man was forty to fifty-nine and 57 percent when he was sixty or over. This gap resulted either from a tendency of men entering second marriages to choose much younger women or from a generational effect. Possibly the choice of much younger brides had been more frequent in 1800 or 1820 than it was in 1850. The social status of husbands made little difference in this pattern; in all social groups, approximately 50 percent of all men and women under forty years of age married spouses within two years of their own age.

The London Irish generally married within their own ethnic group; there was little intermarriage with people of English ancestry or with continental Roman Catholics. While 24 percent of the sampled families listed in the 1851 census and 20 percent of those in the 1861 census contained one English-born and one

Irish-born partner, virtually all of the technically English spouses were second- or third-generation Irish. The "English" men had Irish names and had been born in London; marriage registers from the Catholic churches serving my sample parishes show that most of the maiden names of women marrying Irish-born men were also Irish.[33] First- and second-generation Irish would seem therefore to have intermarried freely.

The first-generation Irish marrying in London chose spouses from their own counties in Ireland or from areas contiguous to them. Of the nineteen couples married in 1810 by priests in St. Olave, Southwark, 80 percent had two Irish-born parents and 63 percent had come from the same or adjoining counties. Of the 188 couples whose parents' addresses are known married in St. Patrick's, Soho, between 1838 and 1856, 41 percent came from the same and 16 percent from adjoining counties. Some of these couples had probably known each other in Ireland. The marriage pool from which spouses were chosen in London was limited geographically as well as ethnically. Nearly all of the people listed in the St. Patrick's marriage registers came from and married spouses from Munster. Moreover, a majority chose partners whose London residences lay within one-quarter mile of their own.[34] Despite the size of London and the possibility of widespread social contacts that the city offered, the friendships that led to marriage seem to have taken place at the level of the ethnic neighborhood.

Marriage among migrants therefore tied them into local networks. Kin and neighbors attended the ceremonies and acted as witnesses, and at least those who chose to be married by a priest went to their parish church, which further integrated them into a local religious coumunity. In the city as in the countryside, marriages were public, ritualized acts that were supported and approved by kin and neighbors. James Greenwood, in his studies of London workers in the third quarter of the nineteenth century, reported the pride of married couples in the legality of their

33. Marriage registers, Church of the Holy Trinity, Dockhead, and St. Patrick's, Soho, 1836–1857.
34. Ibid.

relationship. Marriage certificates were framed and prominently displayed on the walls of workers' apartments.[35]

How did these urban marriages function? The advice of the Roman Catholic church around 1850 on the responsibilities of spouses is both explicit and adapted to Catholic urban populations. "The husband must work for the support of his family, and not spend his wages in drinking, gambling, and the like or spend unjustly what belongs to the wife or children. The wife must take care of the household, and not spend too much money, and she must obey her husband." Desertion without "just cause," cruelty, beating, and the giving of "their affections to another person" were all condemned, as was the passing of time by the husband in "idle or bad company."[36] Men were placed at the head of the household, to be respected and obeyed by wives and children, while women were expected to remain at home to minister to the wants of their families. The church also gave advice on sexual behavior: "The wife must obey her husband in the lawful duties of marriage," but it was not right to do anything before the children which might "scandalize" them. Couples were reminded that abortion was a mortal sin and that "the wrong or improper use of marriage" (that is, contraception) was also a sin and must be confessed.[37]

We do not know to what extent this model of marital behavior was followed by the London Irish. On one level there was certainly conformity. As we saw in Chapter 4, husbands did provide the main financial support while household chores and child care became the primary responsibilities of women. But the way husband and wife divided and exercised authority within the household is a much more complicated matter. No one pattern of male–female relations will fit all cases, of course, and all we can do is to specify some of the options that were exercised. In certain ways, the primary status of the husband was made clear. Nearly all of the meat purchased by South London laborers' families around 1914 was given to the husband and father; women and

35. James Greenwood, *The Wilds of London* (London, 1874), p. 71.
36. Furniss, *What Every Christian Must Know*, pp. 7, 31–32.
37. Ibid., pp. 7, 32.

children had a more restricted diet.[38] The man controlled the initial disposition of income. He could decide what to keep and what to turn over to his family. Husbands' desires for tobacco and alcohol were therefore built into family budgets in a way that sums for women's and children's spending were not. Tales of husbandly abuse of control over income are not difficult to find. Joseph Oppenheim, who visited the St. Giles slums as a Protestant City Mission visitor in the 1860s, describes several nearly destitute households where wives were beaten and starved by husbands who spent most of their wages at the pub.[39] Henry Mayhew describes a family in which the husband, a ballast heaver, was an abusive alcoholic who brought home only 1s. 6d. or 2s. a week.[40] Around 1900 Charles Booth reported much drinking and wife beating in a Camberwell Irish colony. Of the Catholic Irish around 1900 he said, "Drinking and fighting are the ordinary conditions of life among many."[41]

We know little about the way such strains on family life were handled by the Irish. Priests berated those who drank and tried to enroll them in the church's organizations. Some wives seem to have been unable to cope and sank into a demoralized state. One woman who talked with Oppenheim in January of 1862 talked of her feelings about her life: "I cant say that I feel well . . . I got everything to knock me down; I could wish I was dead if it was not for this little baby and he would be much better off if he was dead too. . . . Well, I heard a great deal about heaven and hell, but I am sure I have got my hell here. I need not have another."[42]

Some wives managed to maintain their morale. Tom Barclay, an English-born son of rural Irish who migrated to Leicester during the famine, described his mother as "the grey mare." By day she worked in a rag-and-bone shop or sold wood chips on the streets. By night, while her husband was at the pub, she stayed

38. Laura Oren, "The Welfare of Women in Laboring Families: England, 1860-1950," in *Clio's Consciousness Raised*, ed. Mary Hartman and Lois W. Banner (New York, 1974), p. 229.

39. Joseph M. Oppenheim, "Visitor's Book, 1861-1862," St. Giles in the Fields, London.

40. Mayhew, *London Labour*, vol. 3, pp. 290-291.

41. Charles Booth, *The Life and Labour of the People in London*, ser. 3, *Religious Influences*, 7 vols. (London, 1902), vol. 6, pp. 15-16; vol. 7, p. 244.

42. Oppenheim, "Visitor's Book," p. 58.

home and taught the children how to read English and acquainted them with Irish myths and songs. Her religion taught her that poverty and suffering were the normal lot of the living, and "her consolation was an old Irish lamentation or love song and the contemplation of the sufferings of 'Our Blessed Lord.'" She and countless other Irish men and women found ways of coping with the strains of family life in the city.[43]

Beyond the question of drunkenness and physical cruelty, whose incidence we cannot even estimate, we need to explore in more detail the distribution of power and authority within Irish workers' families. If power is defined as the control over persons or resources, then clearly power was divided in workers' households.[44] Women should have had primary control over children, since men were absent from the mid-nineteenth-century household for most of their waking hours. Even if men initially divided resources between their own needs and those of the family, the wife controlled the daily allocation of funds. The health of the household depended on the wisdom of her handling of family income. Laboring women, in fact, prided themselves on their ability to cover household needs on a small wage packet. In "Fifteen Shillings a Week" and "The Labouring Woman," wives defended in song their spending decisions:

> Threepence halfpenny a week for milk is spent,
> One and ninepence a week for rent,
>
>   .   .   .
>
> A penny a week for cotton and thread,
> Last Sunday tenpence a small sheep's head;
> Ninepence halfpenny a day for bread,
> Out of fifteen shillings a week, sir.[45]

Every farthing was accounted in the purchase of food, clothing, and other consumption items. Moreover, wives commonly handled the chore of staving off family creditors — the landlord, the tallyman, the local shopkeepers.

If these housewifely skills were appreciated, they should have

43. Tom Barclay, *Memoirs and Medleys: The Autobiography of a Bottlewasher* (Leicester, 1934), pp. 3–5, 9, 10, 23.

44. This definition was formulated by Louise Tilly; this part of my argument owes a great deal to conversations with her and with Joan Scott.

45. Baring-Gould Collection, British Library, p. 143.

brought women status in the eyes of their families. But did they? Tom Barclay clearly thought that his mother was a saint, but what his father thought is unclear. There must have been many tensions between husbands and wives in Irish urban workers' families. When Tom Barclay's father came home from the pub, quarrels and blows followed.[46] The pressures of low wages, unemployment, and overcrowded apartments would have made conflict inevitable even if adapting to urban life in another culture had presented no difficulties.

Irish songs describing marriage contrast markedly with generally idealized tales of courtship and romantic love. Balladeers contended that women changed into shrews as soon as the knot was tied.

> A young girl before she gets married
>   You think butter won't melt in her mouth,
> But when she puts on the sweet bands of wedlock
>   Her notebook she soon opens out;
> And in five or six months after marriage
>   Her gentility all is forgot.[47]

Husbands found wedlock the "beginning of all . . . strife" and complained of being ignored, thrashed, and cuckolded, and having their money taken.[48] One such songwriter concluded:

> Tis Oh, the marriage, the marriage,
> Refrain it for goodness sake, do.
> You'll find it no simple matter,
> If you marry in earnest you will rue.[49]

The problems of cohabitation outweighed its pleasures in the world of the balladeers.

Two thorny matters that infuriated men in the broadsheet ballads were women's alleged attempts to get help in child care and housework and to assert their will over that of their husbands.

> The women they are fully bent and every day they are aiming.
> By hook or crook they'll find a plan to give the men a taming.[50]

46. Barclay, *Memoirs and Medleys*, p. 12.
47. James N. Healy, *The Mercier Book of Old Irish Street Ballads* (Cork, 1969), vol. 4, p. 127.
48. Ibid., pp. 122, 123, 128.
49. Ibid., p. 126.
50. Ibid., p. 129.

Women's attempts to alter a sex-based division of labor were particularly resented. Husbands were urged to wear the breeches and not to surrender their authority.

Perhaps these disillusioned views of marriage reflect only age-old conflicts and contests for resources; perhaps these songs could have been written about workers' families in centuries other than the nineteenth. But I distrust the neglect of time and setting that this argument implies. Let us look more closely at the specific claims made by both the male and female sides in these disputes.

In "The Unlucky Fellow," a husband complains of his wife's quarreling and physical abuse. He ends his tirade with the following:

> My wife on Saturday night comes, oh dear!
>   To the place where my wages I take,
> She won't e'en allow me a pint of small beer,
>   And with hunger and cold I oft quake.
> Then the young uns she makes me take out for a walk,
>   Or drag them about in a shay.[51]

Similarly, in "The Wife's Commandments on the Rights of Women," a satirical account of female behavior, a much-caricatured Mrs. Brown claims of her husband:

[Commandment] 4th: Six days you must work from 6 to 6, that you may provide me with the comforts of life, and on the seventh, you must scrub the floor, peel the potatoes, make the dumplings and cook the dinner. In the afternoon, by way of amusement you must take the children to the park, and show the little darlings the ducks.

. . .

6th: You must not crib a shilling from your wages on Saturday night, but fork it all out, and be contented with the pocket money I shall think fit to give you.

. . .

10th: You must not covet to be trusted with a latch key in the evening.[52]

In addition, he was enjoined from getting drunk, looking at other women, or complaining about his wife's cooking or sewing. In "The Wife's ABC's," which was written for a woman to sing, a more favorable version of female attitudes is presented. Men are advised to marry if they want to lead happy lives, but the fact that "it isn't quite all honey" after the wedding is freely admitted.

51. Crampton Collection, British Library, vol. 4, p. 89.
52. Ibid., vol. 8, p. 139.

Again, the wife claims "a share" of "the old man's wages" and says he should help with the baby when he's home.[53] All through the song the wife asserts both her right to do things jointly with her husband and his obligation to come home early from the pub and recognize his duties toward wife and children.

D   stands for dancing, if you want a spree,
    You neednt join the shakers but shake at home with me.

E   stands for excursions, to Putney or to Kew,
    When a husband has a holiday the wife should have one too.

W   stands for weaning — when the baby makes a riot,
    Its the husband's duty to nurse it till its quiet.

X   stand for ten o'clock, I think it only right,
    It is the time for working men to be home at night.[54]

Several issues recur in these ballads: the turning over to wives of wages, men's desire to spend evenings and money in the pub rather than at home, and the extent to which men were to help with household chores and child care. Two competing sets of values seem to have triggered domestic battles. Men demanded their rights to come and go freely, to determine the allocation of their earnings, and to be free of domestic duties. Women demanded that family needs take precedence over individualistic male desires; men ought to contribute both time and money to children and spouse, and they ought to participate occasionally in the child-rearing process. What men perceived as an attempt to rule the roost seems to have originated in claims made to maintain the nuclear family. Men's drinking, spending, and retreating to the pub when wages were not high enough to cover both household needs and husbands' consumption desires were threats to the survival of the family.

Movement into the city surely intensified these conflicts. While the drinking of poteen was widespread in Ireland before the famine, liquor could be brewed at home.[55] Although heavy drinking was an accepted social activity among the peasantry, landless laborers lacked the ready cash to purchase alcohol

53. Ibid., p. 565.
54. Ibid.
55. Connell, *Irish Peasant Society*, pp. 26, 49.

regularly. In the city, both money and pubs were ready to hand. Husbands began to increase claims over income in a situation where automatic brakes on individual consumption desires were removed. The urban environment increased both pressures and opportunities to spend, thus intensifying competition within the family for resources.

Irish migrants' households in 1850 were somewhere between Philippe Ariès' vision of families closely linked to a local community and the self-enclosed nuclear family of the present. Their values and habits were in a state of transition as they learned to cope with an urban environment. Marriages based on romantic love and individual choice were not the creation of the city, but perhaps the strains on those relationships were. Peter Willmott and Michael Young call the early decades of the Industrial Revolution a time of disruption for family life, a time when husbands and wives had to accept the consequences of the separation of home and workplace. We should add to this sequence the pressures of migration. Households were stripped of economic resources — gardens, animals, women's by-occupations — at the same time that the city forced changes in patterns of recreation and consumption. Migrant families had to adapt to a new urban world; domestic roles could no more remain static and unchanging than could economic and social relationships.

Over time, different patterns of family life developed. By the mid–twentieth century, many Irish workers' families in England became strongly matrifocal; married daughters brought their husbands and children to live either with their mothers or in nearby flats, creating complex units that functioned as extended families by sharing services and often eating together. Not only was the mother the main center of family life; she maintained considerable psychological and economic power over her spouse, children, and sometimes grandchildren. While some couples reported good relationships between husbands and wives, women seemed to have been far closer to their mothers than to their husbands. Men in turn were close to their peers in the neighborhood. In consequence, marital bonds were comparatively loose.[56]

56. Madeline Kerr, *The People of Ship Street* (London, 1958), pp. 12–14, 40–47, 80–83; B. E. Harrell-Bond, "Conjugal Role Behavior," *Human Relations* 22, no. 1

An alternative style of marriage and family relationships resembling Willmott and Young's symmetrical family has been described by Elizabeth Bott. In socially and economically heterogeneous neighborhoods, sex segregation, male solidarity with peers, and the density of local social networks all decrease; many couples in this situation depend more on one another than on kin or peers and look for emotional satisfaction to their marriage partner rather than to their family of origin, partly as a result of personal needs and partly in response to their social environment. In this second style of family life, which is correlated with geographic and social mobility, ties with kin loosen and sex roles shift toward greater equality and interchangeability.[57] Such an arrangement among workers' families became much more common in this century, after fertility declined and women reentered the labor force in large numbers. It also required a certain time to develop among Irish rural-to-urban migrants. Among those who moved into Dublin during the 1950s and early 1960s, little change could be found by 1965 in either ideology or family organization.[58] Couples maintained similar definitions of sex roles, although parental control over children declined and women took on greater responsibility for child rearing. Contact with kin also decreased, since there was less opportunity for sharing of labor and goods in a fixed seasonal cycle. The early effects of urbanization on recent migrant families were primarily organizational. Families had to adapt to urban patterns of education, social services, and community life, which took away certain accustomed functions.

Irish families have therefore not changed linearly or uniformly into strong, relatively private conjugal units in which emotional and practical ties to other kin have become minimal. In the nineteenth century, migrants continued to recognize long-term obligations to their families of origin. Their residential units remained flexible as people entered and withdrew from the labor force and migrated from place to place. The uncertainties of the

(1969):77–91; Peter Willmott and Michael Young, *Family and Kinship in East London* (London, 1957).

57. Elizabeth Bott, *Family and Social Network,* 2d ed. (London, 1971), pp. 218, 303.

58. A. J. Humphreys, *New Dubliners: The Urbanization of the Irish Family* (London, 1966), pp. 230–251.

early industrial urban environment forced upon them adaptations that restrained the growth of individualism and the rigid assignment of work and sex roles. In the twentieth century, no single pattern of family organization has developed. Instead, different arrangements suited to the personal needs, socioeconomic environment, and subculture of individual couples have emerged. There is no single "urban Irish family."

CHAPTER 7

The Reforging of an
Irish Catholic Culture

The migrant Irish were neither disorganized nor culturally impoverished. Perhaps the links between physical and cultural poverty are closer in an urban society than they were in the traditional societies of times past; nevertheless, the Irish urban poor had many cultural resources at their command and had a vocabulary of symbols and actions through which to express their view of the world. The beliefs and the practice of Roman Catholicism supplied Irish migrants with a vigorous alternative to the secularist ideology of London workers and to the life-style of the Evangelical Protestant. A Catholic workers' culture was slowly built by migrants and priests amid the London slums. The locus of this culture was the Catholic parish, which issued an unceasing call to the faithful to reaffirm their religious and national heritage by returning to the arms of Mother Church. It drew the worshiper into a fervently nationalist piety that bridged the gap between the secular and the sacred, the political and the spiritual, and it provided an alternative to assimilation into the English working class. Through the work of the priests, thousands of Catholics were reintegrated into local communities where raggedness and dirt did not mark them as pariahs and where Catholicism was a sign of grace rather than of superstition and error. The Roman Catholic church functioned therefore as a major agent of social and cultural change among the migrant Irish and helped them to convert their vestiges of traditional culture into an urbanized, nationalist variant compatible with church orthodoxy. While the hierarchy's attempts to spread an ethic of self-help and sobriety were only marginally successful, clerics hastened the process of cultural and social transformation within the Irish community, turning migrants away from their rural past and toward participation in local urban neighborhoods. The cost of this transformation for individual psyches is impossible to estimate; yet whatever the initial impact of migration, the church cushioned the shock of change for many by providing a measure of institutional and cultural continuity. We may lament the virtual disappearance of the rich and fascinating system of beliefs whose origins reached back into the pre-Christian past; but this system of beliefs was decaying under the impact of social change in Ireland, too. Once migrants had left the communities that had fostered and enacted this ethos, they had to adapt to the urban, industrial civilization of an English-speaking world.

Popular Catholicism in Prefamine Ireland

An imaginative world based on religion infused with magic and magic strengthened by religion survived in rural areas of Irish-speaking Ireland into the twentieth century. Undeterred by the Reformation, the Counterreformation, and the Enlightenment, popular Catholic culture in Ireland retained until at least 1850 its links to pre-Christian ritual and to magic; belief in fairies, ghosts, witchcraft, and magical healing seems to have been widespread in the west of Ireland until at least the First World War.[1] Rural Irish folk beliefs and popular religion during the nineteenth century bear an uncanny resemblance to the mental world of pre-Reformation England.[2]

Before 1850, the Catholic church in Ireland had succeeded only partially in imposing upon the Irish population acceptance of the religious practices decreed by the Council of Trent. While the French and Italian Catholic churches reformed religious practices in their areas during the seventeenth century, the prefamine Irish Catholic church was not well enough organized to enforce its

1. Lady [Isabella Augusta] Gregory, *Visions and Beliefs in the West of Ireland* (New York, 1970); W. Y. Evans-Wentz, *The Fairy Faith in Celtic Countries* (Secaucus, N.J., 1966), pp. 17–84.
2. Keith Thomas, *Religion and the Decline of Magic* (London, 1973).

norms upon the mass of the population.[3] In Ireland, the effort to encourage individual conformity to a system of parochial devotions that entailed weekly attendance at mass and regular confession and communion foundered on the inability of the clergy to teach and to minister to the Catholic population. Not only was the church deficient in personnel and physical resources before the potato famine of the late 1840s, but penal laws severely restricted clerical activities. Since it was illegal to operate Roman Catholic schools in Ireland until 1782 and their financing was restricted until 1829, the church did not educate its adherents and barely taught its clerics. Since each priest served on the average 3,000 people in 1840, clergymen outside the cities found it all they could do to give last rites to the dying and to say mass irregularly at stations set in farmhouses and cottages throughout their districts. They had neither the time nor the training to teach much of the catechism to their flock.[4] The result was a low level of participation in the cycle of parish rituals and general ignorance of orthodox Catholic doctrine. A census of church attendance in 1834 showed that in Irish-speaking areas of the west and southwest, between 20 and 40 percent of eligible Catholics went to mass on the Sunday investigated. While rates were higher in English-speaking rural areas, in the cities, and in eastern counties, rural rates of attendance ranged generally between 30 and 60 percent.[5] Outsiders found the Irish woefully ignorant of their faith. Marist priests in the East End of London in the mid-1850s deplored the lack of awareness among the first-generation Irish of "the most essential truths of our Religion," and added that almost no migrants had taken their first communion.[6]

Popular Catholicism in the early nineteenth century centered on ceremonies and devotions in which one finds an unfamiliar mixture of the secular and the sacred. Patterns (celebrations of patron saints' days) were staples of communal life. They often

3. John Bossy, "The Counter-Reformation and the People of Catholic Europe," *Past and Present*, no. 47 (May 1970), pp. 52–58.

4. Emmet Larkin, "The Devotional Revolution in Ireland, 1850–75," *American Historical Review* 77, no. 3 (June 1972):627, 635.

5. David W. Miller, "Irish Catholicism and the Great Famine," *Journal of Social History* 9, no. 1 (Fall 1975):86.

6. Father S. E. Chauvrain, "Rapport sur la mission de Ste Anne, Spitalfields, Londres," February 2, 1857, E61–331, Marist Archive, Rome.

involved a pilgrimage to a holy well or some other sacred site. St. Patrick's Purgatory, a pilgrimage to a holy well on an island in Lough Derg in Donegal, was said to draw 10,000 persons annually in the early nineteenth century.[7] At all of the patterns there were prescribed rituals. Since many of the sites of the patterns were thought to have the power of healing, rituals intended to cure penitents of diseases were common. Pilgrims had to circle holy wells a certain number of times (often three) on their knees, always going from east to west, in the direction of the sun, while reciting paters and aves. At the end of each circle they were to erect a pile of stones, one stone for each prayer, which the angels would count on judgment day, giving the highest places in heaven to those who had said the most prayers. Finally the votary was to bathe the face and hands in holy water, after which his cure was to begin. While these devotions were carried out, tents were pitched and food, drink, and relics were sold in a carnival atmosphere. By evening, dancing, drinking, and faction fights replaced the prayers of the devout.[8]

Appropriate sites for patterns and pilgrimages could be found all over Ireland. There are 3,000 known holy wells; county Kerry alone has 143.[9] These sites have been venerated for centuries; the early Christians merely added a cross and a saint's name, thus appropriating the site's sanctity for the Catholic church. Visits to the wells remained popular in the early nineteenth century.

Some of the most important Irish religious festivals linked religious devotions, pre-Christian practices, and folk rituals. Many of the saints' days that dot the Irish calendar were celebrated in ways that reveal their ancient origins. St. John's Feast is a partly Christianized version of the Celtic celebration of midsummer. The practice of lighting fires on hilltops survived until

7. E. Estyn Evans, *Irish Folkways* (London and Boston, 1957), pp. 262, 266. This pilgrimage, during which penitents were locked overnight in a cell after fifteen days of fasting, was probably a survival of pagan initiatory rites; see Evans-Wentz, *Fairy Faith*, pp. 443–444.

8. Lady [Jane Francesca Speranza] Wilde, *Ancient Legends, Mystic Charms, and Superstitions of Ireland* (London, 1888; reprinted Galway, 1971), p. 237; see also Evans, *Irish Folkways*, p. 298; Mr. and Mrs. S. C. Hall, *Ireland: Its Scenery, Character, etc.*, 3 vols. (London, 1841), vol. 1, pp. 282–284.

9. Evans, *Irish Folkways*, p. 298; prefamine religion exhibit, Muckross House, Killarney, county Kerry.

at least the mid-1950s in Galway and was claimed to be universal in the mid- and late nineteenth century. A variety of traditional activities intended to bring luck and fertility were practiced around the fires. Evil influences were supposed to be rampant at midsummer, working against human beings, crops, and animals; strong measures to combat them were considered indispensable. Walking three times around the fire on one's knees while saying prayers supposedly brought a year without sickness. When the flames had died down, young men and women would leap over the fires. Three jumps back and three forward were to bring a speedy marriage and many children.[10]

Lammas (or Garland) Sunday, which marked the beginning of harvest, was celebrated in part with more explicitly religious rituals. Offerings of fruits and flowers were made at holy wells, and various popular pilgrimages and patterns were held on that day. But there also was a tradition in hilly districts of climbing to an appropriate spot for a picnic with berrying, dancing, and games. On that Sunday unmarried women decorated wreaths with ribbons and flowers, which were then deposited in the church and later in the graveyard. The day that began with sacrifice in honor of the harvest and of the dead then terminated with dancing, the young being given free license to court.[11] Irish religious festivals in the nineteenth century thus combined pre-Christian practices, folk beliefs, religious rituals, and recreation.

Just as the saints were credited with miraculous powers, so too were Irish priests. A curse pronounced by a priest would produce its fulfillment because "the doom of the priest is as the word of God."[12] Priests could be used as conjurors or exorcists to chase out devils or lay the wandering spirits of the dead.[13] Priests were also credited with magical powers to heal. In the southwest in the early and mid-nineteenth century, fire was asked of a priest when

10. Evans, *Irish Folkways*, pp. 274–275; Lageniensis [Rev. John O'Hanlon], *Irish Folk Lore: Traditions and Superstitions of the Country* (Glasgow and London, 1870; reprinted Darby, Pa., 1973), p. 203; Wilde, *Ancient Legends*, p. 113.
11. Evans, *Irish Folkways*, pp. 275–276; Sean Ó Súilleabháin, *A Handbook of Irish Folklore* (Wexford, 1942), p. 342.
12. Wilde, *Ancient Legends*, p. 69.
13. Ibid., pp. 80–81; James Berry, *Tales of the West of Ireland*, ed. Gertrude M. Horgan, 3d ed. (Dublin, 1975); Ó Súilleabháin, *Handbook of Irish Folklore*, pp. 383–384, 158.

any epidemic or disease threatened. The hearth fire would be rekindled with a priest's flame in order to drive away infection. In 1849, the population of Carrick used clay from a priest's grave to cure several diseases.[14]

The study of popular Catholicism in nineteenth-century Ireland quickly leads to the study of belief in Celtic magic. One finds in Irish popular beliefs a large amount of syncretism, Catholic rituals and dogmas having been built into the devotions to pre-Christian deities and accommodated to belief in witches, ghosts, and fairies. Irish peasants combined their Catholicism with belief in a non-Christian world. Some folktales are built around encounters between priests and fairies in which two different but similar forms of power and knowledge are demonstrated. The saying of a mass was believed to release a person from a fairy spell.[15] Sean Ó Súilleabháin argues that both fairy lore and the belief in ghosts are "inextricably confused" in Irish folklore and linked to a Catholic view of the world, since ghosts were thought to be the wandering souls of those in Purgatory.[16] Fairy lore gave Irish peasants an explanation of death, disease, and misfortune, partly independent of Catholicism. Witches could cause sudden sicknesses, which only a fairy doctor or wise woman could cure.[17] Fairy kidnappings served to explain the deaths of the young and apparently healthy. Although fairy magic and religion appear to an outsider to offer alternative analyses of both natural and supernatural forces, in the cultural world of Irish-speaking Ireland in the nineteenth century there was a fusion of many forms of popular belief, which expressed itself in hybrid forms of folktale, ritual, and symbol.

How extensively accepted was this imaginative world of magical Catholicism and fairy sprites? Until the end of the century, available evidence is fragmentary and consists of travelers' and amateur ethnographers' opinions. Although not ideal sources, these observers had excellent eyes for other aspects of traditional culture, so their views cannot be automatically dismissed. For the

14. Lageniensis, *Irish Folk Lore*, pp. 206–207; George Henderson, *Survivals in Belief among the Celts* (Glasgow, 1911), p. 335.

15. Gregory, *Visions and Beliefs*, p. 11; "The Priest's Supper," in *Fairy and Folk Tales of the Irish Peasantry*, ed. William Butler Yeats (London, 1888), pp. 9–13.

16. Ó Súilleabháin, *Handbook of Irish Folklore*, p. 450.

17. Gregory, *Visions and Beliefs*, pp. 31–49.

moment, let us use the belief in fairies to stand for acceptance of a world view based on magic and Celtic folklore.

The persistence of this world view among the Irish was closely linked to their social status, language, and area of residence. In addition, substantial changes over time seem to have taken place. T. Crofton Croker, who wandered about in southern counties in the early 1820s recording folklore, thought that the traditional belief in fairies still existed.[18] Later observers had doubts. Mr. and Mrs. S. C. Hall thought that by 1840 many Irish peasants had become skeptical of fairy beliefs and were reluctant to talk about them.[19] William Wilde, one of the early collectors of Irish folklore, said that by 1850 discussion of fairies and stories about them were dying out,[20] and a Dingle farmer in the 1880s told Jeremiah Curtin, another early collector, that although when he was a boy "nine men in ten believed in fairies, and said so, now only one man in ten will say that he believes in them. If one of the nine believes, he will not tell you."[21]

The growth of skepticism was part of a larger process of social change. A national system of education, which used English exclusively, was organized in 1831 and spread rapidly. At the same time, the Catholic church reformed itself. Priests disclaimed the ability to cure; patterns were forbidden or discouraged because of the drunken brawls that often resulted.[22] The commitment of the Catholic church both to temperance in the 1840s and to the "devotional revolution" after 1850 resulted in a direct attack on popular rituals and beliefs. Other changes were less direct, but the increasing dissemination of books and ballads in English, the impact of seasonal migration, and the improvement of transportation helped to undermine the Irish culture of rural areas and to spread a modernized, demystified replacement. Contact with the

18. T. Crofton Croker, *Researches in the South of Ireland Illustrative of the Scenery, Architectural Remains, and the Manners and Superstitions of the Peasantry* (London, 1824), p. 78.

19. Hall, *Ireland*, vol. 3, p. 237.

20. W. R. Wilde, *Irish Popular Superstitions* (Dublin, 1852; reprinted Totawa, N.J., 1973), p. 14.

21. Jeremiah Curtin, *Tales of Fairies and of the Ghost World* (Dublin, 1895; reprinted 1974), p. 2.

22. Gregory, *Visions and Beliefs*, pp. 298, 300; Hall, *Ireland*, vol. 1, p. 279; vol. 3, p. 422; Wilde, *Irish Popular Superstitions*, p. 16.

English language drew the rural Irish into a larger society as it distanced them from the imaginative world of their ancestors.[23]

Tales of fairies and folk magic circulated primarily in an Irish-speaking world, and at least some types of folklore were not translated into English. Folktales told in Irish seldom passed into English, and the rich oral literature of prayers and religious poetry could not survive in another language.[24] It therefore seems plausible to confine the imaginative world of fairy lore and magical religion to Irish-speaking Ireland. The Irish language faded fast during the nineteenth century. Although a recent estimate indicates that half of the population spoke Irish in 1800, by 1851 this proportion had fallen to 25 percent.[25] Since most Irish speakers lived in rural areas of the west and southwest and belonged to the poorest social groups, the Irish-speaking population was drastically reduced by the deaths and emigration of the late 1840s. But the language survived in western Munster and Connaught among the rural population. Despite the drastic national decline in the proportion of Irish speakers, in parts of Kerry, in Clare, Galway, and Mayo, 60 percent or more of the population spoke Irish in 1851.[26] Because of this uneven distribution of Irish speakers, the Irish oral tradition was able to survive. The belief in fairies remained alive in the west, southwest, and parts of northern counties well into the twentieth century.[27]

The complex mixture of fairy beliefs and skepticism that circulated in Ireland by the middle of the nineteenth century is a good indicator of the progress of social change. Mentalities as well as economic and social structure were being transformed. In modernizing areas, traditional Irish culture was a victim of this process, but slow decline rather than death was its fate. Different social groups learned to react in different ways to the legacy of the

23. On the consequences of change in language, see Clifford Geertz, *The Interpretation of Cultures* (New York, 1973), pp. 242–243.

24. Sean O'Sullivan, *The Folklore of Ireland* (London, 1974), p. 15; Douglas Hyde, *The Religious Songs of Connacht* (New York, 1972), p. xi.

25. I cannot vouch for the reliability of these data on continued use of the Irish language. Some pressure probably existed to inflate the extent of knowledge of English and to deflate the numbers of those who spoke Irish.

26. Great Britain, *Parliamentary Papers* (Commons), "Census of Ireland for 1851," 1856, 31:xlvi, xlviii.

27. See Gregory, *Visions and Beliefs*, pp. 182, 227.

Irish past. In Limerick by the 1860s, the children of prosperous farmers were sent to church schools where they learned an orthodox version of the Catholic religion, and their parents branded as "imaginary and untrue" the tales of fairies and witches told them by farm laborers and dairymaids. While all went to mass, the uneducated relied not on Catholic saints for protection but on a strange mixture of charms and popular lore, which were said to keep away witches and other evil spirits lurking about, eager to do harm.[28]

Alternative vocabularies of ritual and symbol were therefore available to Irish Catholics in the nineteenth century. Orthodox practice had to contend with ancient beliefs and the many particularistic customs of each locality. Those who went to England probably brought with them a host of traditional beliefs leavened with amounts of Catholic orthodoxy that varied according to their place of birth and social status. After migration, these sets of beliefs had to be adapted to a different physical and cultural environment.

The Building of a Roman Catholic Community in London

As in other English towns, the Roman Catholic church in London was small and haphazardly organized as late as 1800. Only limited opportunities for religious observance existed. Ambassadors from Roman Catholic countries maintained chapels that could be used by English Catholics, and a small network of secret mass houses supplemented these embassy chapels. But attendance was permitted only at the pleasure of the government, and the practice of Catholicism remained hazardous in the eighteenth century, particularly for the clergy. Priests were forced to wear lay dress, and they and their bishops had to move frequently to conceal their activities. As late as 1767, police seized Father John Baptist Moloney and sentenced him to life imprisonment for operating a chapel in south London. Yet even under these conditions, the English Catholic church began to grow. Mass centers appeared in the alleys of the Irish poor. By 1741, records of the vicar apostolic list five such secret mass houses in London, and by the time of the Gordon Riots in 1780, three

28. Mary Carbery, *The Farm by Lough Gur* (Cork and Dublin, 1973), p. 158.

permanent chapels had been built. All, however, were destroyed by anti-Catholic mobs.[29]

A pattern of rebuilding and slow growth accelerated with the pace of Irish migration. Appropriately enough, the man who provided the major impetus for Catholic expansion in London was himself an Irish migrant. The son of a Catholic merchant who had emigrated to Spain, Nicholas Wiseman was sent to London as vicar apostolic in 1849. Although he was by instinct and training a scholar, Wiseman strongly believed in the possibility of reconverting England to the Catholic faith. This belief led him to adopt a policy of expansion and active missionary work. In 1850 he became archbishop of Westminster, the first head of the newly reorganized hierarchy of the English Catholic church. In his new position, Wiseman worked to revitalize English Catholicism and to expand the facilities of the church in areas where the Irish resided. What Wiseman began, his successor, Henry Manning, an Anglican convert, continued. Manning worked closely with Wiseman from 1854 and then in 1865 became the second archbishop of Westminster.[30]

Wiseman and Manning discovered thousands of Irish migrants in London who were Catholics by birth but who did not participate in church rituals. And who could blame them? There were neither enough priests nor enough churches. Priests from all areas of the metropolis regularly sent in reports describing whole colonies of the nominally Catholic. When the Marists moved into Spitalfields in 1850, they found thousands of nonpracticing Catholics:

The seven or eight thousand Catholics who live here are devoid of all Religious instruction, living and dying without the sacraments, and, if one omits several families, less poor than the others, who go to Moorfields [chapel], all the others live without any Religion.[31]

In 1851 the priests of Richmond found it impossible to get the poor Catholics living two or three miles from their chapel to

29. Douglas Newton, *Catholic London* (London, 1950), p. 225.
30. Denis Gwynn, *A Hundred Years of Catholic Emancipation, 1829–1929* (London, 1929), pp. 6–7; Denis Gwynn, *Cardinal Wiseman* (Dublin, 1950), p. 39.
31. Letter of July 22, 1852, from Father T. Bernin to his superior in Lyon, "Epistolae superiorum," Marist Archive, Rome.

participate in Catholic rituals.[32] The priests who attempted to start a mission in Rotherhithe in 1853 described the religious state of local Catholics as a mixture of "indifference, apathy, and neglect."[33] Similar complaints could be multiplied, for priests judged the Catholicity of their charges in terms of their knowledge of doctrine and attendance at mass. Since priests and chapels were few and far between, it appeared that Irish Catholics were abandoning their religion. Yet Catholics in rural prefamine Ireland had similar habits of nonobservance, and their level of participation in London differed little from the level of church attendance in Ireland at the same time. The standards of the English hierarchy, however, demanded a different pattern of religious activity.

The attempt in mid-nineteenth-century London to make migrants into "good Catholics" necessitated the transformation of their religious behavior. The first step was to provide the proper settings for Catholic devotions. This was accomplished in the metropolis during the second half of the century. Under the two cardinal archbishops, the London Catholic church expanded rapidly as a network of chapels, schools, and convents were built. Although restrictions on the building of Catholic churches had been removed as early as 1791, it was only during the late 1840s that church facilities were built to meet the needs of thousands of arriving migrants. This building boom brought the church into the neighborhoods of the poor. The area in south London that had been served by two Catholic chapels from 1780 to 1847 supported eight missions by 1860, and in the East End, two extremely large congregations subdivided several times between 1840 and 1870.[34] Although some of the chapels listed by the *Catholic Directory* were probably only mass stations served intermittently by a priest attached to another mission, each represented a foothold of the church in a neighborhood inhabited by many nonpracticing Catholics.

These new parishes were established slowly. When a colony of

32. *Catholic Standard* 4, no. 98 (August 23, 1851).
33. Ibid., vol. 8, no. 187 (May 7, 1853).
34. Newton, *Catholic London*, p. 159; *The Catholic Directory and Ecclesiastical Register for the Year 1860* (London, 1860); *The Catholic Directory . . . for 1870* (London, 1870).

unchurched Irish was discovered, either the bishop or the local clergy would send a priest there to revive interest in religion. Wiseman decided early that local missions in the midst of Catholic residential areas were the only means of turning migrants into active Catholics. In an attempt to intensify and speed work among what he called "the dense, sinful masses," Wiseman brought thirty-four religious orders, ten male and twenty-four female, into London by 1860.[35] The nuns worked primarily as teachers, assisting the parish priests by taking over the girls' and infants' schools and various charitable organizations. Although some of the male communities were prohibited from parish work by the rules of their orders, the Marists were active from 1850 in the East End, and the Fathers of the Oratory ran a chapel in the Strand from 1849 to 1853 and schools for the poor in Holborn between 1851 and 1863. The Oblates of St. Charles settled into West London, in Notting Dale and the Potteries, building churches near the tumbledown cottages of the pig keepers, brickmakers, and laborers.[36]

The initial stages of parish building were difficult. Priests often found themselves preaching in attics or sheds, and they used tumbledown factories or stables to avoid high rents. The poverty of the migrants made the collecting of money for a permanent church slow and difficult, but the priests seemed always to succeed and in so doing to give the parish added status in its own eyes and in those of its English neighbors. The building of SS. Mary and Michael, a large Victorian Gothic pile along Commercial Road in the East End, was a great victory for Father William Kelly and his ministry:

This splendid new church has doubled my congregation; . . . it beats hollow in beauty the finest of the [gin] palaces . . . and has, in the eyes of

35. *Catholic Directory . . . for 1860*, p. 50; Archbishop Nicholas Wiseman to Father Frederick Faber, October 27, 1852, in E. J. Purcell, *The Life of Cardinal Manning*, 2 vols. (New York, 1896), vol. 2, p. 3.

36. Rev. W. J. Battersby, "Educational Work of the Religious Orders of Women, 1850–1950," in *The English Catholics, 1850–1950*, ed. George Andrew Beck (London, 1950), pp. 340–352; Rev. W. Salmon, S.M., *A Short History of the Parish* [St. Anne's, Underwood Road, London] (London, 1950), p. 4; John Edward Bowden, *The Life and Letters of Frederick William Faber, D.D.* (London, 1869), pp. 361–362, 380–381, 402; Francis J. Kirk, *Reminiscences of an Oblate of St. Charles* (London, 1905), p. 54.

our protestant neighbors, raised this poor congregation at least fifty years
in social position and consideration.[37]

Learning from Italian priests, English clerics added colorful
statues and side altars, making their buildings as attractive as
possible to the poor.

Once a chapel was built, priests began an unceasing series of
devotions.

We bring our people to the chapel every evening, Saturday excepted. On
Monday, Wednesday, and Friday, we say prayers after which one of us
teaches catechism until ten o'clock; Tuesday and Thursday there is
family instruction, and every Saturday, we preach at High Mass and
Vespers. Every evening from six until ten o'clock, three of us hear
confessions.[38]

In order to interest migrants in these devotions, skilled preachers
would be brought into a parish to conduct a mission in the
revivalist style of the Methodists and other Evangelicals. Sermons,
candlelit ceremonies, processions of clergy, and calls to repen-
tance were brought to the doorsteps of the Irish. Wiseman
preached at one such mission in a court in central London:

I found the place crammed from end to end, all round and behind the
platform. Every window was filled with tiers of faces, the whole line of
roof covered with legs dangling over the parapets — most with candles in
their hands, and every window illuminated, while against the wall were
illuminations with lamps.[39]

Wiseman's sermon concluded the mission:

After a hymn, I addressed the people, who listened intensely. I preached
on perseverance, especially in sobriety, going to their duties, peaceable-
ness and not sending their children to Protestant schools. They all with
one voice promised fidelity.[40]

The missions created such an atmosphere of religious revival
that the Irish flocked to confession and communion. When in
1852 Father Frederick Faber and the Oratorians held a mission in

37. *The Tablet,* January 6, 1844, quoted in Sheridan Gilley, "The Roman
Catholic Mission to the Irish in London," *Recusant History* 10, no. 3 (October
1969):129.

38. Letter of July 22, 1852, from Father T. Bernin to his superior in Lyon,
"Epistolae superiorum," Marist Archive, Rome.

39. Denis Gwynn, *Cardinal Wiseman,* p. 144.

40. Ibid.

Dunne's Passage, Holborn, the opening sessions drew about a thousand people. At first the congregation did not respond to the priests; then Father Faber knelt before them and said, "I will pray to *you*, my dear Irish children, to have mercy on your own souls." The congregation then "fell on their knees, and for some minutes nothing was heard but their sobs and prayers." By the end, "many most unhappy women . . . were on their knees before the crucifix, sobbing and beating their breasts."[41]

After a revival of religious feeling was generated by a mission, priests moved into the district, renting rooms in Irish courts. Every evening they called out the flock with a school bell to bring them to meetings, at which they learned doctrine, sang hymns, and said the rosary.[42] As familiarity with orthodox Catholicism spread, the flock was encouraged to attend special rituals and celebrations. Religious holidays were marked by special sermons and services. At least in some cases these holiday services generated large amounts of religious enthusiasm. The typical service for the feast of the Assumption as usually celebrated in Dunne's Passage in the mid-1850s was described by one of the Oratorian Fathers:

The procession will go ten times round the room at least — All the hymns the F. ever wrote to Our Lady will be sung twice over — The children will all go to Communion several times, the preacher will stand & shout till he is hoarse, promising all who hear him eternal salvation & no Purgatory & they will all join with him in giving three cheers for the Madonna. . . .[43]

As staff and congregation grew, each London Catholic parish founded several confraternities to woo the faithful with their trappings and ceremonies. In 1861, St. Patrick's, Soho, had a chapter of the Confraternity of the Blessed Sacrament, the Confraternity of Sorrows of the Blessed Virgin, the Brotherhood of St. Patrick, and the Confraternity of Mt. Carmel. Several children's organizations were added to the list by late in the century. Members of the St. Patrick's Confraternity of the Blessed

41. Bowden, *Life and Letters*, pp. 391–392.
42. Ibid.
43. Father Hutchison, "The Oratory in London," p. 102, London Oratory Archives, quoted in Raphael Samuel, "The Catholic Church and the Irish Poor," unpublished paper, Past and Present Conference, London, 1966, p. 39

Sacrament pledged to attend mass, communion, and benediction frequently, to make a monthly offering to the church, and to visit the Blessed Sacrament.[44] In general, members promised to participate in certain rituals in return for indulgences and special prayers. They also gained recognition and an honored place in church rituals. Groups regularly had banners, cards, medals, or scarves that members were encouraged to wear at appropriate times — for example, at the masses dedicated to the patron saint of the society or when they had a special function to perform. Members often sat together or marched in procession on such occasions.

Apparently these groups successfully integrated their members into parochial life and produced the active participation in church rites thought necessary by the priests. The clergy of St. Patrick's declared in 1869, "We say now what we cannot say too often, an individual regular to the rules of a Confraternity can scarcely be lost; a congregation without a thriving confraternity can never be sound."[45] But whatever their success among the already converted, these societies appealed to only a minority of Catholics. The St. Patrick's clergy who praised the effects of confraternities complained at the same time that few joined them. Membership took time and money, both of which were in short supply among Irish laborers' families. Nevertheless, the Marists of Spitalfields claimed that almost 1,000 of 7,000 parishioners had enrolled in their various religious societies. They kept a list of men who joined between 1858 and 1860, giving us a record of the type of person to whom the confraternities appealed. Most had low-skilled jobs and presumably low incomes. Of the forty men whose records have survived, almost two-thirds were laborers, and most of the rest followed simple crafts such as shoemaking, tailoring, and paving. Only two members had middle-class occupations. A specific type of man joined the confraternities. About two-thirds of the new members were married and over the age of thirty; virtually all were Irish-born. About three-quarters could read and write, and one-quarter had taken the pledge and were teetotalers. The young and the single who belonged had

44. St. Patrick's Soho, *Report for 1861* (London, 1862), p. 5.
45. St. Patrick's, Soho, *Report for 1869* (London, 1870), p. 5.

generally attended Catholic schools. Second-generation Irish and those who preferred the pub as the center of their social world were notably absent from these associations.[46]

Confraternities, colorful statues, altars, and the lively round of parish rituals encouraged the pious to build Catholic devotions into their daily lives. Tom Barclay described himself when about twelve years old as a "voteen" (devotee of religion). Every morning after awaking, he made the sign of the cross and said prayers, "Our Father, Hail Mary, the Apostles Creed, and an invocation to the Holy Family." He chalked an altar on the bedroom wall and wore a religious medal and "the blessed cord of Angelic Warfare" to help defeat temptation. Regular attendance at mass, confession, communion, and the rosary were part of his life.[47]

What proportion of all Irish migrants were drawn into a Catholic community through participation in Roman Catholic activities? Priests had little or no contact with either lapsed Catholics who lived far from their churches or the Protestant Irish, and their influence over the nominally Catholic who ignored their call remains to be demonstrated. Before we can estimate the hold of Catholic norms and social institutions, we need to know more about the size of the nominal and effective Catholic populations.

Most of the London Irish were Catholics by birth and by heritage. Although there is no direct record of each migrant's religion, their counties of origin were overwhelmingly Catholic. In both Munster and Connaught, the areas from which most London migrants came, 94 and 95 percent of the population were Catholic in the middle of the nineteenth century. Even in Dublin, where the proportion of Protestants was far higher than in the west, over 80 percent of the population was Catholic.[48] The strongholds of Protestantism in Ireland were the northern counties of Ulster — Antrim, Down, Armagh, and Londonderry — areas that sent few people to London. While there were certainly Irish Protestants in London, they were vastly outnumbered by

46. St. Anne's, Underwood Road, confraternity books, 1858–1861.

47. Tom Barclay, *Memoirs and Medleys: The Autobiography of a Bottlewasher* (Leicester, 1934), pp. 26–27, 31, 40.

48. Ruth Dudley Edwards, ed., *An Atlas of Irish History* (London, 1973), p. 128; Edward Wakefield, *An Account of Ireland, Statistical and Political*, 2 vols. (London, 1812), vol. 2, pp. 630–631.

their Catholic compatriots. The number of Irish Catholics in London in 1840 was probably between 110,000 and 125,000. Priests' estimates of congregational sizes in 1839–1840 totaled 146,000, but several thousand European and English Catholics (I estimate between 25,000 and 35,000) are included in this figure and must be subtracted.[49]

But we need to know far more than the estimated size of the Catholic Irish population. What proportion of London Catholics participated actively in the rituals or organizations of their church? Unfortunately, quantitative evidence on religious observance is limited. In the 1830s, priests sent the vicar apostolic of the London district reports on the numbers of Easter communicants and baptisms in their parishes, and in local parish files the numbers of baptisms, marriages, and deaths per year can be computed by totaling the entries in the registry books. A steadily growing number of baptisms, which reached 4,722 in 1839, was recorded by the London diocese during the 1830s.[50] Since the number of baptisms multiplied by an estimated crude birth rate yields a number for the total London Catholic population close to that of my estimated size for the London Irish population, it would seem that even in the 1830s, before the expansion of clergy and chapels, virtually all Irish Catholics brought their children to the priest to be baptized. This pattern continued through the 1850s and 1860s, when Roman Catholic parishes in the east and south of London recorded high and increasing numbers of baptisms of the second-generation Irish.

But few of these Irish parents and professed Catholics participated regularly enough in church rituals to make their Easter communion. Even if a low estimate of the total Catholic population is used (125,000), only 10 percent of the Catholic parishioners fulfilled their Easter duties in 1837.[51] We must remember that there were relatively few priests and only twenty-six Roman Catholic churches in London in 1840, and that Irish migrants imported low standards of religious observance from prefamine

49. The priests' estimates seem roughly correct, for the total of reported baptisms in the London district multiplied by a crude birth rate of 35 per thousand population is close to their totals. See "Letters Principally to Rome," Westminster Archives, London, folder B-4, pp. 34–37, 46–51.

50. Ibid., pp. 34–37.

51. Ibid.

Ireland. There is some evidence that this ratio increased markedly as the Catholic church expanded and increased its work among the Irish. The church of SS. Mary and Michael, Commercial Road, reported 7,500 communions during Lent of 1858 for a congregation of approximately 16,000.[52] Without comparable figures for other parishes, it is impossible to judge how typical was this increase in participation.

Other kinds of evidence cast doubt on the argument that a majority of Irish migrants soon became active Catholics. The returns of the 1851 religious census and the 1902 survey taken by the *Daily Mail* allow us to calculate the proportion of the Catholic population that went to a Sunday service at the middle and end of the nineteenth century. Although far more London Catholics went to mass in 1851 than had made their Easter communion in 1839, only a minority showed up at church on census Sunday. If we count only those who attended a morning service, we find that 35,994 attendances were recorded. If we add another 1,750 to compensate for those chapels that sent in no returns to the census takers, a corrected figure of 37,744 is obtained.[53] A comparison of this figure with the size of the total Catholic population yields a lower attendance rate (approximately 30 percent) than the Protestant one that shocked the nation. The supposedly devout Irish were apparently even worse churchgoers than the total London population (37 percent attendance) or the total English population (41 percent attendance). But this comparison of English and Irish propensities to go to church is misleading. The census was taken at a time when the Catholic church had only begun to rebuild its position in England. In 1851 there were not enough priests and churches to accommodate any more Catholics. Almost 20 percent of the Irish-born in London lived in census districts without any sort of

52. *The Tablet*, April 24, 1858.
53. Great Britain, *Parliamentary Papers* (Commons), "Census of Great Britain: Religious Worship," 1852-3, 89:cxlvii. Missing returns are compensated for on the assumption that a chapel would have been filled at least once; therefore the number of seats it held can be used as a minimum figure for attendance. On the accuracy of the census, see W. S. F. Pickering, who concludes in "The 1851 Religious Census — A Useless Experiment?" *British Journal of Sociology* 18, no. 4 (December 1967):386–387, that the census was "fairly reliable" and "substantially correct."

Catholic chapel, and Catholic churches in heavily settled Irish areas were filled to capacity.[54] The lack of space helps to explain the low Catholic attendance record. For the census to have been a fair test, it would have had to be held ten or fifteen years later.

The only other survey of religious attendance in London was made in 1902 and 1903. By then the number of Catholics who went to a morning mass had risen to 73,680 — an increase of 95 percent over the figure for 1851.[55] Yet the rate of participation remained low. Using the number of Catholic baptisms for that year, Charles Booth estimated that there were 200,000 Catholics in London in 1900; this figure yields a ratio of mass attendance of approximately 1 to 2. But Booth's method of determining the Catholic population excluded lapsed Catholics. If all the surviving Catholics of mid-century plus children and grandchildren and the newly arrived Irish migrants had been counted as part of the Catholic fold, the proportion of those going to mass would have been much lower. Clearly the pattern of nearly universal mass attendance that existed in Ireland by 1900 was never accepted by the London Irish community.[56]

We can conclude that in nineteenth-century London most migrants as well as their English-born children took part in the major Catholic rituals marking birth and probably death, but that far fewer had either the opportunity or the interest to sustain the pattern of regular parochial devotions recommended to them by their priests. Although the churches were filled, many remained outside. The question of the Catholic church's influence in London must therefore be judged in terms of two Catholic populations: a minority of active participants and the majority, whom the priests saw irregularly between the ceremonies consecrating birth and death or not at all.[57]

The influence of the church over the behavior of the second group is very difficult to estimate, for the evidence is ambiguous. Priests deplored what they considered to be the "loss" of those

54. Great Britain, *Parliamentary Papers* (Commons), "Census of . . . Religious Worship," p. cxlvii.

55. Richard Mudie-Smith, *The Religious Life of London* (London, 1904), p. 271.

56. Larkin, "Devotional Revolution in Ireland," p. 636.

57. Hugh McLeod, *Class and Religion in the Late Victorian City* (London, 1975), p. 34.

souls who would not heed their call. The Marist fathers worried about their Irish population in the East End: "Defections are not as numerous as one might fear, but are still sufficient to make us lament the loss of many souls whom religion alone could save."[58] The priests of St. Patrick's, Soho, complained in 1869: "Indeed, it is an appalling fact that we have so many merely nominal Catholics among us. It is an appalling fact that hundreds and hundreds habitually miss Mass and never approach the Sacraments."[59] Priests made similar complaints when they spoke to Charles Booth around 1900.[60] Mixed marriages, irreligious parents, Protestant schools, and the anti-Catholicism of Poor Law guardians worked together to produce what one Catholic writer called "the perpetual draining away of the children of the poorer classes."[61] By the mid-1880s, alarmed Catholic journalists regularly wrote articles about the vast losses of the Catholic population under the influence of life in English cities:

In all our great towns, there is a large body of people, beyond and above those of whom the local clergy have personal cognizance; who ought to be Catholics, and who might be brought within the Church were it possible to look after them. But the work of hunting them up, in addition to the other labours of keeping their acknowledged parishioners to their duty, visiting the sick, administering the sacraments, and collecting funds for various purposes, is altogether beyond the physical powers of the clergy.[62]

Yet the sources and the purposes of these accounts of leakage must be remembered. Priests seeking the monetary and physical help of middle-class Catholics had every reason to exaggerate the numbers of the unchurched. Also, the unrealistic hopes of earlier decades for the reconversion of England made more modest levels of achievement seem low indeed. Moreover, many complaints of Irish nonparticipation in the church originated with French

58. Chauvrain, "Rapport sur la mission de Ste Anne."

59. St. Patrick's, Soho, *Report for 1869* (London, 1870), p. 5.

60. Charles Booth, *Life and Labour of the People in London*, ser. 3, *Religious Influences*, 7 vols. (London, 1903), vol. 7, pp. 254–255.

61. "The Measures of Catholic Progress," *The Month* 21, no. 2 (August 1874):472.

62. Edward Lucas, "The Conversion of England," *The Month* 44, no. 1 (July 1885):310–311. See also Kenneth S. Inglis, *Churches and the Working Classes in Victorian England* (London, 1963), pp. 122–130.

Italian, or English clerics, who used different standards of religious fidelity from those of prefamine Ireland. And it is most important not to confuse indifference to Catholic ritual with indifference to Catholicism. Nineteenth-century accounts of the Irish stress their religious fidelity. Henry Mayhew described the street Irish flocking to the priest when he walked nearby, the women curtseying, the boys touching their hair in salute. Quarrels and noise stopped until he passed.[63] Langton Vere reported that the Irish of central London had much the same response to priests who entered their courts during the early 1870s. The Irish obeyed their orders to stop wakes or quarrels and showed much deference.[64] The Marists of Spitalfields who complained of their flock's ignorance of doctrine and ritual also maintained that they were "Catholic by instinct" and would not deny their faith.[65] Charles Booth also judged that the Irish "are generally attached to their religion, are almost universally submissive to its authority when that authority can be exerted . . . even lapsed Catholics rarely deny their own faith."[66] It is therefore difficult to maintain that Catholics who remained outside the round of parish activities for the faithful were indifferent to the norms and attitudes of the Roman Catholic church. Moreover, active Catholics were in a position to influence others. The pattern of religious observance reported by the *Daily News* for 1903 indicates that women and children, rather than entire families, made up the bulk of the people at mass. Almost two-thirds of the Catholic adults counted on census Sunday in 1903 were women: adult males made up only one-third of the total.[67] The person in an Irish household most responsible for child rearing was therefore the most likely to be a devout Catholic. Far more families and individuals had contact with Catholic norms and rituals than the low attendance rate at mass indicates.

63. Henry Mayhew, *London Labour and the London Poor*, 4 vols. (London, 1861–1862; reprinted New York, 1968), vol. 1, p. 108.

64. Langton George Vere, *Random Recollections of Old Soho* (Barnet, 1908), pp. 15–17, 44–45.

65. Letter from L. M. Petit, S.M., dated St. Raymond's Day, 1853, in "Lettres addressées à la procure mission," Marist Archives, Rome.

66. Booth, *Life and Labour*, ser. 3, *Religious Influences*, vol. 7, pp. 243–244.

67. Mudie-Smith, *Religious Life of London*, p. 271.

The Transformation of the Irish Catholic Mentality

A comparison of nineteenth-century rural Irish religion and folk beliefs with the popular Catholicism of Irish migrants in London reveals two very different worlds of imagination and action. Catholic rituals, symbols, and expressions of belief were transformed in the city. The rural St. Brigit was pictured as a cowherd, a figure who was derived from the Celtic goddess of fire and the hearth, Brigid. Her saint's day, February 1, was said to be the beginning of the pastoral year, the date from which the weather began to warm up because the saint supposedly appeared and dipped her feet in the water. She also had magical powers. On St. Brigit's Eve, crosses were fashioned out of straw and hung anew over the door to protect both the house and the livestock from evil spirits. Ribbons or cloth left out overnight on St. Brigit's Eve were believed to acquire healing power, and tales of the saint's appearance in her holy well in Burren in the guise of a fish to heal the faithful circulated in Connaught as late as the 1890s.[68] The urban St. Brigit lost all links with agriculture and the provision of food. In London in 1880, Brigit was honored by a women's confraternity, whose members had medals and membership cards. They said the rosary together and pledged to attend monthly confession and communion.[69] The saint herself had changed character; from the patroness of cattle to a symbol of female virtue and chastity. Along with her pre-Christian origins had vanished her active intervention to control the weather and heal the sick. The urban St. Brigit had been largely demystified and distanced, to become one of many holy intercessors with God for the protection of the faithful. Her worship was shifted into the church and supported by a specialized organization. Yet she related migrants' rural past to their urban present, easing Irish acceptance of an orthodox Catholic culture.

The cultural world of Irish Catholicism gave migrants an

68. Evans, *Irish Folkways*, pp. 267–268; Lady [Isabella Augusta] Gregory, *A Book of Saints and Wonders* (New York, 1907), pp. 11–16; Ó Súilleabháin, *Handbook of Irish Folklore*, pp. 324–325; Charles Squire, *Celtic Myth and Legend, Poetry and Romance* (London, n.d.), p. 56.

69. Father Sheridan, "About St. Brigit's Confraternity," MSS of St. Patrick's, Soho, quoted in Samuel, "Catholic Church and the Irish Poor," pp. 1–2.

essential resource in their struggle to adapt to urban life. It provided a vocabulary, a set of beliefs about the world. Direct transference of traditional Irish culture was impossible, if only because migrants resided in a different social system where the possibilities for action were not the same. Sidney Mintz argues that culture is actively used in the arena of society to "confirm, reinforce, maintain, change or deny particular arrangements of status, power, and identity."[70] Irish migrants kept their Catholic identity and their generally subordinate economic and social status vis-à-vis the English, but they had to redefine that identity and status in terms of an urban milieu. One avenue of cultural adaptation was provided by the Catholic church in England, which worked to reshape Irish Catholicism to both orthodoxy and the modern world.

The process of change in rural Irish culture, which many began to experience at home by the second half of the century, was vastly accelerated for those who moved into foreign cities. Whether in Philadelphia, Boston, or London, Irish-speaking migrants found themselves in a greatly changed world. The back-alley "urban villages" in which most Irish workers lived in the major American and British cities provided only partial insulation from the transformations necessitated by rural-to-urban migration and by residence in a different culture. While kith and kin could re-create an Irish cultural milieu to some extent, major changes in migrants' ways of life were immediate. A greatly altered Catholic church ministered to them; the Irish language all but vanished. The nature of work and its daily routine were transformed.

A brief balance sheet of cultural disappearances and survivals in the London Irish community between 1840 and 1870 should clarify some dimensions of the changes that took place. Only a few communal rituals survived transplantation. The wake, common all over Ireland, was the one major folk ceremony brought to London. After death, the corpses of Irish migrants were dressed in the best clothes that could be obtained and laid out on the bed or a

70. Sidney W. Mintz, Forward to *Afro-American Anthropology: Contemporary Perspectives*, ed. Norman Whitten and John F. Szwed (New York, 1970), pp. 9-10, quoted in Herbert G. Gutman, "Work, Culture, and Society in Industrializing America, 1815-1919," *American Historical Review* 78, no. 3 (June 1973):542.

board in the family's quarters; candles were burned and sometimes a plate of salt was placed beside the body. When enough
money for burial was collected, a wake commenced. All the
neighbors and friends came to smoke, drink, and talk together
until the store of liquor and tobacco was exhausted. A reference
by Father John Furniss to "mock marriages" and dancing suggests that wake games were sometimes played.[71] Some Irish
beliefs about the dead were also brought to the city. The corpse of
a pious young woman was thought to have magical powers.
Rosaries and medals could be sanctified if touched to the dead
girl's hands or throat.[72]

Traditional belief in the magical power of the clergy was not
shed automatically with migration. Priests found that, while
Irish Catholics remained attached to the church in their new
surroundings, their idea of Catholicism differed markedly from
that of their spiritual guides. A Marist priest in the East End of
London remarked in the mid-1850s, "The Irish never lose their
faith or respect for the priest. . . . The faith of the Irish frees us
from proving our power over souls; more likely we must protest
that we do not have the gift of making miracles! . . . They are a
unique people, Catholic by instinct."[73] Belief that priests could
cure or exorcise devils or lay ghosts persisted, but to an unknown
extent. Epidemics were said to bring crowds of Irish to confession,
and priests were regularly summoned to the bedside of the ill.[74]
But these importations from Ireland came under constant attack
from the Catholic church in London. Clergy did what they could
to discourage belief in their healing powers and banned wakes.
Priests in the 1880s even kept watch when a death occurred and

71. Great Britain, *Parliamentary Papers* (Commons), "Supplementary Report
on the Practice of Interment in Towns: Report on the Sanitary Condition of the
Labouring Population," 1843, 12:33; Board of Guardians of Whitechapel, Stepney, "Signed Minutes," vol. 10, December 13, 1848; Vere, *Random Recollections
of Old Soho*, pp. 44–45; Father John Furniss, *The Book of Young Persons*
(London and Dublin, 1861), p. 7.
72. Lady Georgiana Fullerton, *Faithful and True: The Life of Elizabeth
Twiddy* (London, n.d.), p. 9, cited in Gilley, "Roman Catholic Mission," p. 140.
73. Letter from L. M. Petit, S.M., dated St. Raymond's Day, 1853.
74. *The Rambler* 4 (1849), p. 434; 9 (1852), p. 446; Frederick Oakeley, *The Priest
on the Mission: A Course of Lectures on Missionary and Parochial Duties*
(London, 1871), p. 151, cited in Gilley, "Roman Catholic Mission," p. 140.

visited the home frequently in order to interfere with any attempt to begin a wake.[75] In this and other ways, the Catholic church worked systematically against the perpetuation in London of what they considered superstitious beliefs and practices. The links between Celtic magic and religion were being broken.

The belief in witches and fairies seems to have declined after migration, but it did not vanish. The Irish who came to the United States brought fairy lore with them and used it creatively to shape and to comment upon their social experiences. In Paterson, New Jersey, Irish residents dubbed a local well the Dublin Spring. An Irish fairy was said to have brought the water for it from the lakes of Killarney in her apron. Fairies were declared to walk in the streets of Paterson, usually in the guise of an old woman with a cane begging.[76] Irish residents of New York as late as fifty years after migration believed in the banshee and in the presence of ghosts and spirits in the city.[77] While I have not been able to discover similar tales about the London Irish, it seems likely that some fairy lore was brought to England too. A Marist priest living in the East End during the 1850s complained of the "superstitious" nature of his flock.[78] It is more probable that commentators failed to record or to note migrants' fairy beliefs than that this manner of describing the world disappeared entirely. I would guess that fairy beliefs were imported into London and then died slowly. In any case, by the 1880s priests in the metropolis read fairy stories at Catholic social hours to entertain rather than to frighten or edify the flock.[79]

The staple forms of popular religious festivities — the patterns, the pilgrimages, and the treks to holy wells — were not imported into London, nor were the celebrations of saints' days in the forms common in Ireland. There was no leaping over fires on St. John's Eve in London, no hanging of crosses in honor of St.

75. Vere, *Random Recollections of Old Soho*, pp. 44–45.
76. *Paterson Evening News*, October 27, 1900, quoted in Gutman, *Work, Culture, and Society*, p. 563.
77. Elsa G. Herzfeld, *Family Monographs: The History of Twenty-four Families Living in the Middle West Side of New York City* (New York, 1905), p. 22. I am indebted to Herbert Gutman for this reference.
78. Chauvrain, "Rapport sur la mission de Ste Anne."
79. Samuel, "Catholic Church and the Irish Poor," p. 2.

Brigit. Nor did the popular parades and pageants held on religious holidays by costumed men or by the Christmas mummers survive migration. Much of the physical context that had supported Irish rural culture and sustained it against changes in a wider world disappeared for those migrants who moved into a city. The agricultural setting in which the forces of nature had demanded regular propitiation vanished. The bushes and trees associated with the fairies and with the possession of magic powers — whitethorn, holly, rowan, and elderberry — were to be found on Irish hills, not in the minuscule backyards of London slum houses. Moreover, Irish rural culture was highly localized; each area had its own set of sacred places, its own particular way of celebrating festivals. Although a pattern of chain migration existed among the Irish, I doubt that the critical mass of villagers with the same version of a particular ritual in their heads could have been found living next to each other in London. Why reenact before strangers, even Irish strangers, the communal rites of a now-vanished agricultural past?

The linguistic medium of folktales and traditional Irish culture did not disappear immediately after migration, but it atrophied in the city. In the 1850s, London journalists and clergymen noted the use of Irish by migrants when talking with each other, but the effects of educational changes in Ireland were even then apparent. While their Irish was said to be better than their English, their origin in a bilingual society with an inadequate educational system meant that they knew neither Irish nor English very well.[80] Under these conditions, Irish died a lingering death. It is doubtful that it was used much outside the homes of the first generation. The one institution that might have helped to save the language, the Roman Catholic church, had no real interest in doing so. Schools taught exclusively in English, and the London Catholic hierarchy did very little to encourage the continued use of Irish by the clergy. Both Cardinal Wiseman and Bishop Griffiths, whose authority over the London Catholic church stretched from the early 1840s to 1865, were reportedly reluctant to use Irish priests

80. Rev. Samuel Garrett, *Motives for Missions* (London, 1853), p. 192; John Garwood, *The Million-Peopled City* (London, 1853), p. 306.

in the diocese. Only 5 of 106 priests in 1842 in the London diocese could speak Irish.[81] The presence of an Irish-speaking priest was so unusual that an Irish congregation in 1853 fought the transference of one who they said could make "the Truths of our Church . . . more forcible and more beautifully intelligible to our ears and hearts by clothing them in the language of our Fatherland."[82] Residual loyalties to the use of Irish for confessions and sermons continued to exist, but no provision for transmission of the language was made.

Facility in English spread rapidly. Joseph Oppenheim, who went from room to room in the St. Giles slums in the early 1860s trying to convert Catholics to Protestantism, had no difficulty speaking with Irish migrants.[83] Tom Barclay, who grew up in a Leicester slum in the 1850s and 1860s, probably learned some Irish as a child; in any case he understood it, and his mother told at home the centuries-old myths of Ossian and Finn and read Irish sermons to her children and neighbors. But as a child Barclay turned away from both the language and the culture transmitted through it. After describing his mother's recitation of "the old bardic legends and laments," he went on: "But what had I to do with all that? I was becoming English. I did not hate things Irish, but I began to feel that they must be put away; they were inferior to things English. . . . Outside the house everything was English: my catechism, lessons, prayers, songs, tales, games. . . . Presently I began to feel ashamed of the jeers and mockery and criticism."[84] Barclay's rejection of Irish language and culture must have been repeated by many second-generation migrants, particularly those who were drawn into an urban Roman Catholic community. The Catholic church in England actively fought continued attachment to the cultural world of the Irish countryside.

At the same time, priests helped migrants to adapt Irish popular culture to an urban setting. The parish church provided a lively social and cultural world organized to give Catholics a

81. *The Tablet*, April 21, 1843; *Ordo recitandi officii divini et missae celebrandae* (London, 1840), p. 17; Gilley, "Roman Catholic Mission," p. 141.

82. *Catholic Standard* 8, no. 185 (April 23, 1853).

83. See J. M. Oppenheim, "Visitor's Book," 1861–1862, St. Giles in the Fields, London.

84. Barclay, *Memoirs and Medleys*, pp. 23–24.

religious alternative to the staple forms of urban working-class recreation. Catholic London supported a colorful variety of social clubs, lectures, benefit dinners, and bazaars. A form of popular recreation different from those of both the Irish countryside and English workers grew up within the Roman Catholic urban parish. In place of pubs, penny gaffs, and trade union meetings, Catholics were expected to join in the confraternities, clubs, and temperance groups of the local church. Priests organized festivals, musical evenings, church suppers, and steamboat excursions for the entertainment of the faithful, while those who wanted more active pastimes could join one of the Catholic choral societies, bands, or drill teams.[85]

Let us look at one heavily Irish parish in central London, St. Patrick's, Soho, and see what members could join. In addition to the confraternities, there were several other clubs, each intended for a particular age and sex group. By 1861 a Mother's Meeting "for the religious and domestic improvement of the married women of the labouring classes" had been formed. Members made and sold clothes below cost while they got helpful hints on low-budget homemaking. The women of the parish also had an annual tea party and could participate in several charities. Adolescents could join either the boys' or the girls' club. Each had its own activities, which ranged from the religious and didactic to the purely entertaining. The parish magazine reported occasional evening parties held for members, which mixed songs, social hours, and "light refreshments." In January of 1898, young women from the convent of St. Aloysius presented "The House That Jack Built" and "The Legend of the Mountain Flowers" as musical entertainment for the St. Patrick's Girls' Club.[86]

Within the context of both the clubs and the parish schools, the clergy organized regular parties, particularly at holidays. Children were fed and amused while they were kept off the streets and out of the penny theaters. Father Vere, who ran a school for the parish in the Seven Dials area around 1870, described the school feasts:

85. *The Catholic Standard* was filled with reports of Catholic social events; see vol. 23, no. 601 (March 16, 1861).

86. St. Patrick's, Soho, *Report for 1861*, pp. 6–7, 13; *St. Patrick's Catholic Magazine*, March 1890, p. 73; February 1898, p. 49.

After a glorious tea, there was plenty of amusement and fun. What the children liked most of all was a good organ that played jig tunes. Once or twice we had a fiddle, but it was not to the taste of the children. 'May we have an organ Father?' was the general request. Then to see how those children danced. None of your new-fangled step dances with high kicks and whirligigs, but plain wholesome honest modest Irish jigs.[87]

Fruit and cakes were given out with an open hand, and prizes were awarded to the virtuous. Sometimes the children themselves would entertain with songs and stories; at least once there was a magic show.[88] Particularly in its work with children, the church played the role of Lady Bountiful, dispensing gifts and religion with a gentle discipline.

When applied to adult males, this strategy contained fewer sweets and more strident calls for behavioral reform. In addition to the confraternities, the major clubs for men were the Total Abstinence Society, the Catholic Association for the Suppression of Drunkenness, and the Brotherhood of St. Patrick, founded in the late 1840s. The Brotherhood had multiple aims, being both a confraternity and a friendly society that paid sickness and death benefits. But the primary function of the group was to redeem the Irish poor, to keep them "from evil combination," and to return them "to almighty God." The men were to take communion monthly, to attend all "festival processions" wearing the insignia of the society, and to "maintain order" in the church.[89]

The operation of a highly similar Society of St. Patrick, founded in 1849 in the Lincoln's Inn Fields area by an Irish priest, Father Kyne, indicates the sort of moral reformation that was supposed to take place in members. Any Irish Catholic "determined to give up his negligent, sinful career" could join and be given a badge and wand of office. A reading room decorated with an oratory of the Virgin Mary, an altar, and religious pictures was established in a back court; members met there after work to read or learn to read and to say the rosary. Father Kyne, who was the first president of the society, worked

87. Vere, *Random Recollections of Old Soho*, p. 38.

88. *St. Patrick's Catholic Magazine*, February 1890, p. 49; March 1890, p. 73.

89. St. Patrick's, Soho, *Report for 1861*, p. 5; *Report for 1867* (London, 1868), pp. 1–2; *Report for 1876* (London, 1877), pp. 9–10; *Rules of the Confraternity of the Brotherhood of St. Patrick* (London, n.d.), pp. 1–3.

out a list of rituals and parish duties for the men. They were to attend local funerals and to say the office of the dead, besides marching in procession every Sunday to mass. When special missions were held, the brothers went from house to house to bring out tardy Catholics. Father Kyne called the men his "special constables" and claimed that "in a short time, the dancing houses were closed, the low gin palaces quiet at night; and in place of the drunken revelry over the dead, the Rosary and Prayers for the Dead were said by the Brothers."[90]

Roman Catholic culture as it touched the Irish thus contained heavy doses of social discipline. But it also helped migrants to adapt to urban society and to develop wider loyalties. Catholic relief organizations helped the poor to survive bad winters and periods of long unemployment. Church schools and clubs taught reading and sometimes offered job training. There was a Catholic emigration society and a bureau to place unemployed servants. Parish excursions gave migrants the chance to travel cheaply to nearby resorts and to see something of London outside their neighborhoods.[91]

But whatever the practical skills taught and help offered, the larger impact of Roman Catholic culture was ideological. The religious symbols of the Roman Catholic church in England sanctified the ideals of work, poverty, virginity, and a moderate Irish nationalism. Hymns sung by the Irish in veneration of several saints helped to propagate the ideals of "holy poverty"[92] and "holy toil." Martha, "saint of the busy hand and heart," was to teach "the will to work, the heart to pray"; but rewards were not to be granted on earth. Her adherents would remain in a state of "lowness" in this life, but through her find a place beside Mary in heaven.[93] St. Joseph was recommended to Londoners as the model of a holy working man. The most explicit enunciation of the ethic of holy poverty can be found in Catholic devotional writers who compared the poor with Christ. Their sufferings reenacted those of the crucifixion, an act by which they expiated

90. *Catholic Standard* 8, no. 189 (May 1, 1853); 8, no. 193 (June 18, 1853).

91. *Catholic Standard* 11, no. 274 (January 6, 1855); 12, no. 293 (May 19, 1855); 6, no. 153 (September 11, 1852); 10, no. 252 (August 5, 1854); 4, no. 91 (July 5, 1851).

92. The term is Sheridan Gilley's; see "Heretic London, Holy Poverty, and the Irish Poor, 1830–1870," *Downside Review* 99, no. 294 (January 1971):64–89.

93. Barclay, *Memoirs and Medleys*, p. 24.

the sins of the rest of society. The poor were "the Holy Family living in the slums of London."[94] In the sight of God, therefore, poverty was better than riches. Despite the existence of Catholic penny banks, friendly societies, and literary societies, a message of endurance rather than self-help was preached to Catholic workers. For them poverty was not a sin but God's will, part of the natural order of life, and bearing it cheerfully was a sign of grace and blessedness. And these ideas were not rejected by Catholic workers. Tom Barclay's mother accepted her poverty patiently, at least in part because of her interpretation of Catholic teachings: "Why shouldn't we suffer when Our Blessed Lord Himself suffered? Didn't he say blessed are the poor? What matters what we may suffer in this miserable life. . . ?"[95]

The figure of Mary helped to spread a rather different ideal. In prefamine religious songs Mary appears predominantly as a mother, while London Catholic hymns stress her virginity. Verses about Mary written by Father Frederick Faber in the 1850s identify her as a "mother-maiden," whose virginity is one of her chief glories. Not only is her "sinless conception" exalted; the believer is asked to sing. "Thou who wert pure as driven snow,/ Make me as thou wert here below." The hymns identify sex with sin. Mary as Blessed Virgin symbolizes and ratifies an ethic of sexual repression that pervaded Irish urban workers' view of the world.[96]

Support for an ultramontane church and for moderate brands of Irish nationalism permeated Roman Catholic rhetoric, rituals, and social life. Church history and the ties to the papacy and the Italian church were staple themes in the semieducational entertainments of Catholic clubs. The Metropolitan Catholic Young Men's Society heard weekly lectures in 1856 on such topics as "Rome Pagan and Rome Christian" sandwiched between "The

94. *Tablet*, March 27, 1852, and F. C. Devas, *Mother Mary Magdalen of the Sacred Heart, Foundress of the Poor Servants of the Mother of God* (London, 1927), p. 74, both cited in Gilley, "Heretic London," pp. 72, 86.

95. Barclay, *Memoirs and Medleys*, p. 24.

96. Father Faber's hymns were widely circulated in England and Ireland; 10,000 copies of the first two editions were sold. The collection from which these lines were taken (a much-expanded fourth edition) was designed "chiefly as a book of spiritual readings" (Frederick William Faber, *Hymns*, new ed. [London and New York, 1861], pp. 146, 154).

Electric Telegraph" and "The Gunpowder Plot." After the local Catholic Association made a pilgrimage to Rome in 1898, Father Vere of St. Patrick's gave a lecture on the papal city, illustrated with lantern slides.[97] Many Catholic hymns sung avidly by Irish congregations invoked Italian saints or praised the pope:

> Holy Mother, guard our pontiff,
> Raging billows round him foam.
> Saint seraphic, still the tempest,
> Aid the Church and pray for Rome.[98]

Father Faber of the Oratory preached sermons on devotion to the pope and founded an Association of St. Peter, whose only purpose was to pray for the "Sovereign Pontiff."[99] Irish Catholics were urged both indirectly and directly to develop loyalties to European Catholicism and to the rites and leaders of the Italian Catholic church.

At the same time, migrants were encouraged to retain their identities as *Irish* Catholics. Priests consciously used Irish symbols to draw migrants into church activities. Through the naming of associations and parish churches for Irish saints and the elaborate parish celebrations of St. Patrick's Day, they united the appeal of religion with that of nationalism. In the rhetoric of March sermons, generally delivered by Irish priests, faith and fatherland were inextricably linked. Migrants would disgrace their country if they showed a "want of love for practical religion." Political struggles against the English were subsumed under religious struggles, and the national character of the Irish was defined in terms of religious loyalties.[100] Their tenacious Catholicism supposedly marked the Irish as a holy people because they had refused to compromise their faith.

Church literature and social life regularly had an Irish flavor. Irish priests came to speak in London, and bits of Irish news were printed in English Catholic papers. The *Catholic Standard*

---

97. *Catholic Standard* 13, no. 330 (February 2, 1856); *St. Patrick's Catholic Magazine,* January 1899, pp. 49, 51.

98. Barclay, *Memoirs and Medleys,* pp. 18–19.

99. Bowden, *Life and Letters,* pp. 429–430.

100. *St. Patrick's Catholic Magazine,* April 1890, p. 96; the Very Rev. Thomas Burke, O.P., *Lectures and Sermons* (New York, 1873), p. 527; see also *The Tablet,* March 21, 1857; October 13, 1860. I am indebted to Sheridan Gilley for the last two references.

regularly carried advertisements of such plays as *The Emerald Isle* and *The Lakes of Killarney,* and Catholic literary magazines sometimes printed fiction on Irish themes. A biography of Daniel O'Connell was one of "The People's Books," a Catholic series designed to be sold to workers for a penny a copy. Topics in Irish church history and Irish songs and poetry in the English language were staple items on the programs of church lecture series and literary evenings. Father Sheridan, a priest at St. Patrick's, Soho, recorded the titles of the light fiction and poetry with which he used to entertain the female members of St. Brigit's Confraternity in the early 1880s. Virtually all of it was Irish material; bits from *Irish Pleasantry and Fun,* such as "The Donnybrook Spree," the much-romanticized folk tales of William Carleton, and Irish comic sketches delighted his audience. Irish Catholics clearly loved to hear the songs and stories that evoked their national culture, even when presented in bowdlerized or comic forms.[101] They made their preferences known when given the chance. Father Hutchison of the Oratory described in 1853 a free concert given on Boxing Night to parishioners in the Covent Garden area to tempt them away from the pubs.

There were about 800 present. Some of the music was too good; . . . we admitted too much of Beethoven's symphonies, etc. This was quite over the heads of the people, though at every pause they applauded loudly hoping that it was the end of the piece. But when we came to the one or two Irish melodies there was no mistake, they encored them, and stamped and shouted to the singers, 'Long Life to your throttle, Sir!'[102]

Within the Roman Catholic church, therefore, migrants found both a national and a religious identity. Whatever their loyalties before migration — perhaps to a parish, a county, or Irish culture — they found something rather different within London Catholicism. They were led into a highly religious popular culture that evoked Ireland through English-language songs and stories and through the assertion of national rather than local claims. The

---

101. *Catholic Standard* 9, no. 210 (October 22, 1853) (see *St. Patrick's Catholic Magazine,* 1891-1911, or *The Rambler,* 1851-1852), and 11, no. 266 (November 11, 1854); Sheridan, "About St. Brigit's Confraternity," quoted in Samuel, "Catholic Church and the Irish Poor," pp. 1-3.

102. Father Hutchison to Lady Arundel, January 5, 1853, in "Letter Books," vol. 30, London Oratory Archives, quoted in Samuel, "Catholic Church and the Irish Poor," p. 6.

Catholic revival in England helped to draw migrants into a modernized Irish culture.

Over time, Irish workers in London created a subculture within English society out of the diverse materials of past and present, out of the religious, national, and social identifications that they brought with them and then adapted to urban life. This process was complicated by the sometimes contradictory models of behavior that they found around them and by the constraints imposed by their economic and social position at the bottom of a hierarchical society. Outside influences such as the Catholic church helped to shape this subculture, although it is difficult to measure their importance in relation to pressures coming from within the Irish community. The Irish brought with them many cultural patterns identical to those of English workers with similar occupations and incomes, thus allowing easy entry into aspects of English working-class culture. The heavy use of the pub for both drinking and recreation, the street life and street fighting — activities that characterize many lower-class urban populations — remained part of the life-style of many Irish Catholics despite the conflict created with the ideals of behavior recommended by the Catholic church. But this life-style did not necessitate the rejection of Roman Catholicism. Although drinking, wife beating, and street fighting were rife among the St. Giles Irish, they retained an allegiance to Catholicism even if they did not attend mass. Joseph Oppenheim dutifully recorded his unsuccessful encounters with Irish Catholics who slammed doors in his face, cursed him, or refused to listen to his Protestant message. Day by day he noted that his listeners, *"as usual,"* countered his threats of the "Wrath to come" with invocation of "the Holy Church" and the "Virgin Mary."[103] Their identity as Irish Catholics was expressed through the symbols of their religion.

The Education of a Good Catholic

One of the major channels through which the ideological and behavioral norms of orthodox Catholicism were inculcated was the church's school system, which was intended to produce both good Catholics and good citizens. Cleanliness, obedience, and

103. Oppenheim, "Visitor's Book," p. 87.

honesty received at least as much attention as arithmetic, for a middle-class ideology of sobriety and self-help was thought necessary to the preservation of the spiritual as well as the social order. "The principal object" of a Catholic education should be "the preservation or correction of the morals of the lower orders," announced Dr. William Poynter, vicar apostolic of the London district in 1816.[104] This view changed little during the remainder of the century, although the commitment of the English Catholic church to providing such an education for its flock increased steadily. Catholic leaders gradually realized that without a church educational system, they could not retain the loyalty of Catholics raised in a Protestant society; so the need to educate the poor became widely appreciated by the 1830s. English Catholic gentlemen who contributed lay support to church schools were particularly concerned with the possible social benefits of religious education. They argued that "the education of the Catholic Church . . . can, and, as far as that education is diffused, will convert these masses into useful citizens, loyal subjects, and good men." As far as they were concerned, secular education was an adjunct to religion. "Mere literary or scientific knowledge" had to take second place to Catholic teachings.[105] At mid-century, the state inspector of Catholic schools agreed:

. . . that the children of the poor should possess more or less knowledge of grammar or geography is really, in itself, a matter of very small concern either to themselves or to the state; but that they should be so trained as to become hereafter lovers of justice, purity, patience, and industry, to be, in a word, good men and good citizens, — this is worthy of any expenditure, however costly, —. of any toil, however laborious . . .[106]

This combination of religious, social, and political motives made it imperative for Catholic clergy and laymen to build their

104. Great Britain, *Parliamentary Papers* (Commons), "Third Report from the Select Committee on Education among the Lower Orders in the Metropolis," 1816, 4:532.
105. Catholic Poor School Committee, *First Annual Report* (London, 1848), p. 14; *Sixth Annual Report* (London, 1853), Appendix E, p. 72.
106. T. W. Marshall, "General Report for the Year 1852 . . . on the Roman Catholic Schools in Great Britain," in Great Britain, *Parliamentary Papers* (Commons), "Minutes of the Committee of Council on Education for 1852," 1852–1853, 80:715–716.

own schools. Since the religious stamp of virtually all education in the nineteenth century made it certain that non-Catholic schools would draw children away from the Roman Catholic faith, priests were forced to compete in the educational field. After the final legal restrictions on Catholic education were repealed in 1829, the number of Catholic schools in England expanded rapidly. In 1835 a parliamentary committee counted 86 day schools and 62 Sunday schools scattered throughout the country, and a Catholic survey eight years later listed 236 day schools, 33 of them in London. According to an informal estimate at that time, however, education was provided for only about 30 percent of the eligible Catholic children.[107] In 1848 the Catholic Poor School Committee estimated that accommodation for at least 40,000 more children in Catholic schools was needed. The situation in London was even worse than that in England as a whole; only 7,643 children attended Catholic schools there in 1845, although the total Catholic population could scarcely have been less than 100,000 people.[108] And most existing schools were badly equipped and understaffed. One of the Christian Brothers' schools opened in 1844 in an old coach house near Lincoln's Inn Fields. A tiny yard held both playground and privies, and the first teachers complained of the polluted air as well as the horrendous teaching conditions:

There were two rooms, one over the other. The lower room was lighted at both ends by small windows, and a large opening in the floor of the upper school filled in with strong plate glass. So dark and dungeon-like was this room that for the winter months gas had to be lighted for the greater part of the day. . . . Again close to the schools was a very large forge, in which [were] not less than fourteen anvils and, of course, twenty-eight blacksmiths, with fires and bellows blowing, blasting and hammering from morning till evening; the only cessation was the dinner hour, which was availed of by us to give religious instruction for a half hour.[109]

The pattern of haphazard local support for education was broken in 1847, when the Roman Catholic bishops of England set

---

107. A. C. F. Beales, "The Struggle For the Schools," in *The English Catholics, 1850–1950,* ed. George Andrew Beck (London, 1950), pp. 366–367.

108. Catholic Poor School Committee, *First Annual Report,* p. 52; *Second Annual Report* (London, 1849), Appendix C, pp. 50–53.

109. "The Lost Province," *Our Province: Journal of the Christian Brothers' English Province,* no. 4 (May 1956), p. 34.

up the Catholic Poor School Committee to collect money and channel it to local schools, as well as to negotiate with the Privy Council for financial aid. In return for a share of the government's education fund, the committee and the bishops granted the state the right to inspect secular education in all aided schools and also complied with various important regulations on the use of certified teachers, a policy that brought financial benefits. The bishops were willing to let the state set the standard for all secular education as long as they remained in complete control of religious training. Individual schools could decide whether or not to apply for state money, thereby opening themselves to inspection, but the clear directive from the school committee was to get as much state aid as possible. Although no building grants were given to Catholic schools for several years, the immediate effect was to supply extra funds for books and apparatus and to furnish extra money for teachers' salaries. Gradually more and more schools allowed themselves to be inspected, more and more teachers passed state certification exams, and a system of teacher training developed which provided competent masters and apprentices for the fledgling Catholic institutions.[110] The best schools soon became the inspected schools, and the Catholic Poor School Committee was aware of the fact. But despite state aid, Catholic schools remained underfinanced in comparison with Anglican and other Protestant denominational institutions. Although amounts of government money increased during the early 1850s, Roman Catholic schools in Middlesex spent in 1856 less than half as much per pupil as did Anglican schools.[111] Even this level of expenditure strained the resources of the church.

In spite of the financial burden, the Catholic church substantially increased the number of school places between 1850 and 1870. When Manning became archbishop, he estimated that about one-half of the eligible children were in Catholic schools. About 11,000 pupils were counted as effectively receiving an

110. Catholic Poor School Committee, *First Annual Report*, pp. 7–15. Within ten years, 197 schools in England and Scotland were under state inspection; their 46,000 pupils accounted for about two-thirds of the total number in all Catholic schools (*Tenth Annual Report of the Catholic Poor School Committee* [London, 1857], p. 18).

111. Great Britain, *Parliamentary Papers* (Commons), "Minutes of the Committee of Council on Education for 1856," 1857, 2d sess., 33:Table XII, 65.

education, and an unknown number, estimated at about 30,000, drifted in and out of various classrooms or were entirely uneducated.[112] By 1870, thirty additional schools had been opened, taking another 3,000 children off the London streets. In addition, church institutions for orphans, delinquents, and other disadvantaged children were provided. By 1875 twenty-four such schools had been opened, and a start was made on the work of furnishing a Catholic alternative to the state's reformatories and industrial and workhouse schools.[113] Nevertheless, the opportunity to have a Catholic education in London in the period between 1830 and 1870 was severely circumscribed. The number excluded because of geography, insufficient space, or parental inclination formed a substantial share of the total. Among children aged six to ten in the Irish families I sampled, only 34 percent were listed as attending school in 1851; the proportion had risen to 57 percent by 1861. At mid-century many fewer children of Irish migrants than of the London population as a whole were in school. In 1851 the census listed 35 percent of all boys under fifteen and 33 percent of all girls under fifteen as scholars; the comparable figures for the sampled Irish were only 28 and 25 percent.[114] Several factors produced this small enrollment; the lack of Roman Catholic facilities and the poverty of Irish parents were probably the most important. There is no clear evidence that the educational aspirations of Irish Catholic parents differed from

112. Canon Edward St. John, *Manning's Work for Children* (London, 1929), pp. 44–45. This proportion was approximately equal to that of students in 1869 among the school-age populations of Leeds, Manchester, Liverpool, and Birmingham. About half were enrolled in school, but many of those on the rolls received no systematic education. Although Roman Catholics were not educating their own people, their effort was no worse than that of the Protestant denominations in the great towns. See *Twenty-second Annual Report of the Catholic Poor School Committee* (London, 1869), pp. 12–13.

113. Under Manning's leadership, the Roman Catholic church cooperated with the Education Act of 1870. In order to secure state funds and to save the inefficient Catholic schools, he led his often bitterly hostile colleagues to participate in local educational affairs, run by the elected school boards. For a detailed examination of the Catholic position on the government's educational policy, see Vincent Alan McClelland, *Cardinal Manning, His Public Life and Influence, 1865–1892* (London, 1962), chap. 3.

114. Great Britain, *Parliamentary Papers* (Commons), "Census of Great Britain, 1851, Occupations of the People," 1852–1853, 88, pt. 1:10, 13; "Census of 1851," manuscript schedules, five-parish sample.

those of low-skilled English workers. Whatever the interest of migrants in education, it was difficult for them to obtain it for their children before 1870. Even when school places were available, priests worked actively to keep Catholic children out of Protestant and nonsectarian schools by identifying Protestant education with apostasy and mortal sin.[115]

The effectiveness of Catholic education was also hindered by the short and irregular attendance of the pupils. Catholic schools were infant schools. Only the exceptional child received more than two or three years of education. Nearly one-half of the Catholic students in 1855 were under eight years of age, and the percentage had not changed by 1866.[116] Not only were the pupils very young, but a widespread drift in and out of the classroom undermined everyone's progress. On the average, the proportion of children at mid-century who had been in the same school for one year or less stood at 30 percent. The school inspector summarized this difficulty in 1851:

Teachers in certain districts are constantly complaining to me, not merely of the early age at which their scholars finally quit them, but that all their efforts are frustrated by the fluctuating attendance of the majority, whose intense poverty leaves them without defense when tempted by the prospect of the smallest conceivable gain. The inducement of 6d per week, to be earned by the sale of chips, periwinkles, or matches, will entirely quench the faint desire for instruction which is its only counterpoise, and reduce a promising class to a skeleton, whilst its members are scattered over the country, often for several weeks together, in pursuance of their vagabond craft.[117]

The same problem persisted through the 1860s and was responsible for the poor attendance records that plagued most Catholic schools. In the southern half of England, the school inspector reported in 1865, only 16,700 children out of 26,300 on the rolls

115. Great Britain, *Parliamentary Papers* (Commons), "Select Committee on Education of the Poorer Classes in England and Wales," 1837–1838, 7:Q. 994, and 400; "Select Committee on Education in England and Wales," 1835, 7:Q. 35.
116. *Minutes of the Committee of Council on Education and Reports by Her Majesty's Inspectors, 1855–1856* (London, 1856), p. 606; *Report of the Committee of Council on Education, 1866–1867* (London, 1867), Table 1, p. 1.
117. T. W. Marshall, "General Report for the Year 1851 . . . on the Roman Catholic Schools in Great Britain," in Great Britain, *Parliamentary Papers* (Commons), "Minutes of the Committee of Council on Education, 1851," 1852, 40:619.

were present on an average day. Although 8,500 under six years of age were listed as pupils in these schools, only 3,300 met the government's standards for minimum attendance.[118] Neither Irish parents nor their children could afford the luxury of more than a minimal interest in education. Not until 1880, when education was made compulsory for children under eleven, did the educational achievement of Catholic children increase markedly.

In one way only was the Catholic educational system able to channel a number of its students into advanced studies and white-collar occupations. The need for teaching assistants and for students who had attended teacher training colleges led the church to recruit a few of the better pupils for such posts in order to qualify schools for state financial support. Since state and parish financial support was available, it was possible for poor children to enter the programs. Apparently the career of a Catholic schoolmaster was so uninviting that few middle-class Catholics considered sending their sons into the profession. The state inspector complained that none of the pupil-teachers came from "respectable" families. Those who became apprentices and then candidates at training schools were overwhelmingly Irish boys who had been laboriously cultivated and prepared to pass state requirements. Large numbers regularly failed their qualifying exams because the standards maintained for their work in the primary schools were so abysmally low. Nevertheless, a great deal of effort was expended at the level of the training college to prepare teachers in a wide range of secular subjects. Although the number who passed through the system before 1870 was quite small, an avenue had been opened up by the church for the movement of Irish migrants into the middle class.[119]

Most Catholic pupils, however, were given only an introduction to basic literacy rather than a passport to higher social status. In nineteenth-century England, mass education was class education; those who could not pay for middle-class training were not

118. Le Page Renouf, "General Report for the Year 1865," *Report of the Committee of Council on Education, 1865–1866* (London, 1866), p. 273.
119. T. W. Marshall, "Report on the Roman Catholic Training College of St. Mary's, Hammersmith," in *Minutes of the Committee of Council on Education, 1856–1857* (London, 1857), pp. 779–780; Scott Nasmyth Stokes, "Report for the Year 1864 . . . on the Roman Catholic Normal Schools . . .," in *Report of the Committee of Council on Education, 1864–1865* (London, 1865), p. 408.

given it. Most Catholic children attended places accurately named "poor schools," where a few pennies a week purchased an overseer for the child as well as snippets of a secular education. Little more than the rudiments were provided. Lessons centered on reading, writing, arithmetic, and religion, with emphasis on the last. There was usually no vocational training, and modern languages were not taught. A very few pupils in higher grades learned geometry or algebra; about 10 percent of those enrolled in inspected schools were taught history. Geography and English grammar were the only other advanced subjects included in the Catholic curriculum.[120]

Most students were led through a series of books published by the Irish Commissioners of Education. Although the volumes were technically nonsectarian, they had been modeled on works by the Catholic Book Society, with secular information added. Children were taught to read by the use of words and sentences containing basic facts about geography, grammar, hygiene, morality, and religion. Students who progressed to the *Fifth Book of Lessons* were exposed to sophisticated statements about science and literature, but few during the 1850s and 1860s went beyond the lower level texts. Only a few bits of history were built into the books: a total of fifteen pages covered the period from 1500 to 1850. Irish history was excluded; the Reformation was not mentioned.[121]

The books of the Irish Christian Brothers, also used in London, were similar. The *First Book of Reading Lessons* introduced children to one- and two-syllable words in such sentences as: "You should not speak loud in the streets"; "A bad life leads to a bad end." Children were told, "Boys should not fight, nor call names. They ought to be kind to all."[122] The books progressed from letters and simple sentences to descriptions of God and

120. Great Britain, *Parliamentary Papers* (Commons), "Minutes of the Committee on Education, 1851," 1852, 39:143.
121. Donald Harman Akenson, "The Irish National System of Education in the Nineteenth Century," Ph.D. thesis, Harvard University, 1967; "Tabulated Reports on Roman Catholic Schools," *Minutes of the Committee of Council on Education, 1852* (London, 1852), pp. 731–753.
122. Brothers of the Christian Schools, *The First Book of Reading Lessons*, 2d ed. (Dublin, 1841), pp. 24–25.

moral lessons directed against lying and stealing. The framework of the book derived from its explication of Christian virtues. As students' reading skills became more sophisticated, they were given a potpourri of excerpts from English, French, Irish, and American writers, many of whom also presented a moral or theological lesson. "Poor Richard" condemned laziness, while Charles Rollin announced that "docility" and respect for their masters were major "duties of schoolboys." The books presented mixed messages. On the one hand, there was a mild exhortation to self-help: "Early to bed, early to rise, makes a man healthy, wealthy, and wise." On the other hand, Catholic children were taught to accept their position in this world: "Do not grieve at the ills of life, for they are brief," and "Time flees, earth fades, with all its pleasures; / The ardent heart attentive hears, / But nought of transient counsel treasures."[123] And while they preached endurance in mortal life, Catholic schoolbooks defended and exalted the status quo:

In England a man of small fortune may cast his regards around him, and say with truth and exultation: 'I am lodged in a house that affords me conveniences and comforts, which even a king could not command some centuries ago. There are ships crossing the seas in every direction to bring what is useful to me, from all parts of the earth. . . .' Such being the miracle of God's goodness and providence that each individual of the civilized millions that cover the earth may have nearly the same enjoyments, as if he were the single lord of all.[124]

The political status quo was accepted too. The Irish nationalism of the schoolbooks was mild and criticism of the English government nonexistent. Ancient and biblical history took precedence over news of modern events. Indeed, theology, geography, and popular science were found to be safer subjects. Students read short paragraphs on barometers, the solar system, electricity, and steam engines in advanced texts, rather than Irish history.[125]

Since the system was designed to produce functional literacy

123. Brothers of the Christian Schools, *The Third Book of Reading Lessons* (Dublin, 1841), p. 75.
124. Ibid., p. 73.
125. Brothers of the Christian Schools, *The Literary Class Book or Fourth Series of Select Reading Lessons* (Dublin, 1840), pp. v, vi.

and piety, it is not surprising that the educational achievement of those who attended was relatively low. Although these primary schools were structured to permit at least six years of training, few went beyond the third year. State examination results in 1865 showed that only 8 percent of the total number of Catholic scholars stayed in school after age twelve, while 12 percent of students in Anglican schools continued beyond that age. In 1851 only a minority of Catholic pupils of all ages could write without the aid of a copy, could read more than easy narratives or monosyllables, or could do more than add or copy numbers. A substantial number failed each year to pass the state examination that tested performance in the standard to which each pupil was assigned.[126] During the next decade student performance in these schools improved markedly, but standards remained low and the curriculum limited.

One suspects that religious teaching was made more attractive and compelling than secular instruction. Nuns and members of male religious orders were preferred and generally used as teachers for the examples they set of discipline and commitment to a Catholic life. The visible link to the church which they provided was augmented by the active efforts of priests to fasten children's attention upon the rituals and recreations of the parish to which they belonged. Clubs, outings, and festivals for school-children drew them into a Catholic community and rewarded their attendance with sweets and social recognition. The singing of a rousing hymn such as "Deep in the Panting Heart of Rome" or the chance to perform in a religious pageant must have had more appeal than the chanting of dull, simple sentences from a beginning reader. Whereas Catholics' secular education was turgid and flat, their religious education was a multimedia effort combining the appeal of music, recreation, and personal example. We do not know exactly what effects Catholic education had upon Irish workers' children, but it may be surmised that those who passed through church schools had their Catholic loyalties reinforced and grew in familiarity with the norms and messages of the church.

126. Renouf, "General Report," pp. 274, 279; "General Summary for the Year 1851," *Minutes of the Committee of Council on Education, 1851–1852* (London, 1852), pp. 142–143.

Self-help and Sobriety

Clerical efforts to educate and mold the flock were not confined
to children. The church sponsored a variety of organizations to
encourage self-help and thrift within a Catholic context. Without
diverting major amounts of energy and time, priests often set up
parochial banks and burial clubs that duplicated in a Catholic
setting the functions of friendly societies and workingmen's
money clubs. In order to teach frugality and to encourage saving
against hard times and pauperism, several middle-class Catholic
laymen worked with local priests in the early 1850s to establish
branches of the Irish Provident Society around the metropolis.
The largest of these friendly societies provided sickness benefits
and burial fees for members. Two groups with meeting places
stretching across the metropolis from Marylebone to Moorfields
were established in 1834 and 1835 by the clergy as exact equiva-
lents of the secular burial clubs. Migrants probably joined the
Burial Society of St. Joseph and St. Patrick and other Irish groups
(such as the Islington United Brothers Catholic Temperance
Benefit Society and the Sons of Hibernia Friendly and Benefit
Society) rather than similar groups dominated by English artisans. The Catholic societies grew up alongside the Protestant
ones, borrowing forms of organization but recruiting from a
different ethnic group. The emphasis on self-help was identical,
however, as was the overriding concern for security. Rules often
excluded men in "dangerous or pernicious trades," and required
that members be healthy, moral teetotalers.[127]

Several types of Catholic organizations preached temperance as
well as self-help. In fact, priests in London regularly attempted to
reform Irish drinking habits. They recognized that drunkenness
was a major social problem both in London and in Ireland
during the nineteenth century. Much Irish social life was built on
the consumption of cheap drink. Weddings, wakes, dances, and
fireside conversations were enlivened by poteen, an illegally
distilled malt whisky. Despite the zeal of police and tax collectors,
poteen was freely available both in the rural districts and in Irish
cities; in Dublin it could be found "as openly in the streets as they

127. F.S. 1-471/B2602; 472/2744; 459/2180, Public Record Office, London.

sell a loaf of bread."[128] Popular songs heaped such praise on whisky and its devotees that in 1840, after one of their tours of Ireland, Mr. and Mrs. S. C. Hall commented that "drunkenness was inculcated as a merit, and almost as a duty."[129] Only in the late 1830s and 1840s, after the temperance campaign of Father Theobald Mathew, did the links between drinking and mass recreation begin to break down.

In London, too, alcohol consumption was high among workers. Brian Harrison has shown the importance of the role played by pubs in urban working-class culture. Pubs dotted the poorer areas of cities, occupying prime corner sites for greater visibility. At mid-century there were more than 5,000 in London — one for every 427 persons — in addition to more than 3,000 beerhouses.[130] The Metropolitan Police took into custody in 1851 more than 23,000 persons on charges of either drunkenness or drunk and disorderly conduct.[131] The Irish were probably well represented among this group. Much of migrants' social life took place in pubs near their neighborhoods, where they sang, met friends, and drank. Irish shoemakers frequented the same central London pubs; Irish ballast heavers used others in the East End.[132] But however strong and popularly sanctioned the links among custom, popular recreation, and drinking, the priests saw the darker consequences of heavy drinking and disapproved. The Marist fathers in Spitalfields reported to superiors the problems of drunkenness ("that distinctive vice of the Irish") among their parishioners and complained that "transplanted in England, too

128. K. H. Connell, *Irish Peasant Society: Four Historical Essays* (Oxford, 1968), pp. 1, 13.

129. Hall, *Ireland*, vol. 1, pp. 34, 36-38.

130. Brian Harrison, *Drink and the Victorians* (London, 1971), and "Pubs," in *The Victorian City: Images and Realities*, ed. H. J. Dyos and Michael Wolff, 2 vols. (London and Boston, 1973), vol. 1, pp. 161-190; Great Britain, *Parliamentary Papers* (Commons), on Criminal and Destitute Children," 1852-1853, 23:Q. 1250-1251.

131. Great Britain, *Parliamentary Papers* (Commons), "Return of the Number of Persons Taken into Custody by the Metropolitan Police Force for Drunkenness and Disorderly Conduct, 1831-51," 1852, 41:515.

132. John O'Neill, "Fifty Years' Experience as an Irish Shoemaker in London," *St. Crispin* 1 (London, 1869):240-241; Mayhew, *London Labour*, vol. 3, pp. 278-279.

often our poor Irish forget the way of the church to learn about that of the cabaret."[133]

The response of the Catholic clergy was to attempt moral reform by both formal and informal means. Mayhew recorded the transformation during the 1840s of "old Norah," probably a street seller of fish in central London. The local priest discovered her drunk in a gutter one evening while young boys were pelting her with mud and orange peel. He took her to the chapel and persuaded her to take the temperance pledge and to begin a savings account, with the result that for several years she lived very well and became the best-dressed woman in her court.[134] Individual clergymen continued to function in this way, although their methods varied; men whom Charles Booth interviewed in 1900 reported that the local priest would not hesitate to go into a public house, drag out the offending drinker, and thrash him in the street. Booth doubted that the priest effected permanent improvement, but he admitted that temporary reform could result.[135]

In addition to these informal temperance campaigns, priests sponsored parish organizations that spread both religion and the pledge. Several local teetotal clubs existed by 1843, when Father Mathew came to London and conducted a week-long temperance crusade. Local Catholic workingmen's associations sent deputations, as did "The Wapping Boys," who declared themselves by their banner committed "to Religion, to Country, and to Honour True." More than 30,000 people attended the first session on Commercial Road in the East End. They flocked to hear Father Mathew's morality tales of Irishmen saved from drink, to take the pledge, and to listen to a Catholic choir sing a specially written temperance hymn. Within the week, Father Mathew drew crowds of 60,000 and 100,000. In the first three days more than 20,000 people were alleged to have taken the pledge, and prominent Catholics and local priests gave public blessings to the cause. As

133. Chauvrain, "Rapport sur la mission de Ste Anne"; letter from L. M. Petit, S.M., dated St. Raymond's Day, 1853.
134. Henry Mayhew, *London Labour*, vol. 1, p. 110.
135. Booth, *Life and Labour*, ser. 3, *Religious Influences*, vol. 7, p. 244.

Father Mathew moved into central and south London, such scenes were repeated.[136]

Thereafter the temperance cause received more publicity and Catholic support. Gradually other parishes set up their own clubs and made them a part of local social life. St. Anne's, Spitalfields, had a temperance club from sometime in the early 1850s to provide nonalcoholic recreation for members. Soon after its founding, it began to sponsor yearly summer outings to Southend for parish families.[137] After local priests preached a series of sermons on drunkenness, 100 Irish workers in St. John, Islington, set up a temperance club in 1860. Their temperance tea party drew several hundred people that year to hear Irish songs and do Irish dances while they sipped nonalcoholic beverages.[138] But despite these efforts, the problem of drunkenness among Catholics does not seem to have diminished appreciably by the early 1860s. After he became archbishop, Henry Manning decided that diocesan efforts in the temperance cause were necessary. As an opening tactic, he proclaimed the "Truce of St. Patrick," arranging a papal indulgence for three days of abstinence on and after the holiday. Apparently his evocation of religion and nationalism worked that time, but a similar attempt to discourage all weekend drinking failed. Then in 1872 Manning borrowed some forms and tactics from the Salvation Army. His League of the Cross, with its brigades, captains, and honor guards dressed in scarlet sashes, combined panache and practical appeal: within two years, Catholics asserted that 28,000 had joined.[139] Manning also organized large open-air rallies for workers in cities all over England, and he spoke frequently in support of temperance. Sometimes 20,000 supporters attended the League's yearly processions at the Crystal Palace, where the cardinal received his temperance soldiers and their brass bands. By 1890 there were forty-two or forty-three branches led by eighty priests in the dioceses of Westminster and Southwark. Drunkenness among the clergy had once been a problem, but the hierarchy had not heard of an intemperate priest

136. *The Tablet,* July 5, August 5, and August 7, 1843.
137. *The Universe,* August 31, 1878.
138. *Catholic Standard* 23, no. 597 (January 5, 1843).
139. McClelland, *Cardinal Manning,* pp. 202–203.

for quite a few years. Moreover, Manning felt that the idea of abstinence had begun to be accepted by many Catholics: "The League [has] taken hold of the people, especially the working men. It was this that gave me a hold in the Dock Strike of last year."[140]

Yet the success of the Catholic church in limiting drinking was mixed. The ethic of thrift, sobriety, and self-help had to compete against other styles of life, which were deeply embedded in the culture of working-class Irish. Charles Booth wrote in 1900 that "drinking and fighting are the ordinary conditions of life among many of their flock." While a priest could easily stop a quarrel or a brawl, the chances were great that it would resume sometime later. Southwark priests claimed around 1900 that many of their parishioners had succumbed to drink, betting, or the moneylender.[141] Within most of the major Roman Catholic parishes in working-class areas, part of the Irish Catholic population still led at the turn of the century rather rough, disorderly lives. They drank, fought each other as well as the police, and frequently moved throughout the district. They remained Catholic in profession, coming into occasional contact with the clergy, but Catholic pressures for behavioral reform had little permanent effect. Charles Booth commented:

It is not possible to trace any persistent improvement either moral or material in their lives, and if a religion which does not secure improvement fails, then success cannot be claimed for these churches. But from day to day, these poor people are greatly helped by their connection with the Church; restrained, controlled and blessed in their rough lives by its care.[142]

Catholic responses to clerical advice and teaching varied enormously in intensity and quality; yet the church did succeed in maintaining ties with the bulk of the migrant community during the nineteenth century, even if the hierarchy's dreams of a perfectly devout and obedient population were not realized. Sheridan Gilley has argued for the relatively greater tolerance

140. Purcell, *Life of Cardinal Manning*, vol. 2, p. 604.
141. Booth, *Life and Labour*, ser. 3, *Religious Influences*, vol. 7, p. 244; vol. 4, pp. 13–14.
142. Ibid., vol. 2, p. 40.

among Catholic clerics than among Evangelical Protestants. This greater willingness to compromise with the life-style of low-skilled workers helps to account for the fact that religion played a larger role in the cultural life of Catholic urban workers than among their Protestant counterparts.[143]

143. Gilley, "Heretic London," pp. 64–74, and "Catholic Faith of the Irish Slums, London, 1840–1870" in *Victorian City*, ed. Dyos and Wolff, vol. 2, pp. 837–849. For a comparative discussion of Protestant and Catholic missionary work among the poor, see Kenneth Stanley Inglis, *Churches and the Working Classes in Victorian England* (London, 1963).

CHAPTER 8

Political Ideas
and Organizations

Political attitudes and the forms of political activity have been transformed during the last two centuries in Ireland, England, and Western Europe. Established national associations with clear criteria for membership have replaced loosely organized groups of neighbors as the major vehicles for the expression of political aims. To use Charles Tilly's typology, competitive and reactive forms of collective action have been supplanted by proactive ones.[1] Increasingly, political parties and trade unions, rather than kin groups or crowds, dominated the field of political action. As parliamentary politicians and sophisticated revolutionaries replaced primitive rebels, political attitudes underwent a marked evolution. Over time in Ireland notions of a moral economy where all received their due according to past "just" practices were exchanged for commitments to peasant proprietorship. By the end of the nineteenth century, ideas of cultural and political nationalism, socialism, and republicanism gained increased currency and support.

Irish migrants also participated in these long-term transformations of political organization and ideology. Although they imported secret societies and faction fights into England, they

1. Charles Tilly, Louise Tilly, and Richard Tilly, *The Rebellious Century, 1830–1930* (London and Cambridge, Mass., 1975), passim, especially pp. 48–51; see also Charles Tilly, "The Modernization of Political Conflict in France," in *Perspectives in Modernization: Essays in Memory of Ian Weinberg,* ed. Edward B. Harvey (Toronto, 1972).

were soon mobilized into a variety of well-organized nationalist groups. This change in their political behavior paralleled a transition taking place in Ireland, but the pace of change for migrants was accelerated. Those who left rural Munster for London exchanged a milieu in which banditry, faction fights, and vigilante groups flourished for a well-policed city with active trade societies and political clubs, and they had to adapt quickly.

But as the Irish were drawn into the forms of modern political life, they faced a choice between old and new loyalties. Would they continue to regard Irish nationalist campaigns as their primary commitment or would they become more involved in the issues and groups that mobilized English workers? Would they define their primary political loyalty in terms of their ethnicity or their residence and their occupational group? Migrants had to choose; their decisions provide evidence of their allegiances as well as their involvement in English society. In the 1840s, their greatest participation occurred in Irish nationalist groups. But as they adapted to English urban life, they slowly began to join English workers' organizations and to vote in local and parliamentary elections. While their ethnicity continued to dominate their political behavior, over time its expression was channeled into the mainstream of English politics, and it was supplemented by other commitments made on the basis of occupation and residence.

The Political Life of Prefamine Ireland

Prefamine Ireland was a conflict-ridden society. Although its parliament was dissolved in 1801 and the country was ruled from abroad, other outlets for political energies existed or were invented in order to express the endemic hostilities of various groups toward one another. Kin group was pitted against kin group. Protestants organized to attack Catholics, who formed defense associations to retaliate. Tenants and laborers joined together to oppose landlords, agents, and clergy. The nationalist cause slowly gained adherents in both the cities and the rural areas. Nationalist clubs mobilized tens of thousands of peasants during years of intense agitation. The political attitudes and experiences of the migrant in England developed in this milieu.

Several types of organization with varying levels of sophistication existed in prefamine Ireland. The most informal local associations sprang to life in rural areas among kin and neighbors. When threatened, families of the men of a given district joined groups called factions, which defended their interests. After a quarrel, the aggrieved parties would recruit relatives or neighbors, who met together at local fairs and markets for tests of strength with opponents. Factions were widely known all over southern and western Ireland. Such groups were endemic in Tipperary in the first quarter of the nineteenth century and could be found in Cork, Limerick, Kerry, and parts of Connaught. Most of these groups were rooted in one small locality, many taking their nicknames from the land on which they lived.[2]

Factions provided the peasantry with extralegal channels for settling personal disputes. The battles of the Dawsons and the Dingens began when the father of a dead woman demanded from her husband's family the right to bury her corpse. They refused, and fighting soon broke out. In upper Ormond, Tipperary, a quarrel in 1805 between two boys over a marble game led to a fight between the adults of each family; soon the Hogans formed a faction called the Bogboys to fight the O'Brien faction, the Bootashees. The two groups were still feuding in 1836.[3] In the 1830s, magistrates generally permitted factions to fight without interference and absolved them of links to local insurrectionary activity.[4] This relative lack of concern by authorities was possible because the targets of faction fights remained within the peasant population and did not include private or public property. Yet these fights kept alive an ethic of confrontation, just as they legitimated direct attacks upon neighbors. The factions thus perpetuated some of the assumptions and methods of agrarian secret societies, which were at the center of peasant political activity and which British authorities feared and actively repressed.

In 1761 bands of men called "Whiteboys" or "Levellers" organized in several parts of Munster to tear down fences and fill

2. George Cornewall Lewis, *On Local Disturbances in Ireland and on the Irish Church Question* (London, 1836), pp. 288–289; Galen Broeker, *Rural Disorder and Police Reform in Ireland, 1812–1836* (London, 1970), p. 16.

3. Lewis, *On Local Disturbances*, pp. 288–289.

4. Broeker, *Rural Disorder*, pp. 15–16; Lewis, *On Local Disturbances*, pp. 290–293.

ditches that enclosed common land. Costumed in white shirts or smocks, they assembled at night to threaten and to destroy the property of those who contravened their rules for the conduct of local social and economic life. Landlords in their areas had granted plots of land to cottiers at high rents but allowed them the right to use waste or common lands. When these rights were rescinded and the common lands enclosed, Whiteboys organized to fight.[5] They quickly found targets beyond enclosers' fences. Like the French peasants who fought the opening of the grain trade, Whiteboys stopped the exportation of grain and flour from their parishes.[6] They tore down granaries and storehouses. They broke into prisons and freed debtors, called upon justices of the peace to lower food prices, and savagely punished local people who did not obey their orders. On their midnight rides they burned buildings, destroyed cattle, and quite prudently extorted money for defense funds.

Groups similar to the Whiteboys were active in several counties of Munster during the 1760s and from 1775 to 1785. Between 1806 and 1840, secret societies under various names reappeared in Tipperary, Limerick, West Meath, Kildare, and several other counties of Munster and Leinster. In 1822 Whiteboys established camps in the mountains of Cork, raiding nearby towns for food and occasionally battling soldiers. Again in 1826, after a bad harvest and rent increases, agrarian societies sprang up in Kerry, Athlone, West Meath, Longford, Roscommon, Mayo, and Galway. Bands of men went on arms raids, set fires, and beat or maimed those who disobeyed the will of the group. During the tithe war of the early 1830s, agrarian secret societies were widespread. "Blackfeet" and "Whitefeet" opposed tithe charges and rent increases. "Terry Alts" flourished in Limerick and Clare. Sizable areas of rural Ireland fell into the hands of these "social bandits" until the spring of 1833, when the groups faded away. By the 1840s police were claiming that such societies had vanished in the southern counties, but small cadres of members continued to operate in some areas as late as the 1850s.[7] Secret societies

5. Lewis, *On Local Disturbances*, pp. 4–7, 10, 12.

6. Ibid., pp. 6, 10; see also Louise Tilly, "La révolte frumentaire, forme de conflict politique en France," *Annales: Economies, Sociétés, Civilisations* 27 (1972):731–757.

7. Lewis, *On Local Disturbances*, pp. 19, 33–35, 41–42, 44; Broeker, *Rural Disorder*, pp. 8, 133, 169, 206, 237.

appeared again during the land agitation of the late 1870s and early 1880s, but their period of peak activity was the late eighteenth and early nineteenth centuries.[8]

These societies flourished in the solidly Roman Catholic areas of the south and west and became most deeply rooted in moderately prosperous counties where population was very dense. Local observers thought that their stimulus to action was less the pressure of grinding poverty than the appearance of specific grievances concerning land or taxes. They arose from and melted back into local peasant communities. Members moved about their parishes at night, visiting all the homes and swearing the adults, particularly the young men, into the group. Those who joined swore to keep activities secret, to come when called, to obey the laws of the group, and not to give evidence against others.[9] Witnesses before a parliamentary inquiry into disturbances in Ireland in 1824 claimed that the participants were chiefly laborers, cottiers, and the smaller farmers, the poorer strata of agrarian society.

The Whiteboys enforced an alternative justice based on a code of behavior different from that of English law. A gentleman residing in Youghall, Cork, near centers of Whiteboy activity, wrote in 1762 of their aims: "They then, and all along, pretended that their assembling was to do justice to the poor, by restoring the ancient commons and redressing other grievances . . . "[10] Arthur Young, who traveled in the south of Ireland in the mid-1770s, asserted that these bands "set up to be general redressers of grievances, punished all obnoxious persons and [took] the administration of justice into their own hands."[11] The Whiteboys rejected the authority of landlords, millers, and larger farmers to dispose of property as they wished. They attempted to substitute a different set of standards, one akin to the "moral economy" of English villagers in the eighteenth century.[12]

George Cornewall Lewis, who investigated secret societies in

8. James S. Donnelly, Jr., *The Land and the People of Nineteenth-Century Cork: The Rural Economy and the Land Question* (London and Boston, 1975), pp. 282–286.

9. Lewis, *On Local Disturbances*, pp. 60–65, 90, 164–165, 194–196.

10. Ibid., p. 6.

11. Quoted in ibid., p. 12.

12. See Edward P. Thompson, "The Moral Economy of the English Crowd in the Eighteenth Century," *Past and Present* no. 50 (February 1971), pp. 76–136.

Ireland during the 1830s as part of his study of Ireland and the Irish for the British Parliament, concluded that the Whiteboys wanted "to keep the actual occupant in possession of his land, and in general to regulate the relation of landlord and tenant for benefit of the latter."[13] The societies were therefore reformist rather than revolutionary. In a rough way, they took from the richer and gave to the poorer, attempting neither expropriation nor the overturning of local social and political orders. Closer to the Mafia than to a trade union, these secret societies grew out of local hostility to landlords, the central government, and a free market.[14]

Similar in form but different in their aims and incidence were secret religious societies, which organized either Protestants or Catholics. These groups originated in Ulster, the stronghold of Irish Protestantism. In 1795, after several years of local conflicts, a major clash between bands of armed Catholics and Protestants in Armagh triggered the formation of a new Protestant league. The Orange Society, with secret initiation rites and an oath of loyalty to the Protestant ascendancy, soon spread throughout Ulster. By 1797, lodges included peasants, administrators, landlords, and gentlemen. After the Act of Union, the society became even more closely linked to British and Irish elites. Lodges were reorganized, members of Parliament and peers being placed at their heads. Thereafter, the political influence of the order rose and fell with the political preferences of English administrators in Dublin and the degree of Catholic militancy and disaffection. Dissolved in 1825 and again in 1836, the order revived in both cases after a few years and continued to express militant Protestantism and equally militant hostility to the social, economic, and political aspirations of Irish Catholics.[15]

As the Orange Society entrenched itself among the ruling elites and the Protestant peasantry, Catholics organized new secret societies to protect their interests. The Defenders, which collapsed along with the abortive rebellion of the United Irishmen, were

13. Lewis, *On Local Disturbances*, p. 99.

14. For European examples of similar phenomena, see E. J. Hobsbawm, *Primitive Rebels: Studies in Archaic Forms of Social Movement in the Nineteenth and Twentieth Centuries* (New York, 1965).

15. Hereward Senior, *Orangeism in Ireland and Britain, 1795–1836* (London and Toronto, 1966), pp. 2–3, 6–8, 12, 16–18, 276–278, 280, 284.

replaced by the Ribbonmen. The Ribbon Society had appeared in several areas by 1814, although it was concentrated in Ulster.[16] It too was a secret society, one whose members pledged that they would not only maintain secrecy and fidelity but also "never spare, but persevere and wade knee-deep in Orange blood."[17] The group spread rapidly around 1820 into counties south and west of Ulster. Groups formed in at least the counties of West Meath, Louth, Longford, Waterford, Limerick, and Dublin.[18] In Ulster, the Ribbonmen served as a Catholic protection force, blocking attacks by Protestant gangs and opposing economic exploitation by landlords. Ribbon societies also made periodic attempts to set up a central organization, to channel money from one group to another, and to have county representatives meet to discuss tactics. The organization of the group was therefore somewhat more sophisticated and more centralized than that of the agrarian secret societies.

A fourth vehicle for political participation emerged with the development of Irish nationalism and resistance to English rule. By the time of the French Revolution, several groups of urban radicals had formed political debating societies. In 1791, under the influence of Wolfe Tone, a new club, the United Irishmen, was organized in Dublin and Belfast to support parliamentary reform and political cooperation between Protestants and Catholics. Leaders were predominantly middle-class professionals and businessmen, although artisans also joined. As the revolution progressed in France, several United Irishmen became more radical in their demands. By 1795, the government arrested two members for sedition and forced Wolfe Tone to flee the country. Shortly thereafter, the United Irishmen were reconstituted as a secret society pledged to support an Irish republic. Within Ireland, a military organization was set up to prepare for the future revolution. Catholic Defenders joined the movement en masse and units formed throughout Ulster and Leinster. As the Orange Society and the Protestant yeomanry began to attack, disarm, and execute Catholics, more and more Catholic farmers

16. Broeker, *Rural Disorder*, p. 12.

17. Lewis, *On Local Disturbances*, p. 165.

18. R. B. McDowell, *Public Opinion and Government Policy in Ireland, 1801–1846* (London, 1952), p. 64; Broeker, *Rural Disorder*, p. 12.

and tenants joined the United Irishmen. How large the group became is not known, but leaders claimed 500,000 members in 1798, and the military commander, Lord Edward Fitzgerald, said that he could raise about 100,000 men for the planned rising. While these estimates are doubtless inflated, they indicate at least that the group was large, capable of causing much trouble for the authorities. And it did. Although the government arrested most of the leaders, in late May of 1798 small uprisings began in Kildare, Meath, Carlow, Antrim, and Down, while a peasant army took over large parts of Wexford.[19]

Repression of the rebels drove Irish republicanism underground and dampened other forms of nationalist political activity for many years. The revival of a mass-based Irish political life took place around the demand for changes in the Penal Laws, which forbade Catholics to vote and to run for public office. Prominent Dublin Catholics began in 1804 to attempt to force the English Parliament to repeal these laws. For the next twenty years, similar small associations of middle- and upper-class Catholics formed, petitioned, and argued about the provisions of proposed legal reforms. Only in 1824, when Daniel O'Connell decided that the campaign must be widened, did large numbers of Catholics become involved. In that year O'Connell formulated a plan for enrolling the rural population as associate members of the Catholic Association. By paying a penny a month to the "Catholic rent," they could show support. Thousands of tenant farmers responded to O'Connell's appeal. Local priests spoke in favor of the movement and supervised village committees of shopkeepers, traders, and farmers who met and drew up lists of grievances.[20]

After repeal of the Penal Laws in 1829, the association faded and with it the political mobilization of the countryside. O'Connell's efforts in the 1830s to secure repeal of the Act of Union remained primarily within the sphere of parliamentary politics. Only in 1840, when he organized the Loyal National Repeal Association, did mass political agitation begin again. Repeal wardens, nominated by the priest or by a parish meeting, led local

19. Gearóid Ó Tuathaigh, *Ireland before the Famine, 1798–1848* (Dublin, 1972), pp. 10–12, 14–15, 19–21.
20. Ibid., pp. 61–63.

branches of the Repeal Association and collected subscriptions. Repeal reading rooms, which served as workers' clubs, appeared in many areas. By 1842 the movement was growing rapidly. Many Irish Catholic bishops expressed support, and priests all over the country took an active part in the campaign. O'Connell toured Ireland in 1843, speaking at more than forty mass meetings before hundreds of thousands of farmers and laborers. Even the Connaught population, which had shown little enthusiasm for Catholic emancipation, was drawn into the campaign. The peak of the movement was reached in 1844. The English government, alarmed at the scale of demonstrations, banned a planned giant rally at Clontarf and arrested O'Connell, charging him with conspiracy. Thereafter, the pace and scale of activities decreased, and the association disintegrated rapidly after O'Connell's death in 1847. Although its successor, the Irish Confederation, struggled on into 1848, agitation collapsed amid the horrors of the potato famine.[21] Despite the group's rapid disappearance, it was the third time in half a century that large numbers of the Irish population had been mobilized in an effort to secure independence. How many people actively participated in the campaign is unknown, but the scale of demonstrations and financial support indicates that a substantial proportion of the Irish population was involved.

Through O'Connell's campaigns and the activities of others, nationalist political ideas spread in rural and urban Ireland. Broadside ballads with a nationalist message circulated widely by the early nineteenth century. The United Irishmen distributed political ballads along the roads. Hedge schoolmasters, thought to be rabid nationalists and republicans, held evening readings at which they discussed Irish history and recited their own patriotic compositions around the fire.[22] Nationalism had been infused into Irish popular culture by the early 1820s. Priests, schoolmasters, balladeers, and urban politicians had brought a message of Irish rights and English wrongs to the Irish population. The

21. Ibid., pp. 184–197; see also Kevin B. Nowlan, *The Politics of Repeal: A Study in the Relations between Great Britain and Ireland, 1841–1850* (London and Toronto, 1965).

22. See Georges-Denis Zimmermann, *Songs of the Irish Rebellion: Political Street Ballads and Rebel Songs (1780–1900)* (Dublin, 1967), pp. 21–23, 30.

result was a spreading political education and the dissemination of patterns of nationalist agitation that ranged from revolutionary secret societies to highly organized, centralized pressure groups.

Irish Politics in England: The Continued Appeal of Religion and Nationalism, 1800–1900

The predominant forms as well as the style of Irish political life in England during the early nineteenth century were imported. Faction fights and secret societies came with migrants across the Irish Sea. Police in English cities complained of the frequent armed clashes among migrants. In London, Glasgow, Liverpool, Manchester, and Birmingham, magistrates and priests noted the regular battles among Irish men and women armed with pokers, sticks, and clubs.[23] But many of these encounters were not just street fights among random crowds of exuberant Irish. The superintendent of the Stockport police reported a high incidence of aggravated assaults among the Irish in his city and commented: "These fights are principally among the Irish of different parties and not so often between English and Irish; the parties depend upon the part of the country whence they come."[24] Tipperary and Kerry Irish feuded in central London rookeries in the early 1860s. While it is not clear that these battles pitted one permanently organized faction against another, the street fights seem to have arisen from the same sorts of local quarrels and territorial pride that triggered periodic confrontations in Ireland.[25]

Secret Irish religious societies also appeared in English cities. In 1830, 391 Orange lodges were reported in England and Scotland. Membership figures indicate, however, that on the average each had only around twenty members. The order had

23. Great Britain, *Parliamentary Papers* (Commons), "Report on the State of the Irish Poor in Great Britain," 1836, 34:xx–xxi; see also ibid., "Select Committee on the Police in the Metropolis," 1817, 20; *East London Observer*, no. 16 (January 2, 1858).

24. Great Britain, *Parliamentary Papers* (Commons), "Report on . . . the Irish Poor in Great Britain," p. xxi.

25. J. A. Jackson, "The Irish in East London," *East London Papers* 6, no. 2 (December 1963):112; Sheridan Gilley, "The Pro-Papal Irish Riots in London, 1862," Prince Consort Prize Essay, 1972, p. 39 (a shortened version of this essay has been published as "The Garibaldi Riots of 1862" in *Historical Journal* 16, no. 4 [1973]:697–732).

been founded in London as early as 1807, but it remained tiny and relatively quiescent. In 1818, only one lodge functioned: a small group of workers met at a pub in Clerkenwell. A lodge for gentlemen was organized shortly thereafter to encourage political contacts among Tories, English peers, and Orangemen. The order grew substantially during the next decade, but the violent clashes that its activities triggered between Catholics and Protestants in Ireland did not occur in London.[26]

Ribbonmen also moved into English cities. In 1841, eight Ribbon delegates representing Manchester, Liverpool, Sheffield, Whitehaven, and Lancaster were reported to the Home Office. They headed a hierarchical organization that reached down to Irish workers via parish masters and local councils. The group seems to have been well organized. Members paid dues and met in local pubs. Their activities are obscure, but they functioned as a Catholic defense association. The groups took an oath similar to the one used in Ireland and also pledged themselves to a campaign of preferential buying among Catholic and Ribbon artisans and shopkeepers. Ribbonmen fleeing the Irish police could find shelter and jobs with society members in most areas of England and Scotland where the Irish had settled, with the possible exception of London. In fact, Ribbon societies were strong only in areas where Orange lodges were active. Perhaps because religious hostilities were much more muted in London than in the north of England, neither group made much headway in the metropolis. Elsewhere Ribbon societies were active until at least the early 1860s.[27]

The political mobilization of the London Irish took other forms. A series of organizations with explicit demands for changes in English laws or constitutional arrangements appeared almost simultaneously in Dublin and in London. Both the form and the timing of agitation in the English capital were derivative. In all cases, the aims of the groups were quite sophisticated: the greater independence of Ireland and the expansion of Catholic political and civil rights. One type of activity that continued throughout the nineteenth century was the secret political society. As early as

---

26. Senior, *Orangeism in Ireland and Great Britain*, pp. 153–154, 172–174, 304–305. By 1830 London had fifteen branches and Woolwich had nine.

27. H. O. 45/PS 184; 45/7522, pt. 1, Public Record Office, London.

the 1790s, Irish workers in London became involved in radical campaigns for an Irish republic. Among the more revolutionary members of the London Corresponding Society were several Irish artisans. And a shadowy organization, the United Englishmen, which also had branches in Lancashire, linked Thames porters, coal heavers, waterfront workers, and sailors into a conspiratorial world of half-planned risings and pike drills. These and later Irish secret societies were vehemently nationalist in their sympathies and wanted to force changes in the constitutional links between England and Ireland.[28]

The numbers involved in the United Englishmen in London were probably not large. A wider mobilization of migrants did not take place until after the end of the Napoleonic Wars, when Irish Catholics expanded their agitation for repeal of the Penal Laws. Within a year of Daniel O'Connell's founding of the Catholic Association, a British Catholic Association was established in London. Led by English Roman Catholic noblemen, such as the Duke of Norfolk and the Earl of Shrewsbury, the group nevertheless depended heavily on Irish Catholics to provide the expressions of mass support that were wanted to influence Parliament. The appeal of the group, however, was clearly pitched to middle-class Catholics. The Earl of Shrewsbury set the tone: their struggle was to gain for the peer, the professional man, and the freeholder the right to serve England "in positions of trust and honor."[29] The mass of the London Irish seem to have remained on the outside of the campaign. No local Daniel O'Connell emerged to capture the imagination of laborers and street vendors. Nevertheless, the agitation in England set a pattern and helped to fuse the causes of Catholicism and Irish nationalism. *The Catholic Journal* filled its pages with reports of O'Connell, the campaign in Ireland, and accounts of charity dinners to aid Irish migrants. Local Catholics were reported to defend Irish nationalism enthusiastically in parish meetings.[30] As the campaign unfolded, Catholic politics in London became more closely identified with Irish politics. This effect was reinforced after 1830

28. Edward P. Thompson, *The Making of the English Working Class* (New York, 1963), pp. 139–140, 167–169, 172, 174, 479–480.
29. *Catholic Journal*, March 29, 1828.
30. Ibid., March 22, 1828; May 3, 1828; May 24, 1828.

when Irish Catholic nationalist M.P.s settled in London. They formed a voluble group of speakers, easily recruitable for Catholic social and charity affairs, who fed the fires of Irish nationalism in the English capital. They, Irish journalists, and other Celtic enthusiasts used Catholic social and literary networks to build support for Daniel O'Connell and repeal of the Act of Union. Catholic migrants provided a ready audience and enrolled themselves in the ranks of the repealers as soon as the opportunity was offered.

Between 1841 and 1848, most of the political energies of the London Irish community were channeled into a campaign for repeal of the Act of Union. Soon after the Dublin founding of the Repeal Association in 1840, Repeal wards were organized in Southwark and Hammersmith. By 1844 the Irish in twenty other parishes scattered throughout the metropolis had formed similar clubs, and 80,000 associates had joined by July of that year.[31] The Repeal Association offered an outlet, albeit narrow, for migrants' political energies. Local clubs met frequently to enroll new members and collect the repeal rent. But control of the wards rested securely with the affluent few who could afford the high fee for voting memberships. Indeed, the men chosen as repeal wardens seem to have been solidly middle-class; those whose occupations I could trace were doctors, lawyers, and tradesmen. Catholic priests often attended meetings, and Fathers Moore, Foley, and Flanigan led the campaign in the Liberator's ward in Shadwell. Priests had a special place within the association: as "unarmed volunteers" they could participate fully and vote, enjoying privileges denied to the working-class members who could afford only the one-shilling fee for associates. Clerics and the Dublin leaders worked together to remove hostile members and to keep Daniel O'Connell's supporters in control.[32]

Nevertheless, the wards provided a forum for political discussion and a tonic for Irish political consciousness. The weekly meetings of such groups as the Grattan ward and the Harp Temperance ward testify to members' energy and aims. An unending stream of resolutions in favor of repeal and temperance,

31. Ibid., August 21, 1841; July 27, 1844. I am indebted to David Goodway for this and other references to the *Northern Star*.
32. Ibid., July 19, 1844; July 27, 1844; December 14, 1844; September 5, 1846.

repeal and liberty, even repeal and democracy were passed "by great majorities" and copies sent along to the *Northern Star.* Speakers read O'Connell's speeches and political articles from Irish and English newspapers.[33] More radical fare was brought into the meetings by London Chartists. Despite the relative conservatism of O'Connell's political program, the wards in London enrolled in their first few years anyone, including Chartists, who would support repeal. Local ties between Chartists and Repealers were also encouraged by the Chartist leadership. Feargus O'Connor and the *Northern Star* sent out a siren call to Irish migrants to support parliamentary reform in England. Throughout the West Riding, O'Connor was able to draw migrants from the Repeal movement into Chartist groups. Several Irish were elected to the executive of the National Charter Association, and Irish radicals, particularly in Barnsley and Manchester, worked within the Chartist campaign. London too had some Irish Chartists. In Marylebone, a Chartist club named itself for Robert Emmet, the United Irishman executed for his part in an 1803 uprising. Several members of Southwark Repeal wards joined the National Charter Association in November 1841.[34]

The attempt by Chartists to attract Repealers into their campaign gained momentum in London through 1841 and produced many self-declared Repeal Chartists who attempted to retain a double allegiance. Through Irish attendance at Chartist meetings, joint membership in the two movements, and Chartist support for Irish home rule, an informal alliance existed for a time between members of the two groups. These halcyon days of cooperation came to an abrupt end in 1843, however, when O'Connell blocked an attempt by Feargus O'Connor and James O'Brien to join a London Repeal ward, and orders were sent from Dublin to exclude all Chartists from the local clubs. Although "much sorrow" was expressed and profuse apologies were made, admission was refused "to any person professing himself an

---

33. Ibid., November 30, 1844; December 7, 1844.

34. Donald Read and Eric Glasgow, *Feargus O'Connor, Irishman and Chartist* (London, 1961), p. 93; Rachel O'Higgins, "The Irish Influence in the Chartist Movement," *Past and Present*, no. 20 (1961), pp. 89–90; *Northern Star*, November 13, 1841, and May 25, 1844.

O'Connorite Chartist."[35] When forced to choose, the London supporters of repeal remained loyal to O'Connell and his Dublin-based organization. Later, in 1846, when tensions over policy and the extent of control by O'Connell's supporters led to mass resignations from the association in London, the politically active remained separate from the London Chartists. Those who left the Repeal movement in 1846 were drawn into Irish Confederate clubs. In the fall of 1846, the *Northern Star* reported that there was "a great prejudice existing between the Chartists and Irishmen in London." Although expressions of Irish support for the Charter were regularly offered to or elicited by the *Northern Star*, Irish militants in London again decided to form their own organizations and to remain separate from the Chartist movement.[36]

By March of 1847, several groups of Irish nationalists in London had affiliated with Young Ireland. Irish Confederate clubs were soon organized at The Green Man, Berwick Street, and at the Cartwright Coffee House in the City. Within a few months, Confederate clubs appeared in five other areas. By July 1847 the group in the City had acquired 109 members.[37] These more militant Irish soon found themselves adopting large parts of the Chartist program. Irish Confederates in the City declared themselves in favor of the National Charter of Ireland. This group also had members who subscribed to Feargus O'Connor's Chartist Land Plan.[38] At a July meeting, the club proclaimed support for the course of international brotherhood, majority rule, Repeal, and the Charter. They pledged "to use our best exertions to obtain Repeal of the Act of Legislative Union between Great Britain and Ireland, and establish a Parliament in Ireland based upon the full, free, and fair representation of the whole people of our country."[39] By September of 1847, this group was calling itself the Irish Democratic Federation of London, clearly identifying with Chartist principles. Feargus O'Connor became president, and the

35. *Northern Star*, June 17, 1843.

36. Ibid., June 10, 1843; June 24, 1843; September 5, 1846; October 24, 1846; June 5, 1847.

37. Ibid., March 20, 1847; March 27, 1847; July 31, 1847; August 28, 1847; October 2, 1847; October 9, 1847.

38. Ibid., March 27, 1847; June 5, 1847; July 31, 1847.

39. Ibid., July 3, 1847.

other officers were a mixture of English and Irish. James Bronterre O'Brien joined in October.[40]

Friendly interest rather than fusion marked the relations of
most Confederate and Chartist clubs until the spring of 1848,
when successful revolution in France and hopes of an imminent
revolt in Ireland brought all varieties of nationalists and radicals
together in a mood of revolutionary euphoria. Thomas Daly, a
furrier from the Davis Confederate Club, expressed the new
mood: he asked that members form a rifle brigade, and he
recommended learning both the Marseillaise and "Fall, Flag of
Tyrants" for use in the coming struggle.[41] Repeal wards and
Confederate clubs forgot their rivalries and planned joint meetings. "Old Irelanders" as well as Young Irelanders decided that
they could support universal suffrage. The Irish Democratic
Federation elected a delegate to the Chartist convention and
marked out a more militant course:

This meeting hereby pledges itself, by solemn oath, to do all that lies in
its power, individually and collectively, by moral force, if practicable, by
physical force, if absolutely necessary, to obtain Ireland for the Irish; and
England for the English people, based upon the divine and glorious
principles of Liberty — Equality — Fraternity![42]

After a few minor problems were resolved, the newly united
Repealers and Confederates accepted a Chartist call for fraterniza-
tion. In April, Irish nationalists agreed to join the great Chartist
parade and meeting in Kennington Common. Local clubs threw
themselves into a flurry of activity, expressing their determina-
tion "to be up and doing," but much of their new fervor came in
response to the prosecution of three Irish leaders from the Young
Ireland movement: Thomas Meagher, William Smith O'Brien,
and John Mitchel, who had been arrested for sedition in Ireland.
At a series of large exuberant rallies, Irish groups proclaimed that
"Liberty, Equality, and Fraternity are now the order of the day."[43]

When the day for presenting the Charter to Parliament finally
arrived in April, the Irish turned out in full array with orange and

40. Ibid., July 4, 1847; September 4, 1847; October 16, 1847.
41. Ibid., February 26, 1848; March 25, 1848.
42. Ibid., April 1, 1848.
43. Ibid., April 8, 1848.

green banners and temperance medals proclaiming their several loyalties. One group joined the column marching in from the East End, while other Confederates and the Emmett Brigade met Chartists from northwest London in Russell Square before proceeding to Kennington Common. But the Irish groups kept a separate identity. They stayed together in one area, apart from the main body of Chartists, and had their own speakers. Only after the debacle of the demonstration, when the Chartist movement was declining rapidly, did local groups of Chartists and Repealers act together. Joint meetings were held in late May and early June in Greenwich, Westminster, Southwark, and Bermondsey. As the sedition trials of Young Irelanders progressed, several mass meetings of protest took place in the East End and Central London. On May 29, their convictions triggered a rally of 3,000 on Stepney Green. After speeches by Confederates and by such prominent Chartists as Ernest Jones, a parade across London began. Another 7,000 people from a Clerkenwell rally joined the procession as it wound toward the West End. Another Clerkenwell meeting, attended by 5,000, ended in a scuffle with police. Within the next week police broke up rallies in Bethnal Green, Victoria Park, and Bishop Bonner's Fields, arresting several people for throwing stones and assaulting officers. Several thousand people came to these protests against English actions in Ireland.[44]

The mobilization of the Irish nationalists in London reached its peak in June and July of 1848 in connection with Mitchel's transportation. New Confederate clubs appeared in Bermondsey, Seven Dials, Kensington, Greenwich, Deptford, and Islington. Islington's Red Hugh O'Donnell Club began with 120 members and rising enrollments were reported in several locations.[45] At this point the government was keeping close watch on the movement. Police spies had infiltrated some of the clubs, and news of threatened insurrection filtered into the Home Office in early June. Reports that pikes were being sold to Chartists by an Irish arms dealer and that Irish laborers were buying guns at

44. Ibid., April 15, 1848; May 27, 1848; June 3, 1848; June 10, 1848; H.O. 45/2410, Public Record Office, London.
45. *Northern Star*, June 17, 1848; June 24, 1848; July 1, 1848; July 22, 1848; August 12, 1848.

small shops throughout London lent substance to the wilder allegations that reached the police. Holborn radicals were reportedly planning to dig a twenty-foot-wide ditch in Farringdon Road. The cavalry was to be lured into the ditch after street lighting was blacked out and then ambushed by Chartists and Confederates.[46] Whatever credence was given to this and other reports of impending revolution, the police decided to clamp down on Irish nationalist demonstrations. A planned meeting in Stepney was banned, and the government arrested the secretary of one of the local clubs after a private meeting of about a hundred nationalists in Soho. He was charged in the Central Criminal Court with giving a dangerous and seditious speech and, as the *Northern Star* explained, advocating the use of arms to wrest the land "from the robbers who held it."[47] With government repression, activity gradually slowed. The Chartists' attention was turned toward the trials of their arrested leaders. Then as cholera moved into the metropolis during the winter, more private concerns and fears appeared in Irish neighborhoods.

Eighteen-forty-eight was the high point of Irish nationalist agitation in London. Thousands of Irish workers had been drawn into participation in Repeal wards and Confederate clubs. They had given money and attended rallies and speeches. Clubs sprang up in the older Irish neighborhoods as well as in areas of more recent Irish settlement outside the central core of the city. In each of these settings, local people demonstrated a strong political commitment to Irish nationalism, in addition to the ability to discriminate among Daniel O'Connell, Feargus O'Connor, and the Young Ireland group. When politics in Ireland became more radical after the death of O'Connell, so did Irish politics in London. A movement that began with strong clerical leadership and limited political aims became more and more dominated by democrats and by those willing to identify themselves with English radicals. The dynamics of mobilization in 1848 led the Irish into a more general campaign for political and social change. Yet they had kept their own organizations and their primary commitment to Irish nationalism.

46. H.O. 45/2410, June 2–4, 1848, Public Record Office, London.
47. *Northern Star*, July 15, 1848; June 10, 1848; H.O. 45/2410, Public Record Office, London.

After 1848, large-scale expressions of support for Irish nationalism disappeared in London for almost twenty years. Nevertheless,
a consitituency that could be mobilized in support of the Catholic
church and of home rule had been created. On several occasions
in London during the 1850s and 1860s, when the Catholic church,
the pope, or Irish nationalists were threatened, Irish migrants
protested. When the restoration of the Catholic hierarchy in
England triggered demonstrations and calls for "No Popery,"
several groups of metropolitan Catholics held parish meetings to
complain, wrote letters to the *Catholic Standard*, and circulated
petitions against the government's Ecclesiastical Titles Bill. In St.
Pancras, a Catholic association that included both Irish and
English parishioners formed in April of 1851 to defend Catholic
civil and religious liberties.[48]

Defense of the pope triggered a more vigorous series of Irish
battles in London in 1862, when the Workingmen's Garibaldi
Committee organized a demonstration in Hyde Park. A crowd
estimated to number from 15,000 to 20,000 showed up to hear pro-
Garibaldi speakers, but several hundred Irish also appeared.
Shouts of "No Garibaldi!" and "The Pope forever!" were hurled
at the leaders of the meeting. Attempts by Charles Bradlaugh and
another man to address the crowd were met by Irish attempts to
take over the speakers' mound. Between 100 and 500 Celtic
assailants, identified as "principally bricklayer's laborers," plus
women and children soon were embroiled in hand-to-hand
combat with guardsmen. On the following Sunday, when a
second pro-Garibaldi demonstration was scheduled, at least 200
Irish clashed with police and the military in the park.[49] Thirteen
Irish were arrested. During the next month, a series of minor
fights took place in pubs and streets of West End areas near the
park, as well as in Irish areas of central London. In Blackheath, a
crowd of about 500 Irish thwarted a ritual burning of the pope on
Guy Fawkes Day. William Totlie Wilie, a Cork Irishman who
was the secretary of the Deptford branch of the Brotherhood of St.
Patrick, organized this demonstration. He promptly followed it
with a call to meet in Bermondsey Square the next Sunday to

48. *Catholic Standard* 3, no. 75 (March 15, 1851); no. 78 (April 5, 1851); no. 80
(April 19, 1851).
49. Gilley, "Pro-Papal Irish Riots," pp. 18–21, 30–31.

show sympathy for the pope. Posters announcing the rally appeared on the doors of Catholic chapels all over London. Although the clergy forbade attendance and the Catholic press denounced the meeting, an estimated 10,000 turned out. After some interference from police, about 2,000 marched to Blackheath for cheers, speeches, and denunciations of Garibaldi.[50]

Each of these confrontations appears to have been a spontaneous response to political demonstrations or political symbols that Irish Catholics opposed. Despite the vastness of London and the dispersed pattern of Irish settlement, crowds of Irish formed and acted together in districts where there were Irish neighborhoods. Only certain sorts of issues could spark the mobilization of an Irish crowd, however; the defense of church, priest, pope, or Ireland could attract supporters easily at a time when the London Irish for the most part remained outside English political organizations and demonstrations. During the 1860s, Irish politics in London operated on several levels. Intermittent street fights and demonstrations by Irish workers coexisted with more complex organizations that formed periodically within the immigrant community. Spontaneous activities by neighborhood crowds came and went with local provocations, while a larger pattern of political mobilization in Ireland continued to produce a London echo.

The growth of the Irish Republican Brotherhood and its revival of conspiratorial nationalism in the early and mid-1860s triggered the formation of affiliated groups in London. Again the organization and its leadership were imported. James Stephen, whose aim was to work for an independent democratic Irish republic, organized a secret society known as the Brotherhood (also called the Fenians and the IRB) in 1858. It spread rapidly in Ireland, Great Britain, and the United States. Although there is no way of verifying the figure, the chief organizer estimated that by 1865 membership in the United Kingdom had reached 80,000.[51] The National Brotherhood of St. Patrick, a front organization for the group, had fifteen branches in London in 1863 and also published there a weekly newspaper, the *Irish Liberator*. One

50. Ibid., pp. 34–35, 38, 79, 80–82.
51. F. S. L. Lyons, *Ireland since the Famine*, rev. ed. (London and Glasgow, 1973), p. 127.

part of the Fenian organization in London was built up by James
J. O'Kelly, the son of a Dublin blacksmith. He moved to London
in 1861 at the age of sixteen to work in an uncle's sculpture
studio. In 1863 he became captain of the London Irish Volunteers. He then reorganized London Fenian circles. Groups were
formed in Camberwell, Notting Hill, and several other locations.
Both first- and second-generation Irish joined the IRB. Among
the London Fenians were Edward Pilsworth, the Birmingham-
born son of an Irish sergeant major in the English cavalry; Dennis
Duggan, a coachmaker from Dublin who worked in London
during the 1860s before returning to Ireland; and John P.
O'Brien, the London-born son of a district postmaster who had
migrated from Tipperary.[52]

After 1875, the IRB in London largely vanished from public
view, although it did not cease to exist. A provisional supreme
council and a hierarchical structure that reached from parishes up
to groups of counties were organized by James O'Kelly with the
help of Joseph Clarke and James Clancy. In London, however,
the group declined both in size and in militancy. By the mid-
1880s its functions were limited almost exclusively to the collecting of money to be sent to Ireland for arms purchases. Its leaders
functioned less as a conspiratorial elite than as proselytizers of
militant nationalism, drawing adherents into a wide variety of
nationalist groups.[53]

During the last quarter of the nineteenth century, Irish nationalism in London was domesticated. Expressions of Irish loyalties
were either channeled into conventional political clubs whose
purpose was to get out the vote or turned toward a revival of Irish
cultural life. The use of mass demonstrations or direct attacks
declined as extensions of the franchise gave Irish migrants and
their descendants a place in the English political process.

By the 1880s, more militant expressions of Irish nationalism
were largely diverted into cultural channels. After the Land
League and the IRB declared their support for Parnell and the
Parliamentary party, London Irish radicals who had belonged to

52. Gilley, "Pro-Papal Irish Riots," p. 88; John Devoy, *Recollections of an Irish
Rebel* (Dublin, 1929), pp. 147, 150, 239, 333–336; Mark F. Ryan, *Fenian Memories*
(Dublin, 1945) pp. 33–34.
53. Devoy, *Recollections*, p. 336; Ryan, *Fenian Memories*, p. 171.

these groups began working for a host of cultural organizations. Frank Fahy, a Galway-born civil servant who worked for the Board of Trade, started a Southwark Irish Literary Club in 1883. By 1893 it had become the Irish Literary Society. Such notable Irish as William Butler Yeats and Charles Gavan Duffy attended its regular concerts, lectures, and meetings, as did many Irish journalists and professionals. A London branch of the Gaelic League formed in 1894; a Gaelic Athletic Association branch appeared in 1895. Then in 1898, Douglas Hyde helped to organize the Irish Texts Society. The Young Ireland Society met between 1882 and 1891 to discuss Irish politics and culture. Organized by a Fenian doctor, Mark Francis Ryan, it served to lead young Irish intellectuals into the IRB. Most of these cultural and political groups as well as Sinn Fein, Cumann na n Gaedheal, and a series of nationalist committees shared the same headquarters in rooms on Chancery Lane and had overlapping memberships. The same people supported Parnell, the revival of the Irish language, and the spread of Irish literary culture.[54]

Over time the cultural component of Irish nationalism in London increased. The relative quiescence of Irish nationalism in Parliament coincided with an outpouring of Irish energy into nonpolitical forms. By the outbreak of the First World War, several hurling and football clubs had regular matches; the Gaelic League sponsored sixty Irish classes a week in schools all over the metropolis, as well as an Irish choir, orchestra, and theater. The Irish Folksong Society collected and published Irish traditional music. *Inisfail*, a magazine of "all matters of national, intellectual, and social interest to Irish people resident in London," began to publish in 1904. The call of nationalism grew stronger and broader over time. The Gaelic League sponsored yearly exhibitions of Irish manufactured goods, and urged migrants to "buy Irish." The Church of the Most Holy Trinity, Dockhead, began in 1901 to celebrate St. Patrick's Day with a high mass in Irish. Soon leaders of various Irish cultural organizations expanded the event into a major London festival with traditional Irish music and ancient Catholic litanies. In 1905, 6,000 were said

54. Ryan, *Fenian Memories*, pp. 157-158, 162, 168-169, 171-172.

to have attended.[55] The pull of nationalism in London extended far beyond the first generation. For many thousands of migrants, their ethnicity was reaffirmed in the religious and cultural institutions of the London Irish community.

The Slow Pace of Political Integration, 1820–1914

In contrast to the extensive participation by migrant Irish in nationalist politics and cultural organizations, their activity in English-led, English-based political movements remained limited in London before 1914. Paul Thompson asserts correctly that they were "insufficiently assimilated to join in a large measure in metropolitan political life."[56] Not only did the Roman Catholic church work to keep Catholics out of groups dominated by Protestants, but a variety of economic, social, and legal barriers excluded Irish workers from activity in parish and parliamentary politics. Even where the Irish were not debarred from voting or standing for office by local electoral arrangements, they rarely won local positions. Although Thomas Kelly, a City bookseller and publisher, became an alderman in 1830 and lord mayor in 1836, the manner in which the Roman Catholic press exulted over this and similar triumphs indicates that such events derived most of their importance from their infrequency.[57]

Even in central London, where the proportion of Irish-born residents was relatively high, virtually no Irish names appear on lists of vestry members or of Poor Law guardians before 1860, although many of Irish descent were among the resident middle class of small merchants and professionals. Francis Healey, a butcher to "good" families in St. Giles and St. George, Bloomsbury, who made a fortune and retired to become a justice of the peace, chairman of the St. Pancras magistrates' board, and

55. Gaelic League of London, *Zut na nZaedeal,* March 1905, pp. 16–17, and March 1906, pp. 17–18; Gaelic League of London, *Program of Irish Religious Celebration at Westminster* (London, 1906); Gaelic League of London, *Program and Book of Words* (London, 1903), pp. 4–5; *Half-yearly Review of the Gaelic League of London* (London, 1904), p. 11; *Journal of the Irish Folk Song Society* (London) 2, no. 3 (1906):43–48.

56. Paul Thompson, *Socialists, Liberals, and Labour: The Struggle for London, 1885–1914* (London and Toronto, 1967), p. 26.

57. *Post Office London Directory for 1840* (London, 1840); see also *Catholic Standard,* October 11, 1851.

member of the Metropolitan Board of Works before his death in 1872, was an exception to the general pattern of Irish nonparticipation in local government.[58] A systematic checking of vestry membership in Lambeth, Shoreditch, St. Pancras, and St. George, Southwark, between 1830 and 1888 reveals few Irish elected to parish offices. A builder, Mark Patrick, and a plumber, T. G. Mahany, joined the Shoreditch vestry in 1857, but Irish representation in St. George, Southwark, was not evident until 1887. Later in the century, a few Irish Catholics held borough offices, served as guardians of the poor, or were elected to the London School Board. In general, however, the Irish played very limited roles in metropolitan local politics before 1914.[59]

Direct mobilization of the Irish vote waited until the third quarter of the nineteenth century, when Charles Parnell and other nationalist M.P.s helped to organize Irish political clubs in English cities. As early as 1873, the Irish Home Rule Confederation of Great Britain, later known as the National League, was formed. Its earliest club in London began in the riverside community of Southwark, but by 1883 the league had expanded to forty branches, many in suburban areas such as Chiswick, Tottenham, and Highgate. The National League remained strong in London until the early 1890s, when it split at the time of Charles Parnell's implication in the O'Shea divorce case. By 1900 only ten branches survived. Clubs had dual functions: they acted most of the time as social centers for lectures, dances, and excursions, but they also led drives for voter registration. Concern over treatment of Catholics in workhouse or board schools, for example, produced efforts to elect friendly candidates to administrative posts.[60] The ability of the National League to create an Irish voting bloc

58. See *Holborn Journal*, April 24, 1858, and May 22, 1858; Joint Vestry of St. Giles in the Fields and St. George, Bloomsbury, *A List of the Joint Vestry* (Bloomsbury, 1827–1844).

59. The late David Owen very kindly passed along to me these examples of Irish political participation which he culled from local newspapers, vestry reports, and parish records; no other Irish names were discovered; see also *South London News*, July 12, 1850; *North Londoner*, December 14, 1872. See also P. Thompson, *Socialists, Liberals, and Labour*, pp. 26–27.

60. John Denvir, *The Irish in Britain* (London, 1892), pp. 231, 314–316; Ryan, *Fenian Memories*, pp. 150–153; Alan Earl O'Day, "The Irish Parliamentary Party and British Politics, 1880–1886," Ph.D. thesis, University of London 1971, pp. 128–130.

was quite limited, however. In addition to the ineffectiveness of many of its agents, franchise requirements and polling hours kept many Irish out of English elections. To vote in a parliamentary election even after 1885, a person had to be male, over twenty-one, and the head of a household in a separate dwelling or a lodger in rooms worth £10 annually, and to fulfill a year's residency requirement. The receipt of poor relief disqualified one. In consequence, low-paid workers who moved frequently were unlikely to be on the electoral register. In most of the East End in 1910, for example, less than 13 percent of the resident population could vote. The *Pall Mall Gazette* estimated in 1886 that there were only 10,000 Irish voters in London; in virtually all constituencies they comprised fewer than 10 percent of the electorate. Finally, the impact of the Irish vote was limited because of the tripartite political ties of the Irish community. Priests' commitments and the issue of education drew Catholics to the Conservatives; desire for home rule produced loyalty to the Liberals; and the growth of unions among the unskilled fostered ties to Socialist clubs. The Irish vote therefore was split and usually as a bloc politically ineffective.[61]

Radical reform movements provided a more accessible path into the lower levels of metropolitan politics. During the upsurge of political activity in England in the late 1820s and early 1830s, Irish migrants joined or formed several London-based political groups. In 1828, for example, a group of London Irish organized the Association for Civil and Religious Liberty, which had contacts with Henry Hunt, William Cobbett, and other English radicals. In 1830, during the agitation for franchise reform, the police reported the involvement of an Irish solicitor's clerk from Lambeth, a Mr. O'Grady, who met regularly with Henry Hunt and Feargus O'Connor. Also in the early 1830s, an Irish Anti-Union Association was formed in Soho, several of whose members belonged to the National Union of the Working Classes.[62]

61. P. Thompson, *Socialists, Liberals, and Labour*, pp. 26, 70, 399. See O'Day, "Irish Parliamentary Party," pp. 101–111, for an analysis of the Irish influence on the 1880 and 1885 elections.

62. E. P. Thompson, *Making of the Irish Working Class*, p. 440; H.O. 40/25, pt. 1, Public Record Office, London; *Poor Man's Guardian*, March 17, 1832; March 24, 1832; August 11, 1832.

Two Irishmen in north and northwest London took an active part in London parish politics during the 1830s. Thomas Murphy, a Roman Catholic coal merchant "of fair round proportions," gained much notoriety for his leadership of radical artisans who took over the St. Pancras vestry in 1832. Working with a coalition composed of small shopkeepers, minor ratepayers, and Dissenters, he dominated the newly reformed vestry and directed its attacks on church rates and the local vicar until 1838, when, after various minor scandals, his party was driven from office by disgusted ratepayers. Murphy's attempts to gain a seat in Parliament were complete failures, but he successfully injected national questions into local affairs; the St. Pancras vestry often called meetings to debate national issues, such as repeal of the Corn Laws, municipal reform, and extension of the franchise. Their positions were strongly democratic: pronouncements duplicated much of the Chartist program with the addition of demands for recall of M.P.s and reform in Ireland. This last demand was perhaps a reflection of Murphy's loyalties, which remained Roman Catholic and Irish nationalist despite his primary commitment to reform in England. He later joined the Chartists and was a London delegate to the Glasgow convention in 1838.[63]

John Savage, an Irish linen draper who later became a publican, played a similar role in Marylebone politics. In 1833 he organized local resistance to the house and window taxes. By 1834 his pub on Circus Street had supposedly become the rendezvous for the borough's "turbulent politicians." Every Sunday evening, political lectures, sometimes preceded by Irish songs, drew many people to meetings there. At the end of the session, Savage would speak, usually denouncing the monarchy, the Church of England, Parliament, or the House of Lords, according to one unfriendly witness. Savage, Murphy, Feargus O'Connor, and several other men formed the Great Radical Association in 1835. Savage later joined the Chartists.[64]

63. *New Vestryman*, November 14, 1833; James Williamson Brooke, *The Democrats of Marylebone* (London, 1839), pp. 28–29, 60–62, 129–133; Iorwerth Prothero, "Chartism in London," *Past and Present*, no. 44 (August 1969), p. 94.
64. Brooke, *Democrats of Marylebone*, p. 47; Prothero, "Chartism in London," pp. 93–94.

The most notable Irish radicals in English political organizations during the 1830s and 1840s were, of course, Feargus O'Connor and James Bronterre O'Brien. Both spent several years in
London and became involved in a wide range of political activities. O'Brien, son of a Longford wine merchant, came to the
capital during the 1820s to study law at King's and later Gray's
Inn, but his political interests soon led him into journalism. As a
friend of Henry Hetherington and the editor of a series of radical
newspapers — *The Poor Man's Guardian, The Operative, Bronterre's National Reformer,* and the *London Mercury* — he moved
into the mainstream of London democratic politics long before
joining the Chartists.[65] Feargus O'Connor also came from the
Irish upper and middle classes: his family owned a large estate in
Cork. They fled to England temporarily around 1800 because
O'Connor's father had been active in the United Irishmen. Even
though a landlord in his own right, O'Connor chose a different
life and came to London in 1826 to study law at Gray's Inn. He
cemented ties to English radicals at this time. After being elected
to Parliament in 1832, O'Connor began his political challenge of
Daniel O'Connell and built up a following among London
workers.[66] Nevertheless, he appealed less to the Irish community
than to London radical artisans and democrats. At the time of the
Chartist movement, most of the politically conscious Irish remained within Irish organizations.

A more extensive fusion of English and Irish workers' politics
did not take place until migrants began to join and to organize
trade unions. In the 1840s, the strength of London Chartism lay
in the trade societies of skilled workers. But relatively few London
Irish were artisans, and fewer still gained admittance to the ranks
of the society men. Registration papers of mid-century London
friendly societies list almost no Irish names among the organizers.
Despite the large numbers of London Irish tailors, neither the
Journeymen Tailors' Club, founded in 1838, nor the United
Clickers' Benefit Society, registered by 1832, had more than one or

65. For more information on J. B. O'Brien, see G. D. H. Cole, *Chartist Portraits*
(London, 1941), pp. 239–267, and R. G. Gammage, *History of the Chartist
Movement, 1837–1854* (London and Newcastle, 1894), pp. 71–76.
66. Donald Read and Eric Glasgow, *Feargus O'Connor, Irishman and Chartist*
(London, 1961), gives the most complete summary of O'Connor's career.

two Irish names among the registered members listed in government files. The London and Westminster Benefit Society of Warehousemen and Porters, which existed between 1827 and 1858, limited membership to Protestant natives of Great Britain despite the sizable number of Irish in the trade.[67]

During the 1840s and 1850s, Irish membership in London friendly societies was largely confined to a few Catholic or Irish groups, such as the Sons of Hibernia Friendly and Benefit Society, the Islington United Brothers Catholic Temperance Benefit Society, and the Irish Unity Society for healthy Irish of good moral character.[68] Only when laborers began to form friendly societies did Irish migrants take a large part in groups that were not given a specific religious or national affiliation. Most of the trustees and officers of three branches of the Friendly Society of United Laborers, formed around 1835 in central London and the East End, were Irish; the rules specifically opened the society to people of any religion, trade, or national origin. The Central London branches of the Accident and Burial Society of Laborers were also heavily Irish. In the later 1860s and 1870s, Irish names appear with more frequency among the officers of artisans' friendly societies. The Bloomsbury Mutual Benefit Society, which met in Seven Dials or St. Giles temperance halls, listed both Irish and English artisans among its ranks between 1859 and 1891.[69] By the mid-1870s, when trades unions began to register with the government, Irish men belonged to several groups of low-skilled workers. The London Paviors' Burial and Trade Protection Society, founded in 1873 in Holborn, was organized and run by several Irish. Irish joined the Chelsea Union of Hawkers, Dealers, and Costermongers and also formed the bulk of the members and officers of the Amalgamated Society of Riverside Workmen, formed in Southwark in 1883. Several unions in the building trades, such as the General Amalgamated Union of Labourers, had a large Irish component by 1910.[70]

67. F.S. 1/1919; F.S. 1/461/2219 (Middlesex); F.S. 1/444/1818, Public Record Office, London.

68. F.S. 1/478/2744 (Middlesex); F.S. 1/409/338; F.S. 1/476/2830 (Middlesex), Public Record Office, London.

69. F.S. 1/465/2321 (Middlesex); F.S. 1/465/2325 (Middlesex); F.S. 1/487/3872; F.S. 1/488/3973 (Middlesex), Public Record Office, London.

70. F.S. 7/9/378; F.S. 7/5/194, Public Record Office, London; P. Thompson, *Socialists, Liberals, and Labour*, p. 270.

Dockers' unions in the port of London had many Irish members because migrants dominated the most skilled and the heaviest riverside jobs. By the middle of the nineteenth century, when the Irish came to control access to the trade, positions in the better paid branches were passed from Irish fathers to their London-born sons. Unionization of the port began among the docking elite, among the Irish stevedores who loaded and unloaded the ships, and among three other groups: the corn porters, the coal whippers, and the lightermen. The Labour Protection League, created in 1871 as a general union for the port, comprised at its peak over 30,000 people in fifty-four societies. Patrick Hennessey, an Irish tailor and trade unionist from the Land and Labour League, had helped to organize the dockers. Unfortunately, the league collapsed as economic conditions worsened in the late 1870s. Only the stevedores' societies and a branch of the corn porters survived. The stevedores, however, joined their groups into the Stevedores' Union, which was recognized by employers. This union prospered. By the end of the century it had become in effect a craft union that enforced a closed shop and closely controlled its numbers. Admission became almost hereditary; sons were admitted underage for nominal fees.[71]

The great expansion of unionism in the port took place in connection with the 1889 dock strike, which brought together skilled and unskilled, English and Irish. The work stoppage was led by Irish stevedores and Ben Tillett, secretary of the Tea Operatives and General Laborers' Association. Tillett, whose mother was Irish, was born in Bristol but had moved to a sister's house in London when he was seventeen. His later work as a seaman and then as a warehouse worker and dock laborer introduced him to the horrible working conditions at the port, and he became a union organizer by conviction. After a strike was declared, the Stevedores' Union, led by James Toomey and Tom McCarthy, a London Irishman from Limehouse, supported it, as did a series of already organized specialized trades in the port. The Irish component in the strike leadership was large: Tillett and Toomey as well as several other Irish — Patrick and John Regan, Dennis Driscoll, and Michael Tighe — signed the call for a

---

71. John Lovell, *Stevedores and Dockers: A Study of Trade Unionism in the Port of London, 1870–1914* (New York, 1969), pp. 61, 64, 75, 81–82.

general riverside strike. Their headquarters was an Irish-owned
riverside pub. This confrontation combined English and Irish
workers in support of changes in work rules and higher, uniform
rates of wages. The strike signaled not only the increased consciousness of the low-skilled, casual port laborers but a great
increase in Irish integration into organized London labor. The
separatism between English and Irish workers evident in 1850 had
broken under the impact of the unions as they expanded into new
trades. At the end of the strike, the Dockers' Union, with sixty-five
branches, brought thousands of men into one mass organization.
Although the union became virtually extinct during the 1890s,
mass unionism returned to the port with the strike of 1911 in the
form of a reincarnated Stevedores' Union and the National
Transport Workers' Federation. As industrial unionism expanded into the docks, the gasworks, the railroads, and other
trades during the quarter century before the First World War,
Irish laborers had the chance to organize. Occupational loyalties
helped to break down ethnic separatism.[72]

By 1900 the London Irish had become much more integrated
into English social, economic, and political structures than they
had been fifty years earlier. Their political life had become highly
institutionalized, as had that of the English population. A
growing Irish middle class moved haltingly into local and
national politics; Irish and English workers combined in the
same labor unions. Not only were Irish voters organized to participate in English elections, but secret societies and demonstrations had declined in favor of political and nationalist clubs.
Although holding strongly to a commitment to Irish independence, the London Irish found themselves working within the
confines of the English political system. The forms, tone, and
style of Celtic politics in London adapted to the English political environment, which had itself been partially opened to
receive the Irish.

The First World War provided a test case for the political
loyalties of migrant Irish. Despite the rejection of participation in
the war by Irish radicals and the attempts of the Irish Volunteers

72. Ben Tillett, *Memories and Reflections* (London, 1931), pp. 25, 69, 88–89,
121, 134, 143. See Lovell, *Stevedores and Dockers*, chap. 4, for a detailed account of
the strike, and Appendix, pp. 219–221, for a list of Dockers' Union branches.

and the IRB to organize a revolution with German help, the British army raised battalions of Irish migrants in London, Glasgow, Edinburgh, and Tyneside. The London Irish Rifles and the Irish Guards fought in the early stages of the war before conscription was introduced. Their battalion included Catholics and Protestants, Unionists and nationalists.[73] Despite the continued strength of Irish nationalist loyalties in London, the appeal of Irish separatism had declined markedly by the end of the nineteenth century. Migrants in large numbers made political choices in terms of their parish, their trade, and their country of residence as well as their ethnic background. By the end of the century, migrants could be mobilized in causes other than the defense of Ireland or the pope. While these loyalties had scarcely been abandoned, they had been found compatible with a measure of integration into English politics and society.

73. Kevin O'Connor, *The Irish in Britain*, rev. ed. (Dublin and London, 1974), pp. 40–41.

The Urbanization of
the London Irish

As the Irish moved from country to city, their environment and life-style changed dramatically. They traded cabins for crowded London apartments; they came from the fringes to the center of a highly developed money economy. Emigrants exchanged small settlements with relatively simple, static occupational structures for a metropolis whose complex labor market was constantly changing as firms relocated and technology shifted. Irish women who had spent their days caring for animals, spinning, and occasionally working in the fields became street hawkers, seamstresses, and servants in middle-class London households. Small farmers and cottagers who had done agricultural work in lieu of rent turned to the docks or to construction sites for jobs as wage laborers. Migrants went from a political milieu dominated by kinship networks, secret societies, and vigilantes to one in which individuals were organized into craft unions, clubs, and specialized pressure groups.

Moving into a city brought major changes in Irish behavior and attitudes. As migrants became integrated into an urban Irish subculture, they altered their demographic decisions, political behavior, religious practices, and language while they redefined their world view to reflect changes in environment and experience. These shifts required many decades to work themselves out, however, and they took place at varying rates of speed. It is important, therefore, to see the transformation of Irish peasants into urbanites as a complex process having different contours in the short, medium, and long run.

The initial impact of the city was to force the abandonment of parts of a rural life-style along with the acceptance of the working conditions imposed by the London labor market. Immediately upon entering the city, migrants abandoned a wide variety of cultural practices and communal rituals as well as the use of the Irish language. Several kinds of group political behavior characteristic of nonindustrial societies soon became extinct. And given the immediate need to earn money, most adult migrants found themselves forced to accept quickly new work relationships and to handle daily encounters with segments of metropolitan society. These changes made possible others. Being employed, migrants were able to marry earlier and to offer shelter to more recently arrived kin and friends. The practice of chain migration, combined with the availability of housing and jobs, thus created the conditions from which Irish neighborhoods could be built. Perhaps to counterbalance the pressures of London life, the Irish banded together. Most Irish migrants during the early and mid–nineteenth century lived with and near other migrants. During the 1840s and 1850s, this tendency to settle in Celtic enclaves in the city was at its height. The particular help other migrants could give them was especially useful at this time. Indeed, the social distance between the Irish and London institutions catering to the poor remained large until the middle decades of the nineteenth century. The status of the Irish as outsiders in a system in which communities assumed responsibility only for their own members pushed migrants to develop means of self-help. Relatively unserved by churches, schools, and charities and given short shrift by Poor Law officials, the Irish created their own social security system during their early years in the metropolis.

In the medium run, Irish urban villages became less isolated and much more complex in structure, while their inhabitants developed a cohesive life-style within the confines of their working-class communities. First, Irish settlements multiplied and spread throughout the metropolis as migration continued. The increased numbers and visibility of the Irish eventually produced increased contacts with outside institutions. London charities and Protestant missionaries sought to deal with both the physical and spiritual needs they perceived. Indeed, for most of the nineteenth century, the low incomes, high unemployment, lack of education, and family problems experienced by the Irish made them prime candidates for the attention of an emerging army of middle-class teachers, preachers, Poor Law officials, and providers of social services. The most successful of these outsiders in reaching the Irish was the English Roman Catholic church, which built churches and schools in Irish areas. Although the Catholic clergy did win to the practice of orthodox Roman Catholicism a large proportion of the migrant Irish, much of their work to transform Irish manners and mores had only limited success. Despite the regular pressures for behavioral change and cultural adaptation, migrants' life-styles were largely conditioned by the norms of the working-class communities within which they lived and by the social and economic realities of their lives. They developed a cultural shield against much of the outside world. Their ethnic loyalties separated them from much English cultural and social life. Some migrants worked within heavily Irish trades or for Irish employers. Irish pubs, political groups, friendly societies, and other organizations kept migrants from mixing with English peers and fostered their emerging ethnic identity. Their marriages kept the Irish within the community while they created an environment in which an Irish identity could be transmitted to the next generation. Religion, politics, work, and the family thus mutually reinforced an Irish subculture resistant to middle-class messages praising self-control and assimilation.

In the long run, by late in the nineteenth century an Irish workers' subculture had solidified under the impact of an Irish cultural revival and the continued strength of Irish nationalist politics. Some moved from Irish enclaves and drifted away from the Catholic church, but many of the second and third generations found themselves living like their parents and reaffirming ethnic loyalties. Although there was continued and increasingly effective pressure through the mass media for the diffusion of English culture, the central beliefs of the Irish, their allegiance to nationalism, and their Roman Catholicism remained largely intact. Indeed, an Irish subculture still has a recognizable place in the social life of many large British cities. Supported by a wide range of organizations, periodicals, and Catholic parishes and fueled by continued nationalist demands for an end to partition of Ireland and more recently by revival of the Irish Republican Army and open conflict in the North, the Irish sense of a separate ethnic identity has remained strong in Britain.

The effects of rural-to-urban migration upon the London Irish have therefore been different from those that would have been predicted by Louis Wirth, Robert Park, and Robert Redfield. The Irish move from country to city cannot be described as a shift from a stable, cohesive, "traditional" community into an impersonal urban society. Both elements of this common stereotype are inaccurate. Irish migrants abandoned a complex agricultural society for a complex urbanizing one at a time when both were in the throes of massive but rather different processes of change. Moreover, migration into an English city, rather than weakening interpersonal ties and producing individual alienation, brought groups of kin together into neighborhoods where they reconstructed a closely knit social life.

Migrants created a subculture for themselves out of the material of both past and present. This subculture was given both shape and substance by three major factors: the city itself, class, and ethnicity. Although each of these factors had independent effects on migrants' behavior and mentality, together they proved mutually reinforcing, and thus determined the nexus within which migrants built a place for themselves in the metropolis.

London provided both the physical setting and the structure of opportunities within which migrants had to cope. Its great size, density, and continued growth by migration produced a large Irish community regularly replenished by newcomers. Its heterogeneous population confronted the Irish with other groups — the Italians, the Scots, the Germans, the French, and the East European Jews as well as the native English — each having a distinctive religious and cultural heritage. While open conflicts were few, more subtle encounters and expressions of difference were many. In the face of a variegated social world, they asserted their own identity rather than adopt another.

The organization of space in the capital had a strong influence on the location of Irish settlements. The Irish moved into a widely dispersed city but one that had a stock of cheap, decaying housing in central and riverside areas, near the location of many low-skilled jobs. Since inexpensive mass transit was unavailable during the decades of most rapid Irish settlement in London, the Irish had to live within walking distance of their work. The result was the creation of Irish neighborhoods within the territory where there was a high demand for casual labor and where several of London's declining industries were located. The spatial organization of London combined with its transport system and its industrial base to shape both the location and the economic structure of urban villages.

If, during the first half of the nineteenth century, the spatial organization of London helped to create Irish working-class neighborhoods, during the second half of the century the development of the metropolis helped to disperse and to relocate them. As land values rose, railways were built, and the central core of the metropolis became more and more a commercial center, the older areas of Irish settlement were torn down and their inhabitants driven out. Here social policy reinforced the market pressures for urban reconstruction. Since removing the slums seemed an easy answer to the problems of overcrowding, bad sanitation, and contagion, Irish quarters had little part in the design of Victorian London envisaged by social reformers and urban administrators. But if the worst Irish neighborhoods were destroyed to make room for new streets, giant wet docks, and railroads, many survived or reappeared in suburban corners.

The nature of the Irish subculture in London was also fundamentally determined by the organization of English and Irish political and economic systems. Migrants lived within an unregulated capitalist economy in which scarce skills and professional training were highly rewarded, while most simple skills earned little. Moreover, London was the political core of the United Kingdom, a land where economic specialization was far advanced. Peripheral areas of the British Isles, particularly those settled by Celtic peoples, can be viewed as essentially colonial territories dominated by the English for their own benefit. Michael Hechter argues that during the eighteenth and early nineteenth centuries the growing specialization of the Irish economy toward the export of agricultural commodities for the

English market reflected a cultural division of labor in which Celtic areas were made dependent on and subservient to central English counties. His model of internal colonialism predicts that the social stratification of such a state will show the superimposition of cultural distinctions upon class divisions, resulting in the monopolization of high-status positions by those from the dominant culture and the clustering of those native to the peripheral area at the bottom of the social and economic hierarchies.[1] This situation obtained for the Irish both before and after migration. Moreover, the Irish maximized their lack of economic opportunity within the system by their choice of residence in the heart of the colonial capital. By migrating to London, the Irish chose to enter England's most complex labor market, one where they had little to offer but their physical strength, willingness to work, and knowledge of simple crafts; then too, many English thought them fit only for menial positions. The continuing demand for casual labor, servants, and low-skilled workers in London made available large numbers of badly paying jobs disliked by natives with greater skills and different work habits. At the same time, more desirable jobs were reserved for those with qualifications difficult for most Irish to obtain. A few already had or slowly acquired middle-class status. But they were exceptions. For the most part, the Irish move to London merely transformed a rural proletariat into an urban one. The shift of the Irish into skilled occupations that took place in small Welsh, Scotch, and American mining and mill towns was largely absent in the English capital, where an urban variant of a cultural division of labor was replicated.

Throughout the process of adapting to London life, most migrants held resolutely to their ethnic identity. Although a certain amount of cultural diffusion took place over time in London, the Irish resisted assimilation. Their neighborhoods did not dissolve, their ethnic and nationalist commitments did not atrophy, their religion did not disappear. Although Irish participation in London trade unions and local politics grew toward the end of the nineteenth century, the third and fourth generations still clung to the symbols of their ancestors' past and continued to

---

1. Michael Hechter, *Internal Colonialism: The Celtic Fringe in British National Development, 1536–1966* (Berkeley and Los Angeles, 1975), p. 30.

use Irish associations, Catholic groups, and kinship networks to mediate their contact with English urban society. The Irish reworked their cultural heritage to fit the demands of life in an urbanizing, industrializing country.

This maintenance of a distinct cultural identity while adopting many elements of an urban life-style served several important functions. Michael Hechter suggests that in a situation of internal colonialism, pride in an ethnic identity becomes a weapon in the hands of a subordinate people. It becomes a means of resisting political integration and of refusing the designation of cultural inferiority through which political dominance is justified.[2] Even more important was the role of Irish ethnicity in welding together a local community of people whose individual lack of resources was to some extent compensated for by the greater strength of the group. In addition to its intrinsic value, Irish culture helped migrants to survive in an alien, sometimes hostile environment. It was an important tool to be used in rebuilding their lives abroad. Yet just as ethnicity brought people together, it also separated them from others. Its stress upon cultural differences had double-edged effects. By reaffirming their ethnicity within the constraints provided by the economic and political environment in which they lived, the Irish produced a remarkably resilient, tenacious subculture that not only sheltered but bound its members, not only strengthened but limited their ability to adapt to urban life.

2. Ibid., pp. 37–38.

APPENDIX A

Sampling and
Tabulation Procedures

Most of the statistical data on the London Irish presented in this book was obtained from a sample of Irish households drawn from the 1851 and 1861 London census manuscript schedules, which list the name, address, occupation, age, sex, and birthplace of every inhabitant. Since the task of locating and retabulating data on even a small fraction of the Irish families scattered among a population of over two million would have been impossible for one person to accomplish in the time available, I selected five subdistricts of the official census districts and drew a systematic sample from those areas. Several considerations guided my choices. First, districts of very heavy Irish settlement and the oldest centers of Irish residence, St. Giles in the Fields and Whitechapel, seemed to demand attention. But I also wanted the sampled districts to reflect as many as possible of the economic and social differences that existed among Irish settlements in the various parts of London. In choosing my five areas I therefore used the criteria of the proportion of Irish-born residents, the geographical location of the district in the city, and the major industries. Subdistricts of the three census districts with the highest proportion of Irish-born residents were chosen and then supplemented with two additional districts, one of low Irish concentration and one of a medium level of settlement. (An Irish-born population that constituted less than 3 percent of the total population was defined as low; 3 to 5 percent was defined as medium.) Because the districts with the highest proportion of Irish-born were in central

London and along the river in the east and south, I added two suburban areas in the west and south to balance the sample geographically and to widen it to include parishes with different economic bases. The range of districts selected therefore ran from the suburban south (St. George, Camberwell) to a riverside parish (St. Olave, Southwark) and from Kensington in the West End (St. John, Notting Hill) through central London (St. Giles in the Fields) and to the East End (the Aldgate district of Whitechapel). The sample was deliberately biased toward the districts of first reception of migrants and to the largest Irish neighborhoods in the capital. It therefore can not be shown to be representative of the entire Irish-born population of the metropolis. Since published census returns do not include separate tabulations according to birthplace, there were no published distributions of the characteristics of the total Irish-born population residing in London in 1851 and 1861 against which I could check the results of my analysis. I have used the following procedures to help generalize my results and to show the limits on their generality. Separate distributions of the most important variables in the analysis were first compared among the five parishes. When significant differences among the distributions (as in the case of sex ratios) were discovered, the results from each of the districts were reported separately or were compared to the total population of the five districts in addition to figures for London as a whole (in the case of occupations). Since the family structures of Irish-headed households were similar in all five districts, variables relating to family composition and size were aggregated.

After the districts to be studied were selected, a systematic sample of one household in three with an Irish-born member either in the nuclear family of the head or among the lodgers, visitors, and servants of the household was drawn from the data and coded. Information was later punched onto IBM cards. A household was defined as a coresiding group comprising all the names listed by the census taker under and including the designation "Head." When Irish-born individuals lived as nonrelated subordinates within an English-headed household, they were coded by use of a set of categories that allowed the easy separation of the households in which they resided from the main sample of Irish-headed households. All schools, workhouses, and prisons were excluded from the analysis; lodging houses were treated as houses and their members tabulated in accordance with the normal rules of selection. The total sample comprised 819 households and 3,947 individuals drawn from the 1851 census and about the same number drawn from the 1861 census. A large sample size was used in order to keep standard errors low. The same districts were coded from each set of census schedules.

The units of analysis were two: the coresiding group or household and the individual. Every member of a selected coresiding group was described on a separate IBM card. All the information provided by the census — birthplace, age, occupation, name, marital status, family status, sex, and address — was recorded. Identical entries were made for every person within the sample. In addition, the card of the household head included codes for a variety of items describing the household as a whole and the characteristics of the total population of the building in which the selected household resided. For example, the numbers of servants and visitors were tallied and a count of all residents and all Irish-born persons in the building was made. By combining a very simple repeated code for individuals with a more complex one for aggregated data, I could use standard computer programs such as Data Text and SPSS to produce frequency distributions and cross tabulations that tallied material on either unit of analysis. Chi square tests were done on the cross classifications, and standard errors were computed for means and frequency distributions.

A code was designed which reduced information in the census to numerical form. Although most items could be transcribed in a straightforward manner, the codes for occupation and social class required classification of hundreds of discrete categories into broad industrial and social groups. After reflection, I adopted procedures and categories similar to those being used in other studies of English cities in order to aid comparability. The basis for my original division of London occupations into industrial groups was the official census tabulation of 1851 combined with Charles Booth's occupational categories, which he derived from several nineteenth-century censuses (see Bibliography, Works by Contemporaries). Jobs were divided according to the product manufactured, while separate categories were created to handle occupations not involved in production. Although the category titles resemble those used currently to classify the labor force in a modern industrial economy, the specific jobs within each group are those existing in 1851 apportioned according to criteria used in the 1851 census. The system used to categorize social groups was essentially that designed by W. A. Armstrong for his study of York in 1851, which he has described in "The Use of Information about Occupation," an essay in *Nineteenth-Century Society: Essays in the Use of Quantitative Methods for the Study of Social Data,* edited by E. A. Wrigley (Cambridge, 1972). Armstrong has adapted the five divisions used by the English registrar general in 1911 to classify occupations in large categories of social rank. I have used these same five groups for reporting my results, although my initial coding scheme comprised twenty-five categories, which I aggregated in final tabulations.

Tables and Figures

Table A.1. Males per 100 females in Irish sample and in total populations of sampled London districts, 1851

Age	Kensington		St. Giles		Whitechapel		St. Olave		Camberwell	
	Irish sample (N=91)	Total population	Irish sample (N=1,586)	Total population	Irish sample (N=1,176)	Total population	Irish sample (N=813)	Total population	Irish sample (N=280)	Total population
0–19	53.8	85.0	102.2	98.1	98.8	101.1	94.7	103.1	83.6	89.2
20–39	28.6	59.4	82.4	85.0	89.8	106.5	109.2	102.8	96.2	65.2
40–59	70.0	74.0	95.1	93.8	106.1	103.9	86.2	94.9	90.5	75.9
60+	100.0	60.3	78.9	80.0	140.0	77.1	130.0	79.7	50.0	59.2

Source: Enumerators' books and printed returns, Census of 1851 (England).

Table A.2. Occupational status of employed Irish household heads, sons, and lodgers, London sample, 1851 and 1861

Occupational status	Household heads		Sons		Lodgers	
	1851 (N=719)	1861 (N=709)	1851 (N=185)	1861 (N=232)	1851 (N=310)	1861 (N=212)
I. Professionals, top-level managers, industrialists	1.4%	2.8%	0.0%	0.9%	0.0%	1.4%
II. a. Lower ranking professionals and managers	1.6	1.8	0.5	0.4	0.3	4.2
b. Shopkeepers	4.3	3.0	0.0	0.9	0.6	0.0
III. a. Skilled labor	20.4	16.5	15.1	14.2	16.8	16.0
b. Clerks	1.3	1.8	3.8	6.0	1.3	0.9
IV. Semiskilled labor	8.2	8.7	9.2	11.2	16.8	16.0
V. Unskilled labor	62.7	65.3	71.4	66.4	64.2	61.3

Table A.3. Residential status of Irish-born adults and coresiding children, London sample, 1851 and 1861

	1851		1861	
Residential status	Number	Percent	Number	Percent
Living with kin	3,363	85.1	3,003	86.9
Living alone	76	1.9	46	1.3
Servants				
Irish household	24	0.6	33	1.0
Non-Irish household	82	2.1	57	1.6
Solo lodgers				
Irish household	178	4.5	229	6.6
Non-Irish household	45	1.1	22	0.6
Solo visitors				
Irish household	110	2.8	31	0.9
Non-Irish household	28	0.7	8	0.2
Employees	6	0.2	17	0.5
Other and unknown	40	1.0	9	0.3
	3,952	100.0	3,455	99.9

Table A.4. Sex and marital status of household heads in Irish sample and in total London population, 1851

	Irish sample		Total London population	
Sex and marital status	Number	Percent	Number	Percent
Men				
Married	573	75.3	2,814	71.0
Unmarried	29	3.8	207	5.2
Widowers	27	3.5	178	4.5
Women				
Married	19	2.5	141	3.6
Unmarried	9	1.2	136	3.4
Widows	104	13.7	488	12.3
	761	100.0	3,964	100.0

Source for London figures: David Chaplin, "The Structure of London Households in 1851," unpublished paper, Western Michigan University, 1975, Table 2.

Table A.5. Mean family and household sizes in Irish sample and in all London, by age of head, 1851

	Mean family size		Mean household size	
Age of head	Irish sample (N=761)	All London (N=3,967)	Irish sample (N=761)	All London (N=3,967)
15–19	1.0	1.6	1.5	1.8
20–24	2.3	2.4	3.4	2.9
25–29	2.9	3.2	4.0	3.7
30–34	3.5	4.2	5.0	4.8
35–39	3.9	4.7	5.3	5.3
40–44	4.1	4.6	5.6	5.4
45–49	4.4	4.6	6.1	5.5
50–54	4.1	4.4	5.3	5.2
55–59	4.1	3.6	5.7	4.4
60–64	3.3	3.3	5.7	4.3
65–69	2.5	2.9	3.8	4.1
70+	2.2	2.7	3.7	4.0

Source for London figures: David Chaplin, "The Structure of London Households in 1851," unpublished paper, Western Michigan University, 1975, Table 3.

Table A.6. Percentage distribution of Irish households and families, by number of members, London sample, 1851

Number of members	Families (N=761)	Households (N=761)
1	9.1%	5.0%
2	23.9	15.5
3	17.2	14.3
4	19.6	15.8
5	13.3	13.8
6	10.0	12.1
7	3.7	7.2
8	2.1	5.1
9	0.8	3.4
10	0.4	7.8
	100.1%	100.0%

Table A.7. Family structure of Irish households, by life-cycle stage, London sample, 1851

Life-cycle stage	Nuclear families		Multiple and extended families		All families	
	Number	Percent	Number	Percent	Number	Percent
1. Wife under 45, no children	97	82.2%	21	17.8%	118	100.0%
2. Wife under 45, 1 child under 1 year	26	86.7	4	13.3	30	100.0
3. Children at home, none employed	314	90.8	32	9.2	346	100.0
4. Children at home, fewer than half working	34	91.9	3	8.1	37	100.0
5. Children at home, half or more working	118	84.9	21	15.1	139	100.0
6. Wife over 45, no children or only one over 20 at home	59	77.6	17	22.4	76	100.0
All stages	648	86.9%	98	13.1%	746	100.0%

Table A.8. Singulate mean age at marriage in Irish and English populations, by sex, 1851 and 1861

Population	1851		1861	
	Male	Female	Male	Female
Ireland	31.2	28.9	31.0	26.4
Irish sample	28.3	26.2	26.2	24.0
England	27.1	25.9	26.5	25.4
London	27.6	25.9	26.5	24.9

Sources: Census of Ireland, 1851 and 1861; Census of England, 1851 and 1861.

Averages were computed from tables enumerating the Irish, English, and London populations by marital status, sex, and age. Identical computations were performed on similar data for the sample of Irish migrants in five London parishes. The method used is that of John Hajnal, "Age of Marriage and Proportions Marrying," *Population Studies* 7, no. 2 (1953):111–136.

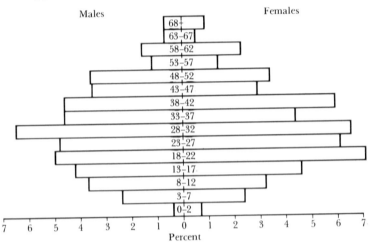

Figure A.1. Age distribution of Irish-born in sampled London parishes, 1851

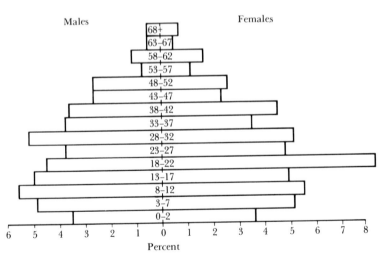

Figure A.2. Age distribution of Irish-born and coresiding children in sampled London parishes, 1851

Select Bibliography

MANUSCRIPT SOURCES

Public Record Office, London

H.O. 107: Enumerators' books, Census of 1851
R.G. 9: Enumerators' books, Census of 1861
H.O. 40: Disturbances
H.O. 45: Home Office papers
Metpol. 2: Metropolitan Police
F.S. 1, 3, 15: Friendly Societies
F.S. 7: Trade unions

Greater London Council Archive, London

S.B. 18, Poor Law records; Boards of Guardians
P. 71/OLA
P. 73/GIS
P. 82/GIS
P. 84/JN 61

Archive of the Holborn Public Library, London

Parish papers of St. Giles in the Fields and St. George, Bloomsbury

Westminster Archives, London

Baptismal registers, St. Patrick's, Soho, 1790–1873. 9 vols.
B 4: Letters principally to Rome.
Marriage registers, St. Patrick's, Soho, 1809–1937. 3 vols.

Church of the Most Holy Trinity, Dockhead, London

Baptismal registers, 1802–1880. 5 vols.
Marriage registers, 1802–1901. 5 vols.

St. Anne, Underwood Road, Spitalfields, London
Baptismal registers, 1848–1870. 4 vols.
Confraternity books.
Marriage registers, 1850–1870. 2 vols.

St. Mary of the Angels, Bayswater, London
Baptismal registers, 1852–1880. 3 vols.
Parish papers, Manning collection.

St. Giles in the Fields, London
J. M. Oppenheim, unpublished "Visitor's Book," 1862.

Archive of the Marist Fathers, Rome
E 61: Correspondence with St. Anne, Spitalfields, London.

Cork Archives Council, Cork
Day papers
Huston–Eedy correspondence, 1826–1834.

Public Record Office of Ireland
Manuscript census returns, 1841.

Trinity College, Dublin
Muniments 5, ser. 78, nos. 47–61. Survey of College Lands, 1843.

PRINTED PRIMARY SOURCES

Ballads

Baring-Gould collection. 7 vols. British Library.
Crampton collection. 8 vols. British Library.
Pitts collection. British Library.
Joly collection. 3 vols. National Library of Ireland.
Ballads. 3 vols. University College Library, Cork.
Ballads. 5 vols. Trinity College, Dublin.

Newspapers and Periodicals

The Builder 12–14 (1854–1856).
Catholic Journal, 1828–1829.
Catholic Standard of London, 1849–1855; continues as *Weekly Register
and Catholic Standard,* 1855–1880.
Inisfail, 1904–1906.
Northern Star, 1838–1854.
Poor Man's Guardian, 1831–1835.
St. Patrick's Catholic Magazine 5–11 (1890–1911).
The Tablet, 1840–1845, 1857–1858.

Parliamentary Papers (Commons)

"Abstract of the Population Returns of Great Britain, 1831," 1833, vols. 36–38.

"Annual Reports of the Registrar General," 1841, 21:341; 1852–1853, 40:1; 1863, 14:1; 1873, 20:1.

"Census of 1841: Enumeration Abstract," 1843, vol. 22; "Occupation Abstract," 1844, vol. 27.

"Census of 1851: Enumeration Abstract and Report," 1852–1853, vols. 85–86; "Population Tables," 1852–1853, vol. 88, pts. 1 and 2.

"Census of 1861: Population Tables," 1862, vol. 50; "Ages and Civil Condition of the People," 1863, vol. 53, pts. 1 and 2.

"Census of Great Britain: Religious Worship," 1852–1853, vol. 89.

"Minutes of the Committee of Council on Education," 1851, 44:1; 1852–1853, 79:497, 80:1; 1854, 51:567, 52:1; 1854–1855, 42:767; 1856, 47:631; 1857, 2d sess., 33:847; 1857–1858, 45:853.

"Reports of the Committee of the Council on Education," 1859, 1st sess., 21, pt. 1:1; 1860, 54:1; 1861, 49:1; 1862, 42:1; 1863, 47:1; 1864, 45:1; 1865, 42:1; 1866, 27:117; 1867–1868, 25:1; 1868–1869, 20:1.

"Reports from the Select Committee Appointed to Inquire into the State of Mendicity in the Metropolis," 1814–1815, vol. 3; 1816, vol. 4.

"Reports of the Commissioners for Inquiring into the Condition of the Poor in Ireland," 1835, vol. 32; 1836, vols. 30, 32, 34.

"Report on the State of the Irish Poor in Great Britain," 1836, vol. 34.

"Reports of the Royal Commission on the State of Large Towns and Populous Districts," 1844, vol. 17; 1845, vol. 18.

"Report from the Select Committee Appointed to Inquire into the Operation of the Law of Settlement and of the Poor Removal Act," 1847, vol. 11.

"Reports of the Royal Commission on the Health of the Metropolis," 1847–1848, vol. 32.

Works by Contemporaries

Barclay, Tom. *Memoirs and Medleys: The Autobiography of a Bottle-washer.* Leicester, 1934.

Beames, Thomas. *The Rookeries of London: Past, Present, and Prospective.* London, 1850.

Beamish, North Ludlow. "Statistical Report on the Physical and Moral Condition of the Working Classes of St. Michael, Blackrock, near Cork." *Journal of the [Royal] Statistical Society* 7 (1844):251–254.

Board of Works, St. Giles in the Fields and St. George, Bloomsbury. *Annual Reports.* London, 1857–1887.

Booth, Charles. *Life and Labour of the People in London.* ser. 1, *Poverty,* 4 vols. ser. 2, *Industry,* 5 vols. ser. 3, *Religious Influences,* 7 vols. London, 1902–1903.

Brewer, James Norris. *The Beauties of Ireland, Being Original Delineations, Topographical, Historical, and Biographical of Each County.* 2 vols. London, 1825.

Brooke, James Williamson. *The Democrats of Marylebone.* London, 1839.

Brothers of the Christian Schools. *The First Book of Reading Lessons.* 2d ed. Dublin, 1841.

———. *Third Book of Reading Lessons.* Dublin, 1841.

———. *The Literary Class Book or Fourth Series of Select Reading Lessons.* Dublin, 1840.

Bullen, Dr. D. "Statistics of an Improved Rural District (the Parish of Kilmurray) in the County of Cork." *Journal of the [Royal] Statistical Society* 6 (1843):352–353.

Burke, Rev. Thomas, O.P. *Lectures and Sermons.* New York, 1873.

Catholic Directory and Ecclesiastical Register. London, 1850–.

Catholic Poor School Committee. *Annual Reports.* London, 1848–1870.

Chadwick, Sir Edwin. *Report on the Sanitary Condition of the Labouring Population of Great Britain.* Ed. M. W. Flinn. Edinburgh, 1965.

Croker, T. Crofton. *Fairy Legends and Traditions of the South of Ireland.* Vol. 2. London, 1828.

———. *Researches in the South of Ireland Illustrative of the Scenery, Architectural Remains, and the Manners and Superstitions of the Peasantry.* London, 1824.

Devoy, John. *Recollections of an Irish Rebel: The Fenian Movement.* New York, 1929.

Furniss, Father John. *Books for Children for First Communions, Missions, Retreats, etc.* Dublin, 1860–1861.

———. *The Book of Young Persons.* London and Dublin, 1861.

———. *What Every Christian Must Know.* London and Derby, 1856.

Garrett, Samuel. "The Irish in London." In *Motives for Missions.* London, 1853.

Garwood, John. *The Million-Peopled City: Or One Half of the People of London Made Known to the Other Half.* London, 1853.

Godwin, George. *London Shadows: A Glance at the "Homes" of the Thousands.* London, 1854.

Hall, Mr. and Mrs. S. C. *Ireland, Its Scenery, Character, etc.* 3 vols. London, 1841–1843.

Hollingshead, John. *Ragged London in 1861.* London, 1861.

Hyde, Douglas. *The Love Songs of Connaught.* 4th ed. London and Dublin, 1905.

———. *The Religious Songs of Connacht.* London and Dublin, 1902; reprinted New York, 1972.

Inglis, Henry David. *A Journey throughout Ireland in the Spring, Summer, and Autumn of 1834.* 3rd ed. 2 vols. London, 1835.

Kirk, Francis J. *Reminiscences of an Oblate of St. Charles.* London, 1905.

Lewis, George Cornewall. *On Local Disturbances in Ireland; and on the Irish Church Question.* London, 1836.

Lumley, W. G. "The Statistics of the Roman Catholic Church in England and Wales." *Journal of the [Royal] Statistical Society* 27 (1864):303–323.

MacGill, Patrick. *Children of the Dead End: The Autobiography of a Navvy.* London, 1914.

Mann, Horace. "Statement of the Mortality Prevailing in Church Lane during the Last Ten Years." *Journal of the [Royal] Statistical Society* 11 (1848):19–24.

Mayhew, Henry. *The Great World of London.* London, 1856.

———. *London Labour and the London Poor.* 4 vols. London, 1861–1862; reprinted New York, 1968.

——— and John Binny. *The Criminal Prisons of London and Scenes of Prison Life.* London, 1862.

O'Leary, John. *Recollections of the Fenians and Fenianism.* 2 vols. London, 1896.

O'Neill, John. "Fifty Years' Experience as an Irish Shoemaker in London." *St. Crispin* 1 and 2 (1869).

Ordo Recitandi Offici Divini et Missae Celebrandae. London, annual, 1816–1849.

Parton, John. *Some Account of the Hospital and Parish of St. Giles in the Fields, Middlesex.* London, 1822.

Pollard-Urquhart, William. "The Condition of the Irish Labourers in the East of London." In *Transactions of the National Association for the Promotion of Social Science* (1862).

St. Patrick's, Soho. *Annual Reports.* London, 1862–1877.

Statistical Society of London. "Report of a Committee Appointed to Make an Investigation into the State of the Poorer Classes in St. George's in the East." *Journal of the [Royal] Statistical Society* 11 (1848):193–249.

———. "Report on the State of the Working Classes in the Parishes of St. Margaret and St. John, Westminster." *Journal of the [Royal] Statistical Society* 3 (1840):14–24.

Sykes, W. H., Dr. Guy, and F. G. P. Neison. "Report of a Committee of the Statistical Society of London to Investigate the State of the Inhabitants and Their Dwellings in Church Lane, St. Giles." *Journal of the [Royal] Statistical Society* 11 (1848):1–18.

Talbot, C. J., Viscount Ingestre, ed. *Meliora: or, Better Times to Come.* London, 1852.

Tillett, Benjamin. *Memories and Reflections.* London, 1931.

Timbs, John. *Curiosities of London.* New ed. London, 1876.

Townsend, Rev. Horatio. *A General and Statistical Survey of the County of Cork.* 2d ed. 2 vols. Cork, 1815.

Wakefield, Edward. *An Account of Ireland, Statistical and Political.* 2 vols. London, 1812.

Wilde, Lady Jane Francesca Speranza. *Ancient Legends, Mystic Charms, and Superstitions of Ireland.* London, 1887.

Young, Arthur. *A Tour in Ireland . . . in 1776, 1777, and 1778.* 2 vols. London, 1780.

SECONDARY SOURCES

Ireland and the Irish

Adams, William Forbes. *Ireland and Irish Emigration to the New World from 1815 to the Famine.* New Haven and London, 1932.

Akenson, Donald Harman. "The Irish National System of Education in the Nineteenth Century." Ph.D. thesis, Harvard University, 1967.

Arensberg, Conrad M., and Solon T. Kimball. *Family and Community in Ireland.* 2d ed. Cambridge, Mass., 1968.

Broeker, Galen. *Rural Disorder and Police Reform in Ireland, 1812-1836.* London, 1970.

Carney, F. J. "An Introduction to Irish Household Size and Structure, 1821." Unpublished paper, Trinity College, Dublin, 1976.

———. "Aspects of Pre-Famine Household Size: Composition and Differentials." Unpublished paper, Trinity College, Dublin, 1976.

———. "Pre-Famine Irish Households: Formation, Size, and Structure. Sec. 2: Household Formation." Unpublished paper, Trinity College, Dublin, 1976.

Connell, K. H. *Irish Peasant Society: Four Historical Essays.* Oxford, 1968.

———. "Peasant Marriage in Ireland: Its Structure and Development since the Famine." *Economic History Review* 14, 2d ser. (April 1962).

———. *The Population of Ireland, 1740-1845.* Oxford, 1950.

Cousens, S. H. "The Regional Variations in Emigration from Ireland between 1821 and 1841." *Transactions and Papers of the Institute of British Geographers* 37 (1965):15-29.

———. "Emigration and Demographic Change in Ireland, 1851-1861." *Economic History Review* 14, 2d ser. (August 1961-April 1962):275-288.

———. "The Regional Pattern of Emigration during the Great Irish Famine," *Transactions and Papers of the Institute of British Geographers* 28 (1960):119-134.

Donnelly, James S., Jr. *The Land and the People of Nineteenth-Century Cork: The Rural Economy and the Land Question.* London and Boston, 1975.

Drake, Michael. "Marriage and Population Growth in Ireland, 1750-1845," *Economic History Review* 16 (1963):301-313.

Edwards, Robert Dudley, and T. Desmond Williams, eds. *The Great Famine: Studies in Irish History, 1845-1852.* Dublin, 1956.

Evans, E. Estyn. *Irish Folkways.* New York, 1957.

Freeman, T. W. *Pre-Famine Ireland: A study in Historical Geography.* Manchester, 1957.

Gailey, Alan. *Irish Folk Drama.* Cork, 1969.

Hechter, Michael. *Internal Colonialism: The Celtic Fringe in British National Development, 1536–1966.* Berkeley and Los Angeles, 1975.

Humphreys, Alexander J. *New Dubliners: Urbanization and the Irish Family.* London, 1966.

Jackson, John Archer. *The Irish in Britain.* London and Cleveland, 1963.

———. "The Irish in London: A Study in Migration and Settlement in the Last Hundred Years." M.A. thesis, University of London, 1958.

Kennedy, Robert E., Jr. "The Persistence of Social Norms: Marriage and Fertility among the Overseas Irish." *Social Demography: The State of the Art,* ed. William Peterson and Lincoln H. Day. Cambridge, Mass., forthcoming.

———. *The Irish: Emigration, Marriage, and Fertility.* Berkeley, 1973.

Larkin, Emmet. "The Devotional Revolution in Ireland, 1850–1875." *American Historical Review* 77, no. 3 (June 1972).

Lawton, R. "Irish Immigration to England and Wales in the Mid-Nineteenth Century." *Irish Geography* 4, no. 1 (1959):35–54.

Lee, Joseph. *The Modernization of Irish Society, 1848–1918.* Dublin, 1973.

Miller, David W. "Irish Catholicism and the Great Famine." *Journal of Social History* 9, no. 1 (Fall 1975).

Nowlan, Kevin B. *The Politics of Repeal: A Study in the Relations between Great Britain and Ireland, 1841–1851.* London and Toronto, 1965.

O'Brien, George. *The Economic History of Ireland from the Union to the Famine.* London, 1921.

O'Higgins, Rachel. "The Irish Influence in the Chartist Movement." *Past and Present,* no. 20 (1961), pp. 83–96.

Ó Tuathaigh, Gearóid. *Ireland before the Famine, 1798–1848.* Dublin and London, 1972.

Schrier, Arnold. *Ireland and the American Emigration, 1850–1900.* Minneapolis, 1958.

Senior, Hereward. *Orangeism in Ireland and Britain, 1795–1836.* London and Toronto, 1966.

Woodham-Smith, Cecil. *The Great Hunger.* London, 1965.

Nineteenth-Century England

Anderson, Michael. *Family Structure in Nineteenth-Century Lancashire.* Cambridge, 1971.

Beck, George Andrew, ed. *The English Catholics, 1850–1950.* London, 1950.

Chaplin, David. "The Structure of London Households in 1851." Unpublished paper, Western Michigan University, 1975.

Dyos, H. J. "The Slums of Victorian London." *Victorian Studies* 11, no. 1 (1967):5–40.

——. *Victorian Suburb: A Study of the Growth of Camberwell.* Leicester, 1961.

—— and Michael Wolff, eds. *The Victorian City: Images and Realities.* 2 vols. London and Boston, 1973.

Gauldie, Enid. *Cruel Habitations: A History of Working-Class Housing, 1780–1918.* New York, 1974.

George, M. Dorothy. *London Life in the Eighteenth Century,* 2d ed. London, 1930.

Gilley, Sheridan. "The Garibaldi Riots of 1862." *Historical Journal* 16, no. 4 (1973).

——. "Heretic London, Holy Poverty, and the Irish Poor, 1830–1870." *Downside Review* 89, no. 294 (January 1971):64–89.

——. "Protestant London, No-Popery, and the Irish Poor, 1830–1860." *Recusant History* 10, no. 4 (January 1970):210–230.

——. "The Roman Catholic Mission to the Irish in London." *Recusant History* 10, no. 3 (October 1969):123–145.

Hall, Peter. *The Industries of London since 1861.* London, 1962.

Harting, Johanna H. *Catholic London Missions from the Reformation to the year 1850.* London, 1903.

Inglis, Kenneth Stanley. *Churches and the Working Classes in Victorian England.* London, 1963.

——. "Patterns of Religious Worship in 1851." *Journal of Ecclesiastical History* 2, no. 1 (1960).

Jones, Gareth Stedman. *Outcast London: A Study in the Relationship between Classes in Victorian Society.* Oxford, 1971.

Lovell, John. *Stevedores and Dockers: A Study of Trade Unionism in the Port of London, 1870–1914.* New York, 1969.

McClelland, Vincent Alan. *Cardinal Manning, His Public Life and Influence, 1865–1892.* London, 1962.

Mackenzie, W. A. "Changes in the Standard of Living in the United Kingdom, 1860–1914." *Economica* 1, no. 3 (1921):211–228.

McLeod, Hugh. *Class and Religion in the Late Victorian City.* London, 1975.

Norman, E. R. *Anti-Catholicism in Victorian England.* London, 1968.

Prothero, Iorwerth. "Chartism in London." *Past and Present,* no. 44 (August 1969).

Redford, Arthur. *Labour Migration in England, 1800–1850.* 2d ed. Manchester, 1964.

Samuel, Raphael. "The Catholic Church and the Irish Poor." Unpublished paper, Past and Present Conference, London, 1966.

Shannon, H. A. "Migration and the Growth of London, 1841–1891." *Economic History Review* 5 (1935):79–85.

Sheppard, Francis. *London, 1808–1870: The Infernal Wen.* Berkeley and Los Angeles, 1971.

Thompson, Edward P. *The Making of the English Working Class.* New York, 1963.

Thompson, Paul. *Socialists, Liberals, and Labour: The Struggle for London, 1885–1914*. London and Toronto, 1967.

Wohl, Anthony S. "The Housing of the Working Classes in London, 1815–1914." In *The History of Working-Class Housing*, ed. Stanley D. Chapman. London, 1971.

Other Works

Braun, Rudolph. *Industrialisierung und Volksleben: Die Veränderung der Lebensform in einem ländlicher Industriegebiet vor 1800*. Zurich, 1960.

Carrier, N. H., and J. R. Jeffery. *External Migration, 1815–1950: A Study of the Available Statistics*. Studies on Medical and Population Subjects no. 6. London, 1953.

Chevalier, Louis. *Classes laborieuses et classes dangereuses à Paris pendant la première moitié du XIXe siècle*. Paris, 1958.

Coale, Ansley J., et al. *Aspects of the Analysis of Family Structure*. Princeton, 1965.

Fischer, Claude S. "Toward a Subcultural Theory of Urbanism." *American Journal of Sociology* 80, no. 6 (May 1975):319–341.

Gans, Herbert J. *The Urban Villagers: Group and Class in the Life of Italian-Americans*. New York, 1962.

Geertz, Clifford. *The Interpretation of Cultures*. New York, 1973.

Germani, Gino. "Migration and Acculturation." In *Handbook for Social Research in Urban Areas*, ed. Philip Hauser (Paris, 1964).

Gutman, Herbert G. "Work, Culture, and Society in Industrializing America, 1815–1919." *American Historical Review* 78, no. 3 (June 1973).

Hajnal, John. "Age at Marriage and Proportions Marrying." *Population Studies* 7, no. 2 (1953).

Handlin, Oscar. *Boston's Immigrants: A Study in Acculturation*. Rev. ed. Cambridge, Mass., 1959.

———. *The Uprooted*. New York, 1951.

Hertzfeld, Elsa G. *Family Monographs: The History of Twenty-four Families Living in the Middle West Side of New York City*. New York, 1905.

Jackson, J. A., ed. *Migration*. Sociological Studies no. 2. Cambridge, 1969.

Kerr, Madeline. *The People of Ship Street*. London, 1958.

Knights, Peter R. *The Plain People of Boston, 1830–1860: A Study in City Growth*. New York, 1971.

Laslett, Peter, and Richard Wall, eds. *Household and Family in Past Time*. Cambridge, 1972.

Lewis, Oscar. *La Vida*. New York, 1966.

Mayer, Philip. *Townsmen or Tribesmen*. Oxford, 1961.

Mendels, Franklin F. "Proto-industrialization: The First Phase of the

Industrialization Process." *Journal of Economic History* 32, no. 2 (March 1972).

Park, Robert E. "Human Migration and the Marginal Man." *American Journal of Sociology* 33 (1928):881–893.

Scott, Joan, and Louise Tilly. "Women's Work and the Family in Nineteenth-Century Europe." In *The Family in History,* ed. Charles E. Rosenberg. Philadelphia, 1975.

Shorter, Edward. *The Making of the Modern Family.* New York, 1975.

Suttles, Gerald. *The Social Order of the Slum: Ethnicity and Territory in the Inner City.* Chicago, 1968.

Thernstrom, Stephan. *The Other Bostonians: Poverty and Progress in the American Metropolis, 1880-1970.* Cambridge, Mass., 1973.

———. *Poverty and Progress: Social Mobility in a Nineteenth-Century City.* Cambridge, Mass., 1964.

———. and Richard Sennett, eds. *Nineteenth-Century Cities.* New Haven, 1969.

Thomas, Brinley. *Migration and Economic Growth: A Study of Great Britain and the Atlantic Economy.* London, 1954.

Thomas, Keith. *Religion and the Decline of Magic.* London, 1973.

Thomas, William I., and Florian Znaniecki. *The Polish Peasant in Europe and America.* 2 vols. New York, 1927.

Tilly, Charles, ed. *An Urban World.* Boston and Toronto, 1974.

———, Louise Tilly, and Richard Tilly. *The Rebellious Century, 1830-1930.* London and Cambridge, Mass., 1975.

Wirth, Louis. "Urbanism as a Way of Life." *American Journal of Sociology* 44 (1938):1–24.

Wrigley, E. A., ed. *Nineteenth-Century Society: Essays in the Use of Quantitative Methods for the Study of Social Data.* Cambridge; 1972.

Young, Michael, and Peter Willmott. *Family and Kinship in East London.* London, 1957.

———. *The Symmetrical Family: A Study of Work and Leisure in the London Region.* London, 1973.

Index

Exiles of Erin

Designed by R. E. Rosenbaum.
Composed by Jessamy Graphics, Inc.,
in 10 point Baskerville, 2 points leaded,
with display lines in Baskerville.
Printed offset by Thomson/Shore, Inc. on
Warren's Number 66 Antique Offset, 50 pound basis.
Bound by John H. Dekker & Sons, Inc.
in Holliston book cloth
and stamped in All Purpose foil.